D1712463

Handbook of
Alligators and Crocodiles

Handbook of
Alligators and Crocodiles

Steve Grenard

Illustrated by
Wanda Loutsenhizer

KRIEGER PUBLISHING COMPANY
MALABAR, FLORIDA
1991

Original Edition 1991

Printed and Published by
KRIEGER PUBLISHING COMPANY
KRIEGER DRIVE
MALABAR, FLORIDA 32950

Library of Congress Cataloging-in-Publication Data
Handbook of alligators and crocodiles
    p. cm
    ISBN 0-89464-435-1
    1. Crocodilia
QL666.C9H26 1990
597.98—dc20   89-71337
                                       CIP

10   9   8   7   6   5   4   3   2

Table of Contents

Acknowledgments

The kind assistance and cooperation of the following individuals, government agencies and private organizations is gratefully appreciated:

Robert T. Bakker, Richard Baker, Penny L. Bartnicki, Patrice Bell, Kathy Boldt, Julius O. Boos, Peter J. Brazaitis, David Burrows, Scott Busa, Carmen Collazo, M. J. Cox, Miguel Alvarez del Toro, Kevin Foster, V. Greenberg, Fred Grunwald, David C. Hayden, Mashiro Iijima, Mark Kaplan, Don Kazimir, Satoshi Kimura, Laurie Krusinski, William W. Lamar, Greg C. Lepera, Helen Longest-Slaughter, Joe Mark, Frank J. Mazzotti, Dixie Lee Nims, David Olson, Antonio V. Ramirez, Juan C. Rodriguez, James P. Rowan, Steve Ruckel, Peter Swiderek, Peggy A. Vargas, Grahame Webb, Jeff Wines and Robert T. Zappalorti.

Alabama Department of Conservation and Natural Resources, Alligator Farm (St. Augustine, FL), American Museum of Natural History (New York, NY), Anthony's Groves (West Palm Beach, FL), Arkansas Game and Fish Commission, Atagawa Tropical and Alligator Garden (Shizuoka, Japan), Aududon Park Zoological Society (New Orleans, LA), Electronic Librarian (Hollywood, FL), Florida Game and Freshwater Fish Commission, Florida Department of Tourism and Commerce, Florida Power and Light Company (Turkey Point, Dade County, FL), Foster (alligator) Farm, Inc. (Okeechobee, FL), Georgia Department of Natural Resources, Herpetological Consultants/Environmental Consultants (Beachwood, NJ), Herpetological Search and Exchange (Lindenhurst, NY), Instituto de Historia Natural (Chiapas, Mexico), Lincoln Park Zoo (Chicago, IL), Louisiana Department of Wildlife and Fisheries, Mississippi Department of Wildlife Conservation, Natures Images (Beachwood, NJ), Nature Images (West Palm Beach, FL), New York Zoological Society/Bronx Zoo (Bronx, NY), North Carolina Division of Wildlife Management, Oklahoma Department of Wildlife Conservation, San Diego Zoological Society, Solar Development (SDI) Inc. (Riviera Beach, FL), The Solar Man, Inc. (Palm Beach Gardens, FL), South Carolina Wildlife and Marine Resources Department, Tennessee Valley Authority, Texas Parks and Wildlife Department, TFH Publications (Neptune, NJ) and the United States Fish and Wildlife Service of the U.S. Department of the Interior.

Thanks are also necessary to Steve Coz, General Articles Editor at the *National Enquirer* for demonstrating that if you need more information just ask for it.

My herpetological friend of some 35 years, Steve Weinkselbaum, helped to locate numerous hard-to-find references. Special thanks also to

Susan Johnson for typing the manuscript and Rose Clark for typing the bibliography.

My early interest in herpetology was inadvertently encouraged by my father, the late Dr. Arthur Grenard. The late Dr. James A. Oliver also fostered that interest and I will always be grateful to him. My mentor at New York University Medical Center, Abe Kaiman, introduced me to the world of human therapeutic hypothermia that was inspired by the American alligator's uncanny abilities to withstand near freezing temperatures. The fact that his name is "kaiman" may or may not be a coincidence.

I wish also to thank my son Kevin for his patience, his understanding and his sacrifices so that this project could be completed. For their unrelenting faith and understanding as well, all the good folks at Krieger Publishing stand out as second to none.

Although this book could not have been completed without the cooperation of so many people, the ultimate responsibility for any errors or omissions remains mine and mine alone.

STEVE GRENARD

Jupiter, Florida

Introduction

Crocodilians arose at the same time dinosaurs ruled the earth—during the Mesozoic Era or Age of Reptiles—so one can't be interested in dinosaurs without also being curious about crocodilians and vice-versa. In fact, who's to say crocodilians are not dinosaurs? Most of the dinosaurs disappeared as a result of a fairly well-documented mass extinction that occurred around the end of the Mesozoic era (Cretaceous period) some 65 million years ago. Crocodilians, however, miraculously survived this extinction, and about two dozen species remain today. How they survived has occupied the minds of naturalists, biologists, zoologists, geologists, and paleontologists ever since fossils were discovered and their significance appreciated. There are almost as many theories regarding the cause of this mass extinction as there are scientists who put them forward. Some say the earth got too hot, others too cold. Others blame huge celestial bodies like comets or giant meteors whereas some researchers say even slight changes in climate or alterations in the food chain were enough to insure the demise of the ruling reptiles. However, this book is about living crocodilians, and it will in no way contribute to that debate.

Alligators, crocodiles, caimans, and gharials are renewable natural resources that are currently being managed by wildlife experts throughout the world in order to prevent their extinction—an extinction that for many species has already occurred in some areas and has become precariously close to reality in others within the last few decades.

Properly managed, farmed and, yes, hunted with realistic controls, these animals will not only go on to serve their environment but mankind as well. Captive breeding, collection, and artificial incubation of wild eggs, captive rearing of hatchlings, stocking of "farms," restocking of natural habitats, and closely monitored, limited open hunting seasons with size and bag limits all form the basis of modern successful crocodilian management programs.

When such programs are given the opportunity (financial and legal resources) to be implemented, crocodilian populations will grow. With that growth they then can be harvested and their valuable leather used to support local economies and their sweet, white tender meat can be an important source of protein-based nutrition for indigenous peoples. Without these management programs they will continue to be hunted to extinction, causing yet another important natural resource to be banished from the face of the earth.

The plan of this book consists of five sections. The first is a general information section followed by three sections representing the crocodilian subfamilies. Each species is accorded its own account based on the latest information available. In some cases this information may be decades old or almost nonexistent. In other cases, such as in the American alligator, a vast amount of recent information is available. In fact the American alligator is probably the most studied crocodilian on earth. The reason is that it is one of the most populous species at present second only to the Spectacled caiman in terms of sheer numbers. It is also one of the most accessible under field conditions. Many species exist in difficult habitats where field naturalists either don't wish or cannot afford to go. Other species remain in such small numbers (*e.g.*, Chinese alligator and Cuban crocodile) that meaningful studies cannot take place, and in some areas of southeast Asia and South America, decades of war, political unrest and the drug trade have made field studies an extremely dangerous occupation at best.

The final section is an extensive but by no means complete bibliography. It includes cited as well as non-cited references so that it may be used as a resource for readers interested in going beyond the boundaries of this book.

PART ONE
GENERAL INFORMATION

Nomenclature and Classification

Zoologists classify all animals by a system originally devised by the Swedish botanist and physician, Carl Linne, whose name has since been Latinized to "Carolus Linnaeus" (1707–1778). While Linne laid down the basic principles by which plants and animals are classified and named, it was Darwin and his supporters who determined that all animals and plants evolved from common ancestors. These principles led people who classify plants and animals (taxonomists) to group them on the basis of their phylogeny or similar characteristics. However such relationships are not always clear and are often subject to debate and a difference of opinion among taxonomists studying these relationships. The field of genetics with its advanced techniques involving the "fingerprinting" of DNA may or may not alter these classifications and, this new science may settle, once and for all, some disputes that exist to the present day.

About 100 years before Linne, Caspar Bauhin in Switzerland and John Ray in England began to classify animals and plants using their system which is called the "binomial system of nomenclature," a system still employed which provides, at the very least, that all animals and plants have two names, a first name and a second name. They also chose Latin as the language in which all species are officially named.

The scientific names of crocodiles and their spelling follow the international rules as agreed upon by the International Commission of Zoological Nomenclature and are obligatory for all publications. The first name of a species is its genus, which is a Latin or Latinized noun and is always singular and capitalized. The second part of the name is the species name. A species may be named after the first person to obtain and recognize a new species, where the type specimen was found (e.g., *Gavialis gangeticus* is named for the Ganges River), or some other distinguishing factor. The species name always is spelled starting with a lower case character. If a subspecies exists, its name follows third and also begins with a lower-case character. Following the scientific name of the animal, another name appears together with a date. This is the name of the person, usually a scientist, who *first* published a scientific description of the species and gave it its scientific name. If that name is in parentheses, it means that the original name has been changed. It is important to point out that the discoverer of a new species is not usually the scientist who was first to recognize it as such or describe it in print. If the discoverer also happens to be the person to first publish the description, he would not name it after himself but would find some other person or factor to name the species. Frequently the first person to collect or obtain a new species is unknown or the name is lost in history or mired in controversy. In such cases the describer may look for Latin words which describe the species or its geographic locale.

The alligators and crocodiles are classified as follows:

KINGDOM: Animal
   SUBKINGDOM: Metazoa
      PHYLUM: Chordata
         SUBPHYLUM: Vertebrata
            CLASS: Reptilia
               SUBCLASS: Archosauria
                  ORDER: Crocodylia
                     SUBORDER: Eusuchia
                        FAMILY: Crocodylidae
                           SUBFAMILY: Alligatorinae
                              GENUS: *Alligator*
                                        Caiman
                                        Melanosuchus
                                        Paleosuchus
                           SUBFAMILY: Crocodylinae
                              GENUS: *Crocodylus*
                                        Osteolaemus
                           SUBFAMILY: Tomistominae
                              GENUS: *Tomistoma*
                           SUBFAMILY: Gavialinae
                              GENUS: Gavialis

This classification constantly changes so one may expect to see variations in other publications.

Common or nonscientific names are based on geographic locations, anatomic features such as color or size, habitat, the discoverer's name, or a host of other factors which may in some way describe the animal. In foreign languages crocodilians are known by names in those languages, and these do not always translate into the English version. Regardless of an animal's common name, the important thing to remember is that it has *ONE AND ONLY ONE* scientific name. This system enables scientists to communicate with each other regarding a species and avoids the confusion that would ultimately result if it were otherwise.

Population Status: CITES and IUCN Definitions

The status of the crocodilians is based on one of two appendices (I and II) of CITES, an acronym for the *C*onvention of *I*nternational *T*rade in *E*ndangered *S*pecies of Wild Fauna and Flora. In addition, the IUCN (*I*nternational *U*nion for *C*onservation of *N*ature and Natural Resources) issues a publication known as the "Red Book" which delineates the following definitions used herein:

1. *EXTINCT*: Species not definitely located in the wild during the past 50 years. This criterion is used by CITES.

2. *ENDANGERED*: Species in danger of extinction and whose survival is unlikely if the causal factors continue operating. Species included in this category are those whose numbers have been so radically reduced that they are believed to be in immediate danger of extinction. Included in this category are species which may already be extinct but which have definitely been observed in the wild within the past 50 years.

3. *VULNERABLE*: Includes species likely to move into the ENDANGERED category in the near future if the reasons for vulnerability continue to operate. This category includes species of which most or all populations are decreasing because of exploitation, extensive destruction of habitat, or other environmental problems such as encroachment by man. Also includes species whose populations have been seriously depleted and whose ultimate security has not been assured, as well as species whose populations are still abundant but are under threat from adverse conditions throughout their range.

4. *RARE*: Species with small populations that are not at present considered either ENDANGERED or VULNERABLE but are at risk. These species are usually confined to a restricted geographical area or habitat as well as those which may be thinly scattered over a more extensive range.

5. *INDETERMINATE*: Species known to be ENDANGERED, VULNERABLE or RARE but where there is insufficient data to determine which category is most appropriate.

6. *OUT OF DANGER*: Species formerly included in one of the above categories but which are now considered relatively safe because of effective conservation measures or where a previous threat to their survival has been removed.

7. *INSUFFICIENTLY KNOWN*: Species that do not definitely belong to any of the above categories because of lack of data.

5

PART 1   GENERAL INFORMATION

CITES—APPENDIX I. Shall include all species threatened with extinction which are or may be affected by trade. Trade in specimens of Appendix I species must be made subject to particularly strict regulation in order not to endanger further their survival and must only be authorized in exceptional circumstances.

CITES—APPENDIX II. Shall include

(a) all species which, although not necessarily now threatened with extinction, may become so unless trade in specimens of such species is subject to strict regulation in order to avoid utilization incompatible with their survival and

(b) other species which must be subject to regulation in order that trade in specimens of certain species referred to in subparagraph (a) may be brought under effective control.

(Note: The concept embodied in subparagraph (b) involves protection of species that are not threatened by extinction but which, because of similarity of appearance to threatened species, make it difficult or impossible for government officials to determine which species are being commercially traded. These species are said to be threatened owing to their similarity to species which are not threatened. Unfortunately, to the untrained eye crocodilians appear superficially similar.)

Integumentary System

The skin of crocodilians serves as a barrier or armor protecting the inner tissues and organs from external elements. It plays an important role in defense and camouflage. It consists of an outer layer or epidermis made of a hard, horny material called keratin. The scales are thickenings of this keratin and are interconnected by hinges of a thinner layer of tissue. Some crocodilian scales may appear to overlap, but for the most part they are distinct structures that form part of a continuous epidermal sheet. They are not separate structures like fish scales.

The inner layer or dermis consists of connective tissue and is traversed by blood vessels and nerves. In crocodilians this layer contains small plates of bone called osteoderms which lie beneath and reinforce the horny epidermal scales.

Crocodilian scales are not periodically shed and replaced as in snakes and lizards. They grow slowly as the animal grows and are replaced gradually as they're worn.

The value of the hide or skin represents the primary reason crocodilians are so severely endangered. The hides of most species are in strong demand to make leather goods such as shoes, boots, handbags, and wallets. The dorsal or back hide of crocodilians is heavily cornified and lies above bony plates and generally is not used for leather. The sides and abdomen, however, are much more supple, and it is these parts of the hide that are commonly used for leather goods. The exceptions are two species of *Caiman* and four species of the subfamily Crocodylinae that have bony plates lying beneath their bellies or ventral scales. These are impossible to remove without forming blemishes during the curing process—although recent technical advances have made this less of a problem than in the past.

The number of scales and their arrangement are used as distinguishing characteristics with the postoccipital and nuchal scales being of most importance. The postoccipital scales are on the dorsal surface at the base of the skull and the nuchal scales are located on the nape of the neck immediately after the postoccipital scales.

The last dorsal scale ends at the posterior margin of the upper thigh of the hind leg. The scales on the tail are similar to those on the back. The tail also has a comb or double-rowed crest of triangular scales vertically along the top, which merge about midway down to form a single fused row of crests. In most species there is a comb-like set of scales on the feet as well.

While the epidermis of most reptiles is devoid of any glands and pores, crocodilians possess a pair of glands on the underside of the jaw and a pair of glands in the cloaca, which emit a musky odor. It is believed, but it has not been definitely proven, that the glands under the jaw are somehow involved in the salt balance,[1] given the penchant for some species to occupy brackish and saltwater environments. The glands near the cloaca excrete a musky substance that is believed to be involved in either mating or defense or both. Johnson and Wellington (1982) say yearlings in the lab clearly respond to scent from adult male cloacal glands.

The armored skin on the head is stretched tight and fused firmly over the skull, which makes a sturdy head and protects it during battle with large prey.

The American alligator, which had become severely depleted by 1970 because of hunting for its hide, has weakly developed abdominal osteoderms which are not linked by joints so that it is especially easy to remove them during processing without leaving any blemishes.

Brazaitis (1987) indicates the following characteristic scale shapes which occur at different parts of the body:

1. Dorsal scales. These are square or rectangular and nearly always ossified. They usually have a well-defined ridge or keel.

---

[1]The glands involved in salt balance are located at the base of the tongue. All species including species living exclusively in fresh water have the jaw glands.

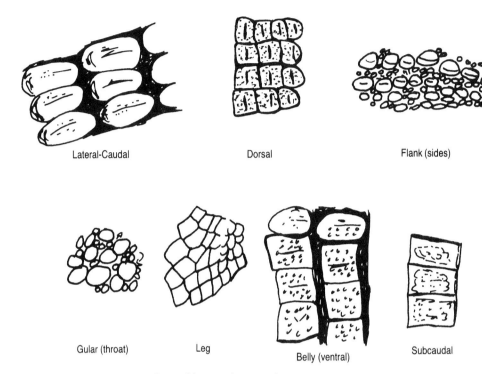

Crocodilian scale types (*after Brazaitis*).

2. Flank scales. The skin of the sides or flank is usually composed of finely creased, soft epidermis bearing a few randomly situated, ovate, or nearly rounded scales. This area may also consist of oval, round, or rectangular scales that may be either keeled or un-keeled. Flank scales may be arranged in either regular or irregular patterns or rows.

3. Gular scales. These are round or ovate scales found on the sides of the throat or under the chin (e.g., snout) extending to the collar region, where they become known as collar scales at the point of attachment to the front leg.

4. Leg scales. These are diamond-shaped scales usually arranged in oblique rows.

5. Lateral-Caudal scales. These scales are found along the sides of the tail and are rectilinear with rounded corners. They are keeled.

6. Sub-Caudal scales. These are the scales found on the ventral or belly-side of the tail. They are smooth (unkeeled) and rectangular.

7. Double-Caudal Verticils. These scales are found on the dorsal surface of the tail between the beginning of the tail at roughly the point of the thighs and extend about halfway down the length of

the tail at which point they fuse and become known as single caudal verticils. These scales form the comb or crest of the tail described previously.

8. Ventral (belly) scales. The belly scales are usually square along the ventral mid-line and are arranged in transverse rows. The ventral scales together with the scales of the flank are the parts of the hide used in making leather goods provided they are not backed by structures known as bony osteoderms.

9. Nuchal scales. These scales, also known as "bucklers" or "plates," are large, almost square scales, the number and arrangement of which varies from one species to the next.

10. Postoccipital scales. These scales lie anteriorly to the nuchals at the base of the skull. They are ovate in shape and their number and arrangement also varies between species.

Crocodilian skin contains pigment cells or chromatophores which are responsible for coloration. While some reptiles such as the chameleons can change color rapidly (metachrosis), crocodilians may alter their

Albino American alligator juvenile (*Courtesy Audubon Zoological Gardens, New Orleans*).

skin coloration in a much less rapid and dramatic fashion. At least one species has been shown, over a period of years, to completely change its adult coloration. In addition the juveniles of several species have colors and patterns which differ markedly from their adult counterparts.

Skin pigmentation varies from light charcoal to brown to olive-green to almost completely black. Belly and lateral scales tend to be lighter, ranging from "off-white" to light brown to various shades of tan. Many species have transverse bands of coloration which are prominent in juveniles but tend to become indistinct in adults. Albinos are known to occur but are extremely rare.

Brazaitis (1987) further indicates that the skin of species from Crocodylinae and Gavialinae can be separated from that of the Alligatorinae on the basis of structures called integumentary sense organs (ISOs). ISOs are absent from all members of the subfamily Alligatorinae (except on the head) whereas they are present among species in the subfamilies Crocodylinae and Gavialinae. ISOs are best seen from the posterior part of nearly

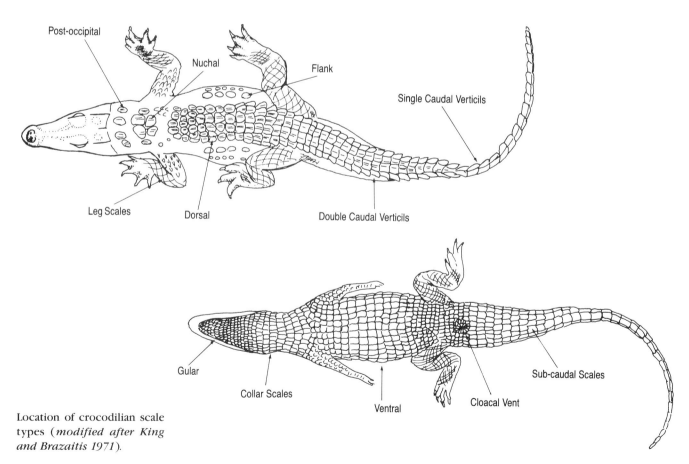

Location of crocodilian scale types (*modified after King and Brazaitis 1971*).

all body scales. However they are most easily visualized on the belly scales, all of which contain at least one ISO although some may contain two or three.

Brazaitis (pers. comm. 1989) says that the role of the ISO is not completely understood but because they contain nerve endings, it is apparent they serve some sensory purpose related to either the tactile senses or the perception of subsonic or underwater vibrations. Some crocodilians produce subsonic sounds by vibrating their sides in the water and ISOs may be the organs used by crocodilians to detect these vibrations.

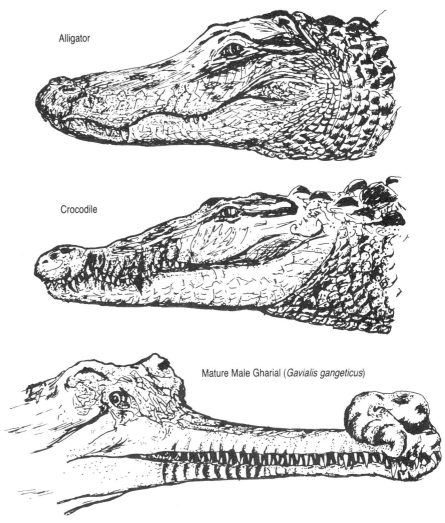

Crocodilian snout types. *Top:* Alligator. *Center:* Crocodile. *Bottom:* Mature male gharial (*Gavialis gangeticus*).

Musculo-Skeletal System

According to Romer (1976) the crocodilian skull is diapsid, meaning it has two openings in the temporal region. The upper opening is smaller and nearly fused whereas the lower opening is larger and forms a trough in which the auditory apparatus is sited. The nostrils lie on the front of the snout set within a bony orifice. These nares can be closed by folds of skin when the animal submerges. A long nasal passage follows the length of the snout from the nostrils to their posterior openings or choanae which open at the rear of the palate. These choanae can also be sealed by muscular flaps in the mouth which permit crocodilians to open their mouths underwater without flooding their respiratory tracts.

Crocodilians have a secondary palate framed by the premaxillary, palatine, and pterygoid bones of the skull. It forms a shelf the length of the snout. They are the first animals on the evolutionary scale to have a complete palate, separating nasal and oral cavities.

The vertebral column is divided into five sections: 9 cervical vertebrae, 12 dorsal (thoraco-abdominal) vertebrae, 3 sacral vertebrae, and some 32 to 42 caudal vertebrae. Each vertebra is convex on its posterior surface and articulates with another by what resembles a ball-and-socket joint. Neill (1971) says that this arrangement affords crocodilians maximum

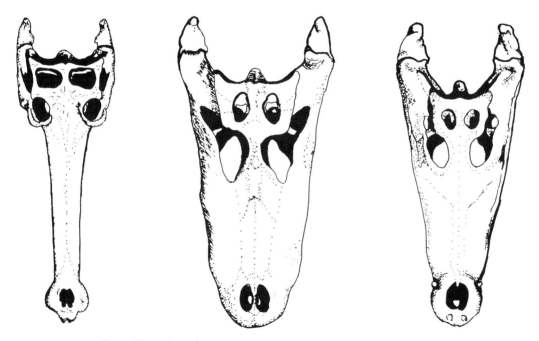

Crocodilian skull shapes. *Left:* Gharial. *Center:* Alligator. *Right:* Crocodile.

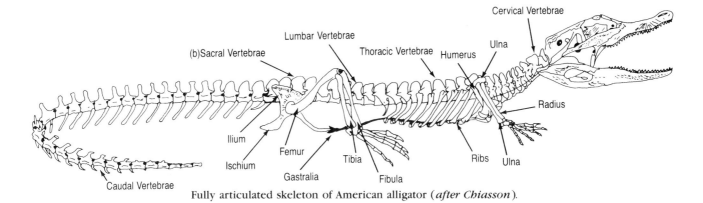

Fully articulated skeleton of American alligator (*after Chiasson*).

flexibility, especially in the tail. It is the serpentine motion of the oar-like tail that enables crocodilians to propel themselves in the water.

Crocodilians have eight pairs of true ribs and an additional eight pairs of floating abdominal ribs or gastralia.

The pelvic girdle has a short ilium, a narrow pubis, and a short, wide ischium.

The front limbs attach to the pectoral girdle which is analogous to the shoulder and collar bones of man. The pectoral girdle consists of paired bones known as the coracoid, procoracoid, clavicle, and scapula. Attached to these are two single elements, the sternum and interclavicle. The bones of the limbs are also analogous to those of mammals. The front limbs consist of a long bone known as the humerus and two shorter bones that work in harmony but anatomically oppose each other—the radius and the ulna. The bones of the front feet include the carpals, metacarpals, and phalanges or toes. The rear limbs consist of the thigh bone or femur, plus tibia and fibula which also oppose each other. The bones of the rear feet are known as the tarsals, metatarsals, and phalanges.

Young wild crocodilians contain very little adipose or fat tissue under their armored hides. Fat tissue is not widely distributed but occurs at specific sites such as at the base of the tail. It occurs on the thighs and bellies as the animal gets older. Crocodilians rank among the most muscular and powerful of the reptiles.

Crocodilians possess a number of tiny, specialized muscles which serve to retract the eyes deep into their orbital sockets—a protective mechanism that goes into action if anything touches the surface of the eyes. In close combat with other animals, the eyes represent a point of vulnerability, so they've evolved this unique way of taking the eyes out of action when appropriately stimulated to do so. Even when not touched directly, the eyes may recede as the animal snaps or bites.

Other small specialized muscles help crocodilians lead their amphib-

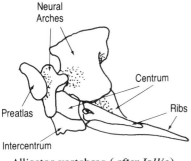

Alligator vertebrae (*after Jollie*).

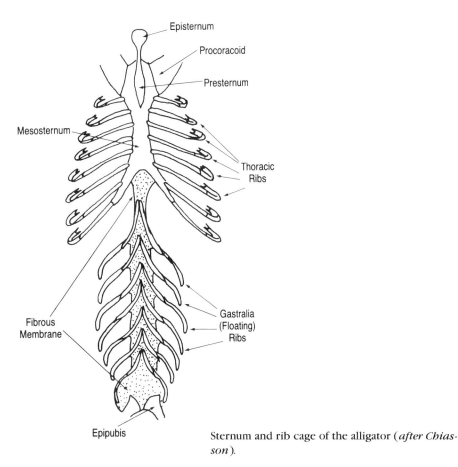

Sternum and rib cage of the alligator (*after Chiasson*).

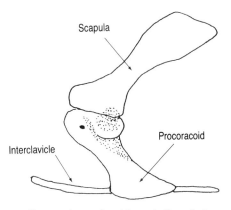

Pectoral or shoulder girdle of the American alligator (*after Jollie*).

ious existence by closing the external nares or nostrils as well as the internal nares or nasal choanae. They can further prevent the trachea and respiratory tract from flooding while underwater by sealing the trachea with the gular fold or glottis.

Specialized muscles work their nictitating membranes or semitransparent eyelids, also put into action when submerged, and special muscles even close off their ear drums to prevent water from entering the auditory canal.

Muscles are described and named by their points of origin, insertion, and function. The nerves which operate the various muscles become a key part of their description.

Locomotion

Given their heavy bodies, the limbs of crocodilians appear relatively small and seemingly useless. With the exception of the gharial, however, this is

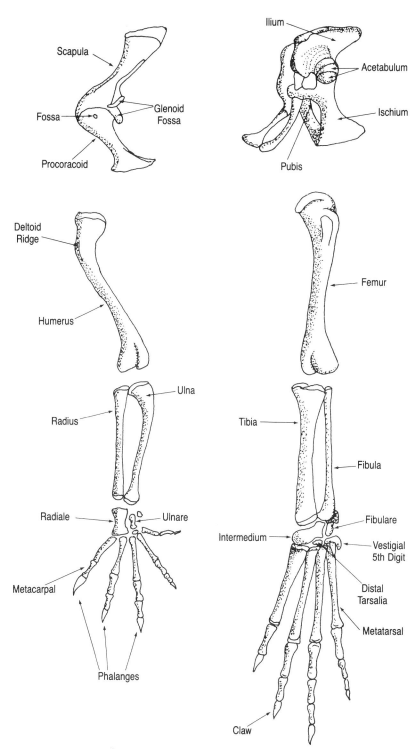

Pectoral (*left*) and pelvic (*right*) girdles with front and hind limbs of the American alligator (*after Chiasson*).

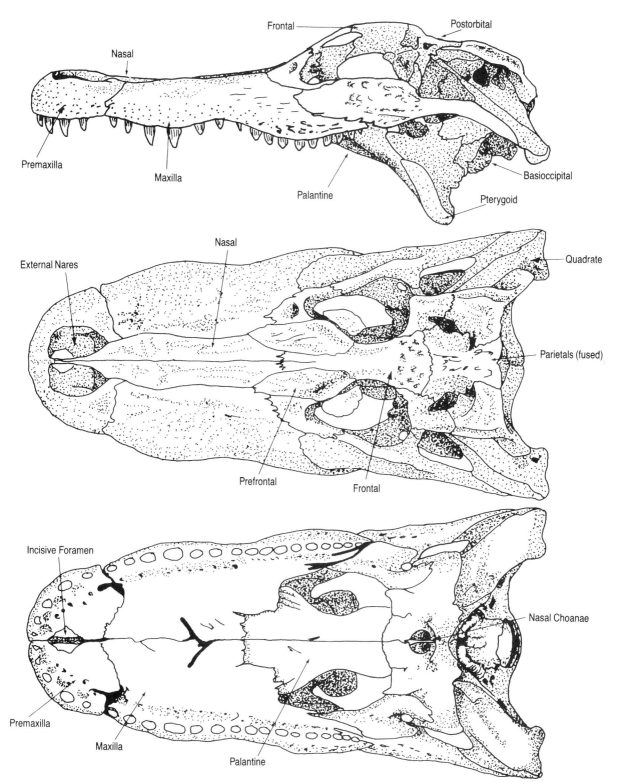

American alligator skull. *Top:* Lateral view. *Center:* Dorsal view. *Bottom:* Ventral view (*after Jollie*).

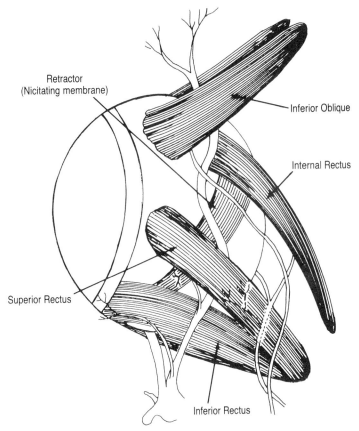

Retractor
(Nicitating membrane)

Inferior Oblique

Internal Rectus

Superior Rectus

Inferior Rectus

Crocodilian eye muscles (*after Chiasson*)

not the case. They not only can swim effortlessly in the water but are capable of a wide variety of effective gaits on land as well.

The hind feet have four toes that are webbed; the inner three toes of the hind foot are heavily clawed as well. The front feet have five toes and are smaller than the hind limbs.

Crocodilians have deep sockets in their thigh bones which serve to articulate the rear limbs. Bakker (1986) points out that crocodilian feet have a "bent-hinge" joint which not only allows a fair amount of forward flexing but enables rotational ability as well.

An extensive analysis of locomotion in crocodilians has been performed by Lewis (1985) while spending over a thousand hours observing three pair-sets of captive juvenile caimans. Lewis catalogued the following modes of locomotion:

1. Belly-run-dive
2. Belly-run-leap-dive
3. High-walk-run-dive

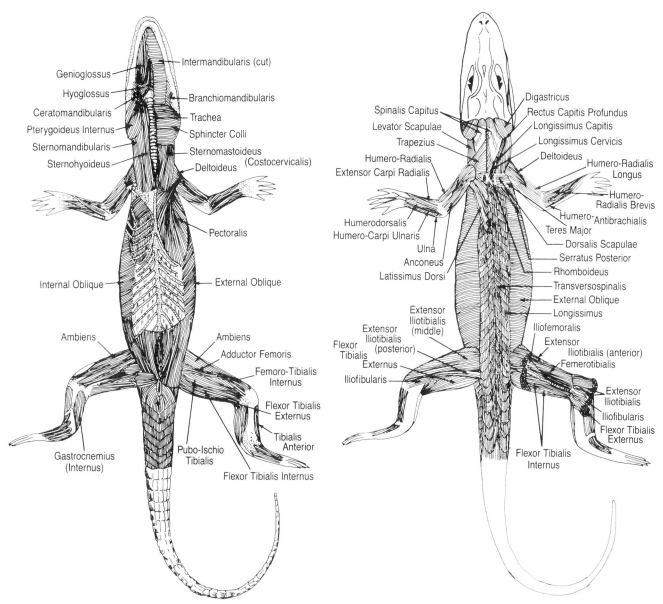

Surface musculature. *Left:* Ventral view. *Right:* Dorsal view (*after Chiasson*).

4. High-walk-jump-dive
5. Surface patrolling
6. Quadrupedal-bottom-walk with horizontal float and tail movements
7. Bipedal-bottom-walk-with horizontal float and tail movements
8. Sinking
9. Surface-dive, head-first
10. Aquatic-leap

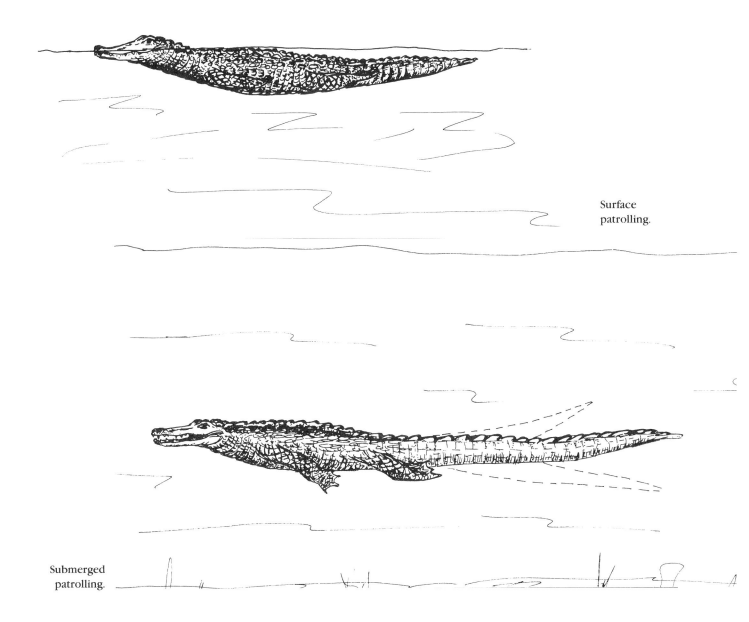

Surface
patrolling.

Submerged
patrolling.

11. Submerged patrolling
12. Surface-torpedo-swimming
13. Submerged-torpedo-swimming
14. Hauling-out
15. Bipedal-bottom-walking with horizontal float and limb paddling
16. Surface-over-the-shoulder-dive
17. Casual-high walk
18. Belly sprint with rapid serpentine tail movements
19. Terrestrial bipedal-stand without support

19

Submerged "torpedo" swimming.

20. High-walk with lateral head movements
21. Bail-out with head thrown back
22. Obstacle climbing
23. High walk-freeze-high walk
24. Belly-slide with limbs tucked

Crocodilians are normally quadrupeds—that is, they walk on all fours, but unless you've seen it, it is hard to imagine any crocodilian leaping into the air and standing on the two hind legs. Yet they do engage in momentary bipedal stances primarily while leaping or jumping to capture prey either from the water or on land. In the water, they have been observed floating in a sort of semi-bipedal stance with the hind legs walking on the bottom and the front half of the body and limbs off the ground. The support provided by surrounding water enables crocodilians to engage in bipedal bottom walking for extended periods whereas such a gait on land is limited to a few seconds, using the tail and front legs to achieve balance.

When swimming rapidly, crocodilians hold their legs tucked in at their sides and move torpedo fashion using the serpentine movement of their tails to propel themselves. When stopped in water they use their feet to doggy paddle. Crocodilians also float in the water with their tails and part of their bodies angled downward, leaving the nostrils, eyes, and ears at just above surface level.

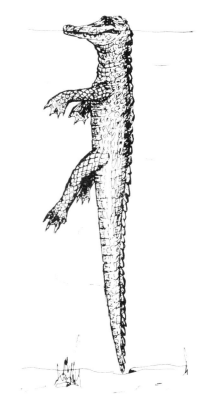

Vertical (bipedal) surface patrolling with limb paddling.

20

Top: High walk with lateral head movements. *Center:* Belly run. *Bottom:* High walk—Freeze.

While their home is clearly the water and they are most efficient there, most species of crocodilians can be surprisingly agile on land and almost as effective in prey capture as in the water, especially when the element of surprise is on their side. Crocodilians will literally jump or leap out of the water and grab prey on the embankment and then drag it back in. On land crocodilians can run or gallop quite fast but only in sprints or bursts of speed, so an animal or person capable of any endurance at all can usually outrun a hungry or angry crocodilian. But if one gets too close, too curious, or doesn't see the animal, then the crocodilian can inflict considerable damage.

Of all crocodilians, the gharial is least effective on land and hauls itself out of the water only to bask, build its nest, and lay its eggs. Its limbs are

Rapid sprint or gallop during which some crocodilians have been clocked at speeds of up to 26 mph (42 km/h).

exceedingly weak, and on land it must resort to sliding around on its belly as high-walking and running are impossible.

Urogenital System

As in other reptiles and birds, crocodilians possess a multipurpose structure called the cloaca which serves as the terminus for the intestinal, urinary, and genital systems. The cloacal vent is a vertical slit-like opening located on the ventral surface at about the level of the hind legs.

Crocodilians of both sexes excrete urine and feces through the cloaca. Females use it as a receptacle by which they engage in copulation with the males. Sperm is introduced into the female cloaca via an erectile penis. The

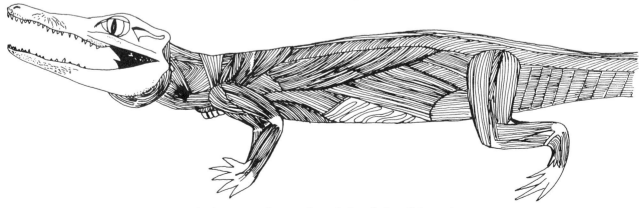

Surface musculature—lateral view (*after Chiasson*).

Quadripedal bottom walking with horizontal float and tail movements. Note: mouth open but no water enters respiratory tract due to nasal and glottic closures.

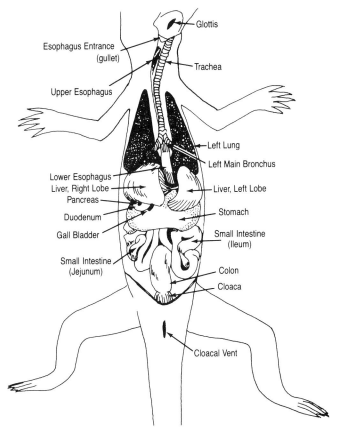

Visceral organs—ventral view (*after Chiasson*).

male is also able to retract the penis which is then housed within his cloaca. The male's sperm is carried from the testes into the penis through the Wolffian ducts or vas deferens. Once fertilized, the female's eggs are passed out of the body via oviducts through her cloacal vent as well.

Crocodilians have no urinary bladder, so urine is excreted whenever it is formed. Urine is formed by a pair of advanced kidneys known as metanephros. These organs are remarkably adept at conserving water and producing a relatively small volume of urinary liquid for excretion. Nitrogen-based wastes are excreted primarily as uric acid rather than as urea and ammonia. Since uric acid is not very soluble and only small amounts of water are excreted, the urine of crocodilians often appears as a white, semisolid paste which consists largely of this substance. Crocodilian urine closely resembles the excrement passed by birds.

Reproduction

Male crocodilians have a single, undivided penis with which they engage in true sexual intercourse. The male reproductive organs also consist of a pair of testes which are suspended internally. In the female, paired ovaries

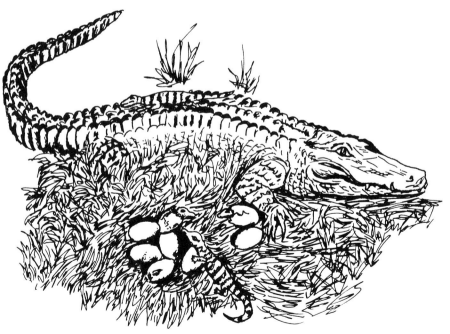

American alligator at nest opening.

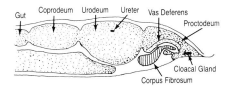

Sagittal section of the crocodilian single, undivided penis (*after Ihle et al. in Jollie*).

produce anywhere from as few as 20 to as many as 90 eggs per season in some species. Fertilization occurs in the oviducts after which the eggs develop shells and are passed out of the female into the nest through the cloaca. As a rule female crocodilians mate only once per year. The female Mugger or Indian Marsh Crocodile may mate twice a year. Courtship goes on for hours and even days whereas mating and intercourse are usually completed in minutes. A single clutch of eggs depletes the female of calcium, lipids, and proteins and in most species recovery to normal levels can take as long as a year. However, males of many species are not monogamous and may mate with more than one female per season given the opportunity to do so.

The mating and reproductive process commences with the onset of warmer weather in areas with seasonal temperature variations. In tropical climates mating may be timed to allow the eggs to hatch just before or after the onset of the rainy season so that the young arrive during times of high water. Specific reproductive patterns are considered under each species account and vary considerably.

Following courtship, mating, and copulation, the male usually departs and leaves the female alone to prepare her nest, lay her eggs, and tend her nest and young. In some cases males have been observed getting involved in the defense and care of the nest and young. Some species build elaborate mound nests whereas others simply deposit their clutch in hole nests excavated for the purpose.

Crocodilians are oviparous, reproducing by means of amniotic eggs incubated outside the body. Unlike the aquatic eggs of fish and amphibians, reptile eggs are not jellylike, are fertilized internally, and are encased in shells composed of fibers laid out at right angles. In addition the shells of crocodilian eggs are reinforced by calcium which renders them especially tough. These sturdy containers serve to protect the eggs during their early development and prevent a host of insects, fungi, and bacteria from damaging them. They also provide at least temporary protection against short bouts of dehydration or flooding.

Crocodilian eggs initially contain albumen, yolk, and a small mass of embryonic tissue which is located toward the top of the egg. As development of the egg progresses within the oviduct, water is drawn from the albumen and is secreted below the embryo onto the internal surface of a structure called the vitelline membrane which surrounds the yolk and embryo. The developing crocodilian embryo is surrounded by a number of membranous structures. The amnion is a fluid filled shock absorber. The chorion acts as a lung enabling some gas exchange to occur, and closely allied to it is the allantois which serves as a receptacle for metabolic wastes. Yolk and the albumen provide nutrition to the embryo, an arrangement identical to that of the birds according to Astheimer et al. (1989).

According to Ferguson (1985), it is irrelevant which way crocodilian eggs are laid because the embryos within always wind up oriented atop the upper surface of the yolk which is where they should be to develop normally. If a crocodilian egg is turned after the embryo has attached itself to the yolk while still young (2nd to 10th day), the embryo remains attached to the yolk but now is beneath rather than atop it. It will drown in the yolk and die. Studies by Webb et al. (1987) indicate that rotation of crocodilian eggs occurring after the first 24 hours but before the respiratory and excretory functions of the chorion and allantois are adequately developed (about the 13th day) will result in embryonic death. Rotation of older eggs (15+ days) appears to be safe. The critical period when eggs should not be handled or rotated appears to be between days 1 and 15. The implications of these findings are obvious for field workers who collect crocodilian eggs for hatching in the laboratory. Each egg should be marked as to its top before being removed from its nest and maintained top-side-up.

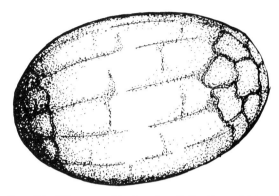

Egg of the Nile crocodile showing distinctive webbing pattern prior to hatching.

Eggs of American alligator. (*Photo by Raymond L. Ditmars; courtesy of American Museum of Natural History*)

As incubation proceeds, acids produced by the bacteria inside the nest start a process of eating away the tough crocodilian egg shell. Pits begin to form in the outer calcium reinforced layer, making the eggs somewhat porous. Ultimately this process exposes the inner shell layer which appears almost honeycomb or web-like. Tiny channels form in this layer which permit respiration to take place between the now almost fully developed fetus and its outside environment. The almost totally eroded shell also facilitates unaided hatching which is otherwise impossible given the construction of the crocodilian egg when it is first laid. In fact, if shell erosion is incomplete, the juvenile will die in its shell unless it is helped to hatch by the female. Many species of female crocodilians have been observed assisting not only in the opening of the nest but in the cracking open of the shells as well. Since eggs incubated in the laboratory are not easily supplied with bacteria which erode the outer shell, such eggs must be opened by the lab staff attending the eggs. When the juvenile is ready to emerge, it loudly emits a "distress" call or vocalization from within the shell which can be clearly heard outside the nest.

Juveniles emerge from their eggs as fully formed versions of the adult except for size and obviously sexual development. In some species both color and color patterns differ between juveniles and adults. Hatching alligators are black and off-white but change to black and yellowish within several days.

The time it takes for eggs to incubate and hatch is indirectly related to environmental temperature and its direct effect on the egg chamber (incubation) temperature. In areas where average temperatures are higher, the eggs incubate more rapidly and hatch sooner than in cooler locales. Incubation times, in general, range from 40 to 90 days or more. Average incubation times for individual species are given in the species accounts.

It has been well established that the sex of newborn crocodilians is not dependent on inherited chromosomes but rather on incubation temperatures. Eggs incubated at higher temperatures are predominantly male; in fact, if the temperature inside the nest remains at least 93° F, more than 75% of the hatchlings are male, but more females are born over a greater range of average temperatures compared to males. It would appear that the sex of the developing crocodilian is determined sometime between the 7th and 35th day.

Ferguson and Joanen (1983) made an exhaustive study of this relationship in the American alligator. They concluded:

1. Alligator sex is determined by the time of hatching and is irreversible.
2. Alligators do not appear to produce sex chromosomes, a fact which precludes any genetic determination of offspring sex.

Captive baby alligators being assisted from shell at Gatorland Zoo, Kissimmee, Florida (*Courtesy Florida Department of Commerce, Division of Tourism*).

3. The sex of alligator offspring is determined by egg incubation temperature: 30°C (86°F) or below produces females and 34°C (93°F) or above produces males.

4. The temperature sensitive period for sex determination is between 7 and 21 days for eggs at 30°C and between 28 and 35 days for eggs at 34°C.

5. Nests constructed on levees tend to be hotter than those built on wet marsh. Levee-sited nests produce 100% males whereas wet marsh nests produce 100% females. Dry marsh nests have more intermediate average temperature profiles so that the hottest part

(top) of the nest produces all males and lower, cooler levels produce females.

Working at the Rockefeller Wildlife Refuge in Louisiana, Ferguson and Joanen also found that female hatchlings outnumbered males by a ratio of 5 to 1. They also determined that females hatching from eggs incubated at 30°C weigh more than males hatching from eggs incubated at 34°C, the reason being that the females incubated at the cooler temperatures tend to absorb more abdominal yolk just prior to hatching. These extra energy reserves enable such females to grow faster and become sexually mature ahead of animals with lighter birth weights. Ultimately, male crocodilians outgrow females, and mature males are longer and weigh more than females of the same age.

Recent research has confirmed that hormone controls prepare crocodilians for reproduction. Other cues that regulate reproductive cycles include day length, rainfall as well as physiological cycles which, over millenia, have improved the chances for reproductive success, and to some extent, the survival rate of hatchlings.

The evolution of seasonal reproductive controls include the timing of adequate food supplies, the availability of appropriate nest sites, ambient temperatures, rainfall and times of low predation risk. These factors coincide with hormonal cycles and become total reproductive control systems which over time tend to coincide with the optimal time and place for reproduction. These are called *ultimate factors*.

Proximate factors are external occurrences that actually induce the onset of reproductive behaviors. These include the correct habitat, ritualized displays such as touching, unusual movements, calling, aggressive displays toward intruders and social stimulation.

For crocodilians it is clearly rainfall that most often defines the breeding seasons in the tropical and neotropical regions. Tropical nesting seasons also may last longer than those in more temperate climates.

Growth and Development

Although it is difficult to generalize, many surveys reveal that up to 90% of newborn or juvenile crocodilians may not survive their first year. Of this number some 50% may not hatch, and of those that do, an additional 40% die as a result of predation by large birds, turtles, fish, carnivorous mammals as well as from pathogenic bacteria, viruses, and parasites. Juveniles occupy a "micro-habitat" or niche distinct from their adult counterparts, and this plus a number of other behaviors, including holing and the use of distress calls, helps some animals survive.

Note: Other effects of higher incubation temperatures

The size of the hatchling is smaller at higher temperatures but there is more abdominal yolk present (Lang *et al.* 1989).

Alligators incubated at intermediate temperatures (30.6°C/31.7°C) grow faster than those incubated at higher or lower temperature extremes.

The color pattern in the American alligator also differs at different incubation temperatures. Hatchlings incubated at 33°C are darker and have less surface area covered by whitish/yellowish crossbands compared to hatchlings incubated at 33°C (Deeming and Ferguson, 1989).

The thermal preferences of juvenile Siamese crocodiles studied by Lang (1987) seemed to be affected by incubation temperature. Males from eggs incubated at 32.5 to 33°C selected higher temperatures.

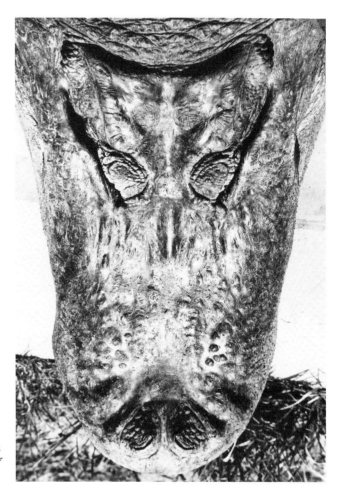

Alligator snout, dorsal view shows flattened duckbill configuration seen in longterm captives. (*Courtesy of Florida Department of Commerce, Division of Tourism*)

Growth continues throughout the life span of all crocodilians. The fastest rate of linear growth occurs during the first two years and declines with age thereafter. Averages for the first five years indicate that most species grow at a rate of between 12 and 18 inches per annum. And while weight increases with length, weight as a percentage of length goes up with age. While linear growth slows down, the crocodilian does not stop adding pounds; in other words, although they are not getting very much longer, they continue to add pounds and get fatter.

Bony epiphyses are secondary centers of ossification commonly found at the end of long bones and on the margins of flat bones. During periods of growth, epiphyses are separated from the main portion of bone by cartilage. They provide a structural boundary beyond which growth can no longer occur. Crocodilian bones do not have epiphyses, and it is believed this is one reason that linear growth continues, although quite slowly, until the animal dies.

Sexual maturity is dependent on size, and it is related to age only insofar as age accompanies growth. Therefore, it is possible for animals of the same size but of different ages to both be sexually mature, and it is possible for a smaller animal not to be sexually mature even though it is the same age as a larger animal.

Growth in captivity depends on an abundance of proper food, optimal ambient temperatures, and sufficient space. If any one of these factors is deficient, then growth in captivity will be retarded. Under ideal conditions captive growth may equal or even exceed noncaptive growth rates.

Arguments over the longest and heaviest crocodilians occur regularly. Tales of exceptionally long or heavy animals tend to be exaggerated like the well known "one that got away" fish story. The oldest known captive specimen was an American alligator that lived in captivity for 56 years. It is doubtful that any crocodilians in the wild could exceed this record given the perils they must face. In addition, crocodilians, even the largest species (*C. porosus*), rarely exceed 20 feet in length, so stories of animals 25 or 30 feet in length are rather doubtful and at best may be unintentional or excited exaggerations. Insofar as weight is concerned, even the largest animals rarely exceed 2,000 pounds, and specimens averaging around 10 to 12 feet usually weigh between 500 and 600 pounds. The maximum sizes given in the species accounts by no means represent the average maximum size, but rather represent all-time world records that have been set down in writing, and in some cases have been verified by the *Guinness Book of World Records*. These animals are exceptions rather than the rule.

Although females may grow faster than males or at the same rate as males during the first five years of life, eventually males outgrow them.

The accelerated growth and development of captive or farm born and raised crocodilians is of special concern to crocodilian farming enterprises for reasons related to financial return. The more quickly animals can be raised to market-ready size, the faster the turnover will be. The financial incentive is coupled with the need to make room for each year's hatch.

The state of Florida is home to a number of such operations and Foster Farms, Inc., in Okeechobee County is a prime example. It is a 165 acre alligator breeding and rearing facility. It has about 55 acres of breeding pens which contain 660 breeding *Alligator mississippiensis*.

Eggs are collected from the pens between May and July and incubated for 60 to 65 days. Hatchlings are nursery reared for the first 10 months, reaching a length of about 24 inches and are then moved to the main raising buildings for the next 10 to 22 months. Within 30 months the alligators reach a length of about 50–60 inches.

The nursery and rearing buildings consist of seven concrete block and prestressed structures with a total area of 32,000 square feet. At any one time they house about 8,000 animals in various stages of development. The buildings are maintained at 89°F year round. At the present time there are two systems used for controlling the temperature. The first is an in-slab heating system which consists of zoned hot water pipes connected to circulation pumps activated by heat sensors in the water. The hot water source is a propane fired boiler. The second system is the washdown and refill water. To insure against thermal shock, which may not only affect growth rate but actually kill some alligators, the buildings are cleaned and filled five days a week using 78,000 gallons of 89°F water each filling day. This system is also heated by a propane boiler.

However, the expense of maintaining a fossil-fuel based temperature controlling system cuts deeply into the profitability of such operations. The cost of raising animals to market size is increased considerably and if market prices for hides and meat do not reflect these increased costs many such farms sustain losses or are marginally profitable at best.

The advantage of being in Florida is that there is considerable environmental heat, but it is not year round, and for three to four months each year even in the more southern parts of the state the temperature drops below optimal feeding levels needed by crocodilians as well as other ectotherms. This temperature imposed fasting period diminishes growth rate and delays the time it takes to bring animals to market. But by providing year round optimal temperatures and maintaining the animals in darkened enclosures, continued, uninterrupted growth can be achieved. The reason for keeping the animals in the dark is related to their feeding patterns in nature. Alligators are normally active at night and this is their usual feeding time although they will feed in daylight given the opportunity. During the day their preferred activity is to bask in the sun, raising their body temperatures which enhances the digestion and metabolism of the evening meal.

The key problem facing Foster Farms and similar operations is how to maintain the alligators at constant optimal temperatures irrespective of ambient temperatures and to do so with as little investment in fossil-fuel generated energy as possible. The answer has been provided by Solar Development, Inc. (SDI) of Riviera Beach, Florida which, based on technical applications developed by the TVA, has designed what is known as a "shallow solar pond" solar energy system to meet alligator temperature requirements.

A 20,000 square foot shallow solar pond system was installed at a textile plant in Georgia at a cost of $11 per square foot. The unit was capable of providing up to 241,000 BTUs per square foot per year and is capable of producing about 200,000 gallons of hot water daily. The plant's savings in coal amounted to an estimated $18,700 per annum as of 1986. This example

Above: Shallow solar energy ponds as seen from within. Black rubber bags hold the water under a roof of corrugated fiberglass. *Below:* Solar-energy ponds as seen from the outside. (*Courtesy Tennessee Valley Authority*).

would pay for itself in about 11 years but other variables including the amount of water needed, the temperature to which it must be heated and the cost of fossil fuel energy at other localities may improve substantially on the cost savings determined for this example. In Florida, fossil fuels and nuclear energy are particularly expensive but solar energy is plentiful. The use of solar energy for alligator farming should be especially profitable, even over the short term.

Digestive System and Feeding

Crocodilians are carnivorous or meat-eating predators that find their
meals both by preying on live animals as well as by consuming dead
organisms or carrion. As predators, they're most successful by using the
element of surprise to their advantage. While appearing to be asleep or
drifting aimlessly along in the water, crocodilians will suddenly lunge for a
bird, fish, turtle, frog, or even a mammal drinking from the shore. This
practice is known as opportunistic feeding. Crocodilians will also stalk
their prey although most stalking is done underwater.

The diet of crocodilians is as varied as the parts of the world they
inhabit. Crocodilians occasionally ingest vegetation but only accidentally
when foraging among water plants for prey that may be hiding.

Aquatic leap and jaw clamp. Graham (*1973*), observing Nile crocodile, noted they would startle a school of fish, which would disperse.
The crocodile gave a wriggle of its tail and thrust its body completely out of the water and then landed among the fish, confusing them
further and then snapping them up in a frenzy.

Jaw clamp toss and throw. Neil (*1971*) observed an American alligator, attacking a cottonmouth moccasin, by biting on it several times, between which it was tossed around several times before it was eaten.

Crocodilians stop feeding at temperature extremes. Optimal feeding temperatures lie between 25°C and 35°C. As temperatures go below these optimal ranges, crocodilians become increasingly inactive and they become stressed as temperatures go above them. Consequently, crocodilians in some geographic locales may spend a considerable portion of each year without feeding at all. It has been estimated that crocodilians can go for as long as a year, if necessary, without food.

The digestive tract of crocodilians begins with their fearsome jaws—jaws which University of Florida experts have determined can snap shut exerting pressures of 1,300 pounds per square inch. This pressure is sufficient to break the limbs or even the neck of large prey, thus disabling or killing the intended victim. Crocodilian jaws can effortlessly crack open the hardest turtle shell in much the same way a human might bite open the tender shell of a peanut.

All crocodilians have what is called "thecodont" dentition and evolved from a group of prehistoric animals known as thecodonts. Theca in Latin means pouch. The teeth of crocodilians are set but not rooted, in pouches or sockets called alveoli. As they are worn, broken, or lost, new teeth grow in. Aged crocodilians may, however, permanently loose teeth. Crocodilian teeth are strong, cylindrical-conical structures angled both horizontally and vertically. They are suitable for grasping and tearing but are incapable of chewing or grinding down food.

Quadrupedal bottom-stand-lunge and open jaw clamp. Once the fish swim within range, the submerged crocodilian lunges forward, with jaws snapping (*Graham and Beard, 1973*).

Terrestrial swallowing.

After tearing a piece of flesh down to manageable bits, crocodilians swallow them whole. Crocodilians have been observed feeding by wedging killed prey or large carcasses of carrion between tree trunks, roots, or rocks along embankments and then tearing them apart—an intelligent and amazing behavior bordering on a primitive form of tool use. The rocks and roots are used as vise grips to hold the prey steady so chunks of meat can be torn off without the meal being thrashed about.

Appetite in crocodilians depends on the availability of heat. To maximize and improve digestion, an animal that has just fed will seek warmer temperatures to help speed up the digestion and metabolism of the meal.

Alligator, partially submerged with head in complete vertical thrust. This posture is used to obtain the benefit of gravity in order to swallow (*Courtesy of Florida Department of Commerce, Division of Tourism*).

Below 22°C, the American alligator will not eat, and some species will regurgitate a meal rather than digest it if heat does not become available.

Swallowing is accomplished by angling the food in the mouth and then lifting or raising the snout so that the head is almost in a vertical line with the esophagus. The tongue has no role in manipulating or pushing the food rearward since it is firmly fixed to the floor of the mouth and is capable of very little motion. It serves primarily as a taste sense organ and contains glands that in some species are involved in salt excretion.

As the food is swallowed, it passes through the gullet or esophagus—a long, muscular tube that terminates in a two-compartmented stomach, which is discussed below.

Adult crocodilians can eat up to 20% of their body weight in a single meal which may take 3 to 7 days to consume and completely digest. If the stomach becomes full, crocodilians may continue to eat, storing food in the esophagus until room is available for it to pass on through the gastrointestinal tract. After the food has been thoroughly processed and digested, the fecal matter remaining is passed out of the body through the intestines and exits via the cloaca.

In his book *The Dinosaur Heresies* (1986), Robert T. Bakker gives the following intriguing account of the crocodilian gizzard which is formed out of the fundal portion of the crocodilian's compartmented stomach.

> A white mouse sacrificed to a hungering alligator posthumously provides a most important clue. The bones of the mouse show up quite clearly in the alligator's stomach on the laboratory's television X-ray monitor. But the mouse's bones are not alone. The alligator's after-stomach is lined with hard, dense objects—gizzard stones. The gizzard stones[1] are convulsed by sudden muscular contractions of the gizzard's walls. The monitor clearly show the mouse is being chewed, not by teeth in the mouth but by stones in the gizzard.
>
> Naturalists who study big 'gators and crocs in the wild find huge masses of gizzard stones when they cut open the animals to study their feeding habits. The stones are found only in one chamber of the stomach—the gizzard—and this one chamber has walls with grooves and folds to permit expansion and contraction. Even without X-ray monitoring, it is obvious that this stomach chamber is a churning compartment designed to crush and pulp the prey's body after the gastric juices begin their preliminary chemical treatment. Crocs usually select very hard stones—quartz and granite pebbles, for example—to line their gizzards. If such materials are lacking in their native streams, they may use angular bits of hard wood, pieces of glass bottles, or whatever else is available. I have also seen one or two near-perfect fossil alligator skeletons containing a neat bundle of hard

---

[1]Technically known as gastroliths.

Semicircular body corral. Crocodilians may create a corral with their bodies to trap and consume fish (*Graham and Beard, 1973; Guggisberg, 1972*).

pebbles clustered between the ribs precisely where the gizzard was in life. These fossilized gastric mills demonstrate plainly that gizzard stones have been an essential functional component of crocodilian food processing for many millions of years. And the study of crocodilian gizzards leads to some intriguing conclusions about evolution both in birds and in the Dinosauria.

Zoos mislead their visitors by the way these species are housed. Birds are in the Bird House, of course, and crocodiles are always segregated to the Reptile House with the other naked-skinned, scale-covered brutes. So the average visitor leaves the zoo firmly persuaded that crocodilians are reptiles while birds are an entirely different group defined by "unreptilian" characteristics—feathers and flight. But a turkey's body and a croc's body laid out on a lab bench would present startling evidence of how wrong the zoos are once the two stomachs were cut into. The anatomy of their gizzards is strong evidence that crocodilians and birds are closely related and should be housed together in zoological classification, if not in zoo buildings.

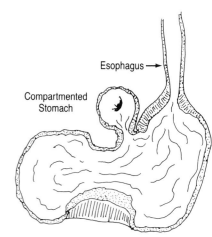

Crocodilian stomach, frontal section (*after Chiasson*).

High walk, freeze and arched lunge. Crocodilians may seize prey such as birds fluttering close to the ground by arching their backs and lunging.

Prey capture: tail strike.

Both birds and crocs have the identical plan to their specialized gizzard apparatus, and this type of internal food processor is absent in the other reptiles—lizards, snakes, and turtles. In both birds and crocs, the gizzard is a thick-walled, muscular crushing compartment with two great tendons reinforcing the walls of muscle (these are shiny sheets of tough tissue you cut off the turkey gizzard before cooking it). In both birds and crocs, the muscular gizzard is just aft of the thin-walled glandular stomach where food is softened by gastric juices.

Since both birds and crocodiles swallow their food without chewing it, this digestive system arrangement makes a lot of sense. Whether this element of the anatomy justifies the grouping of crocodilians as a member

Incipient bipedal stance and jaw clamp to neck of prey. The Nile crocodile has been observed by Guggisberg (*1972*) engaging in this atypical terrestrial means of attack against a donkey.

39

of the Class Aves or Birds is a matter for considerable conjecture. However, crocodilians share many characteristics with other reptiles as well as with the birds.

According to Coulson and Hernandez (1964) crocodilians experience extreme shifts in plasma pH levels on an almost daily basis. When excited or stressed, pH levels drop precipitously, often to levels incompatible with life in other species (e.g., below 7). However, the ingestion of food matter in crocodilians produces a profound alkalemia with pH levels reaching 7.8 to 8 but with no apparent ill effects. Predictably such high pH levels would cause involuntary wavelike muscular contractions called fasiculations, tetany, muscle spasms, irritability, and twitching. In humans, pH levels this high often result in convulsions and potentially fatal cardiac arrhythmias such as ventricular fibrillation.

The alkalemia seen in crocodilians in association with food ingestion is attributed to the production of highly concentrated hydrochloric acid in the stomach. In order for the stomach to produce such large amounts of concentrated HCl, Cl shifts from the plasma NaCl, leaving a large store of

Jaw clamp and bashing. Graham (*1973*) reported a 9-foot Nile crocodile which seized a large fish in the water, came ashore with the animal still struggling in its mouth and then began to bash it on the ground until it was unconscious or dead.

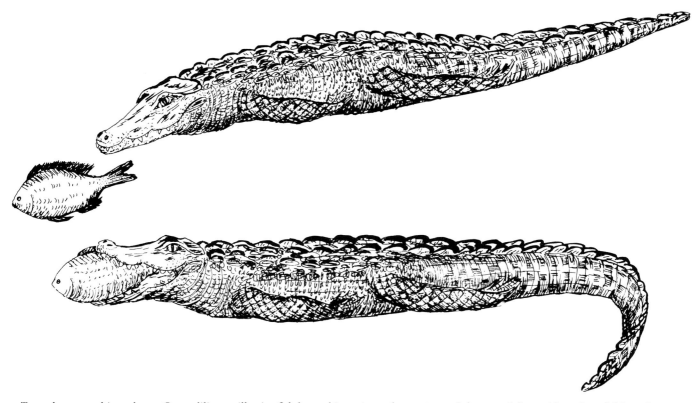

Torpedo run and jaw clamp. Crocodilians will seize fish by making a torpedo run toward the prey followed by a forceful jaw clamp (*Guggisberg, 1972*).

Head jaw clamp and drowning. Prey drinking at water's edge are seized by the head and dragged underwater until it drowns or ceases to struggle (*Guggisberg, 1972*).

Jaw clamp, pull into water. Once the prey is down, crocodilians may clamp their jaws over the head of the animal to drag it into the water.

sodium (Na) to react with plasma carbonic acid (metabolically produced CO_2 in water or H_2CO_3). The sodium (Na) and H_2CO_3 react to form a base, sodium bicarbonate ($NaHCO_3$) in excessive amounts, thus producing what Coulson and Hernandez refer to as the "alkaline tide," and exaggerated to an exceptionally high degree.

Circulatory System

Crocodilians are the only reptiles with a four-chambered heart and separate pulmonary and systemic circulations. Deoxygenated blood is returned from the systemic venous circulation to the right side of the heart. It is received by the right atrium and flows into the right ventricle, which than propels it to the lungs where it releases excess carbon dioxide and absorbs oxygen from the inspired air. From the lungs the oxygenated blood is returned to the left atrium and flows into the left ventricle, which then pumps it into the systemic arterial circulation. Crocodilian heart rates are

Crocodilians are able to swing their heads in a 60° arc.

Foraging behavior: lateral head turn and turn away.

Snout rub, speculative hunting. Neil (*1971*) says alligators may forage by approaching potential prey, swinging the head so that one side of the snout contacts the substratum. Neil believes sense organs on the sides of the snout help it identify prey. Florida American alligators usually forgo snapping at the Florida red-bellied turtle (*C. nelsoni*) because it is unable to crack its very tough shell.

Underwater to surface, seize and drag under. A crocodilian observing prey from below, quickly ascends toward surface, seizes prey by limb and drags it under to drown (*Guggisberg, 1972*).

slow—beating 24–45 times per minute at 28°; 15–16 times per minute at 18°C and only 5 to 8 times per minute at 10°C.

When deoxygenated venous blood is allowed to mix with freshly oxygenated blood, this results in an event known as venous admixture. Venous blood, which is deoxygenated, still has oxygen left in it, but it is roughly 25% to 30% less saturated with oxygen compared to oxygenated arterial blood. When deoxygenated venous blood mixes with oxygenated arterial blood, the volume of oxygen in the oxygenated blood diminishes somewhat by virtue of its dilution with the deoxygenated blood.

In endothermic birds and mammals, including humans, small amounts

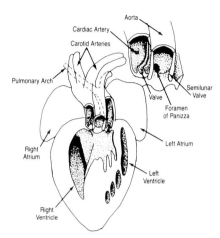

The crocodilian heart (*after Jollie*). There is a complete separation of right and left atria and ventricles. The only connection between the two sides of the heart is through the foramen of Panizza which connects the right and left aortic trunks. The most peculiar feature is that the left aortic and pulmonary trunks leave the right chamber of the heart, while the right aortic trunk, bearing the carotid arches, comes from the left chamber (*Jollie, 1972*).

of venous admixture can be tolerated, but increased amounts are disabling and ultimately fatal. In ectotherms, the metabolism can be more readily adjusted to the presence of deoxygenated blood, which is present in the systemic arterial circulation as a consequence of the three-chambered heart arrangement in amphibians and all reptiles except for crocodilians. The existence of a four-chambered heart in crocodilians, from an evolutionary standpoint, may be one of the predisposing conditions required for endothermy.

In the three-chambered hearts of amphibians, there are two atria and one ventricle. The right atrium receives blood from the venous circulation from where it then flows into the one and only ventricle where a fraction of the volume is then pumped to lungs, gills or epithelial mucosa and epidermis for gas exchange. The left atrium receives the reoxygenated blood from the gills, lungs, and skin from where it flows into the same ventricle where a fraction of the blood therein is pumped into the systemic arterial circulation. The blood in the ventricle at any one time may be considered a mixture of oxygenated and deoxygenated blood.

Crocodilians have four fully formed heart chambers, but there is a small window (foramen of Panizza) located between the aortic blood vessels or arterial outflow tracts. This opening may permit venous admixture, and its operation depends on the pressure in left ventricle. Blood will flow through the opening from the area of higher pressure to the area of lower pressure. While the animal is breathing then, the chamber is effectively open because the left ventricular pressure is higher than the right ventricular pressure. A small amount of oxygenated blood may leak from left to right, but this is of no consequence. However when the animal is submerged, the pressure in the lungs from the air trapped within retards the flow of blood through the pulmonary capillary bed, a condition called pulmonary hypertension. This pressure is transmitted back through the pulmonary circulation all the way to the right heart. When the animal is submerged, the right ventricular pressure is increased. Crocodilians can remain submerged by engaging in anaerobic metabolism, and by remaining very inactive they can tolerate this lack of oxygen for various lengths of time. In most adult crocodilians such times can last as long as six hours.[1] When they return to the surface, the pressure in the right ventricle goes down as normal pulmonary ventilation resumes.

The hemodynamics of crocodilian circulation and the functional anatomy of the heart are extremely difficult to assess and are mostly based on dissections and physiological models rather than on in-vivo hemodynamic measurements which would require cardiac catheterization and the direct monitoring of pressures in various parts of the cardiopulmonary system.

[1] R. A. Coulson et al. (1989) reckon that alligators over 200 kgs. can stay submerged to 12 hrs at 28°C and for several days at 7 to 10°C.

45

Alligators submerge with a lung full of air which consists of four gases: oxygen, carbon dioxide, water vapor, and nitrogen. Nitrogen, which is inert and is not involved in gas exchange, represents the largest amount of gas present both by percentage and partial pressure. As the oxygen in the lungs of the submerged animal is used up, it is replaced by carbon dioxide until the lungs have no oxygen and can hold no more carbon dioxide. This ultimately results in declining oxygen levels in the blood accompanied by rising carbon dioxide levels. In addition, increased carbon dioxide levels and declining oxygen levels lower blood pH. Some of this acid is buffered by various systems in the blood, but eventually these too are over-whelmed. What happens next that permits the crocodilian's most prodigious ability to remain submerged is theoretical or based on empirical observations. It is difficult to perform baseline blood chemistries on restrained adult animals on the surface let alone under natural conditions while they are submerged. Also, it is theoretically impossible to perform cardiac catheterizations and the fluoroscopic dye and pressure studies necessary to confirm the exact means by which the animal shunts blood from now almost totally useless lungs to its peripheral circulation. Anatomical studies on the position of the foramen of Panizza indicate that it swings open or closed, depending on point of view, enabling blood from the right heart to enter the outflow tract leading to the descending or abdominal aorta. This diverts blood from the lungs, which are severely or almost totally devoid of oxygen, to the less oxygen sensitive organs such as the liver and stomach. On the other hand, blood returned from the lungs which may still have oxygen in them, is directed to the more oxygen-dependent organs such as the heart and brain. However, no one has quantified the amount of blood shunted away from the lungs, the amount of blood that remains in the pulmonary circulation and left side of the heart, or the means by which the foramen of Panizza becomes functional. In Ross and Garnett (1989), a simplified diagram and accompanying text indicates that while diving, the foramen of Panizza "closes" and by so doing isolates the outflow tract to the descending aorta away from the left side of the heart. This permits unoxygenated blood from the right side of the heart to pass into the lower portion of the systemic arterial circulation which supplies tissues that are more tolerant of decreased oxygen levels.

Respiratory System

Crocodilians are air-breathing animals and possess a pair of well-developed multichambered lungs located in the thoracic cavity. Ventilation of the lungs is accomplished by both voluntary and involuntary muscle

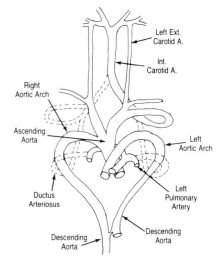

Crocodilian aortic arches (*after Goodrich in Jollie*).

action. The principal ventilatory muscles are the *intercostals* located between the ribs and a large, diaphragm-like muscle that separates the abdomen from the liver and the chest cavity. It is known as the *septum posthepaticum*. By alternately contracting and expanding, these muscles cause a drop in the pressure around the lungs, creating a pressure gradient or difference between the outside air pressure, the intrapulmonary, and the intrathoracic pressures causing air to flow into the lungs until equilibrium is reached. Air can be held in the lungs for prolonged periods by closure of a glottic valve or gular fold, and this is the principal mechanism by which crocodilians can remain submerged for periods of an hour or more. Larger animals are capable of longer breath holds than smaller ones. When the crocodilian returns to the surface, the glottic valve relaxes, and the air in the lungs is expelled as a result of the elastic recoil of the lung tissue. This process is known as passive exhalation.

Crocodilians are perfectly suited for their amphibious existence, and to this end one of their assets is a built-in "snorkel." They can lie in the water, hanging unseen just below the surface with only their slightly elevated nostrils and eyes protruding above the surface. They can close off the mouth, which is underwater, from the entrance to the airways thus preventing any water from entering the lungs. They can rest like this for hours, breathing through their nostrils, without being seen.

An elongated palate, which forms the entire roof of the mouth from the tip of the snout to the gullet, assures the animal that any water taken into the mouth will remain there or be swallowed, but never inhaled. This capability also enables them to swallow prey under water without aspirating water into the lungs. They cannot forcibly spit out water that enters the mouth; some drains by gravity, the rest is swallowed.

The inhaled air traverses a long nasal passage above the palate and exits into the pharynx through two rear openings known as the posterior nasal choanae. From here the air travels down a long windpipe or trachea which divides into the left and right lungs. The plan is similar to that of mammals and functions in the same way.

Blood enters the lungs via the branches of the pulmonary artery pumped by the right ventricle. It then flows into the pulmonary capillary network which carries it to the pulmonary units or alveoli where excess carbon dioxide is expelled and additional oxygen is absorbed. After leaving the alveoli, it is returned to the left side of the heart via the pulmonary veins, and it is then pumped into the systemic arterial circulation.

Seymour et al. (1987) studied the reasons why large crocodilians, on occasion, suddenly die of apparent cardiorespiratory arrest during or immediately after capture. The study measured blood pH and pCO_2 levels and found that during the struggle of capture the pH dropped to such precipitously low levels as to be normally incompatible with life. The normal blood pH of crocodilians falls within the same range as humans, between 7.35 and 7.45. Seymour's study revealed that crocodilians can tolerate remarkably high levels of acidemia or decreased blood pH (pH = 6.6 to 6.8). These levels would kill most vertebrates almost immediately. However, the study revealed that the animals could survive these levels if allowed to recuperate from their struggle. After capture the animals are often quickly tied and bound and dragged behind a boat underwater, and this represents the "straw that breaks the animal's back," pushing the pH to even lower and now certainly intolerable levels of around 6.4 to 6.6 causing the animals to become unconscious and drown.

Further confounding the study of cardiorespiratory dynamics in crocodilians is what is already known in mammals and humans about the effect of cyclic respiration itself on the return of blood to the heart and cardiac output. The late Andre Cournand and co-workers received a Nobel prize for their work on the effect of positive pressure on cardiac output in humans. A crocodilian that dives with its lungs full of air and holds it there against a closed glottis is engaging, in effect, in an event human physiologists call the Valsalva maneuver. It occurs in humans for short periods of time when bearing down during labor and childbirth or during a difficult bowel movement. It serves to raise the intrathoracic pressure (pressure inside the chest wall but outside the lungs) which impedes the blood flow returning to the heart from the systemic venous circulation. At the same time it increases central venous pressure and keeps a fraction of the returning blood away from the right side of the heart and subsequently out of the lungs. As a treatment, this positive pressure is administered (by retarding the exhalation of air from the lungs) to humans suffering from left heart failure and pulmonary edema. Pulmonary edema of cardiac origin occurs because of the failure of the left side of the heart to pump the blood returning from the lungs out to the arterial circulation fast enough. The blood backs up in the pulmonary capillaries and the liquid part spills out into the airspaces (alveoli) of the lungs. In effect this drowns the patient. It would appear that crocodilians expose themselves to their own continuous positive airway pressure whenever they dive. By holding a volume of gas in the lungs constantly while submerged, crocodilians also serve themselves by retarding the flow of blood through the pulmonary capillary bed in addition to preventing the entry of water into the airways and lungs.

If the above factors do not add enough confusion to this subject, then there is another mechanism which may also serve the submerged crocodilian which has been documented in humans. It involves response of the pulmonary capillaries to the presence of hypoxia or lowered oxygen levels. In what is obviously a mechanism meant to also divert blood away from useless lungs, the pulmonary capillaries constrict in the presence of low oxygen levels.

Designing experiments to determine if human responses also occur in crocodilians is not an easy task, and finding the resources and facilities to enable such research may be even more difficult. This discussion is included here only to point out that much more work needs to be done before any thorough understanding of crocodilian underwater physiology can be made.

There is considerable disagreement among observers regarding how long crocodilians can stay submerged. The ability to remain underwater without breathing air depends on size, water and air temperature, the metabolic status of the animal and whether or not it has recently fed. Therefore, no one observation is representative in all situations. In personal communications from field workers in Florida, it has been stated that in particularly cold water some large animals are able to stay submerged, if they haven't eaten recently, as long as 4 to 6 hours. This should be a simple enough area to research, even under laboratory or captive conditions.

As in all vertebrates, the rate and depth of breathing in crocodilians increases with increased metabolism and activity levels and diminishes with lowered metabolic rates and inactivity. At 28°C, at rest, the American alligator breathes at a rate of only 2.5 to 3 breaths per minute.

Other factors concern the wide swings in blood pH of crocodilians which have a profound affect on the affinity of hemoglobin for oxygen, which, in turn, affects the unloading of oxygen to the tissues. A high pH or alklaemia increases the affinity between oxygen and hemoglobin and decreases unloading of oxygen to the tissues. As Coulson and Hernandez (1964) have pointed out, the chief occasion for crocodilian blood pH to increase is during the digestive processing of food matter in the stomach. On the other hand, during times of stress and energy expenditure, many researchers have demonstrated that blood pH decreases. This decreases the affinity between oxygen and hemoglobin and increases the unloading of oxygen to the tissues. The dissociation of oxygen from hemoglobin is also affected by other factors including blood PCO_2 levels, and body, or more accurately, blood temperature levels. A decreased PCO_2 increases hemoglobin-oxygen infinity and decreases dissociation or unloading to the tissues; an increased PCO_2 does the opposite. In the case of temperature, decreased temperatures act like decreased PCO_2 levels and increased temperatures act like increased PCO_2 levels. The implications of these biochemical responses, known as the Haldane and Bohr effects, in terms of crocodilian ability to endure stress or remain submerged, are not clearly understood.

Thermal Regulation

Crocodilians, unlike birds and mammals, are *ectotherms*, which means their temperature is regulated from "outside" the body; environmental conditions dictate crocodilian body temperature although crocodilians and other reptiles selectively engage in behaviors which give them some control over their body temperature. Birds and mammals, on the other hand, are *endotherms*. Their body temperature is regulated internally.

Although *ectothermic* and *endothermic* are the preferred terms, two other sets of terms have been used with respect to thermal regulation. Commonly, birds and mammals are referred to as warm blooded and reptiles, amphibians and fish are called cold-blooded. These common popular terms are not accurate. A crocodilian basking in the sun with a body temperature of 95°F can hardly be called cold blooded. Specialists also disdain the use of two other terms in this respect. Poikilothermic which means "of varying temperature" for reptiles and homeothermic for birds and mammals which means "of constant temperature." While somewhat more accurate than warm and cold-blooded, these terms may *not always be correct*. Crocodilians can maintain remarkably constant body

Crouched, bottom sitting. Crocodilians may lurk submerged in shallow water, ready to lunch, by squatting or crouching like a dog.

temperatures, and birds and mammals can have their body temperatures vary because of fever or extreme environmental hypothermia or hyperthermia.

Crocodilians and other reptiles seek environmental conditions which enable them to have some control over their body temperature and which enable them to maintain favorable temperatures for their activity. Alligators and crocodiles emerge from the water to bask in the sunlight, and in extremely hot weather they can cool their brains and head, at least, by lying for hours with their jaws open. This causes evaporative cooling across their extremely long palate. They can also cool themselves by alternately entering and leaving the water which also produces evaporative cooling, this time to the entire body.

Even under unfavorable temperature conditions, crocodilians can adjust their metabolic rates to stay in tune with prevailing temperatures, so that the relative intensity of metabolism can remain basically unchanged even if temperatures are not ideal. This ability is called temperature compensation. Birds and mammals achieve metabolic homeostasis by internally regulating their body temperature within a narrow range. Reptiles accomplish the same thing by regulating their metabolism internally because they can't do it for their body temperature.

In cold weather, crocodilians will retreat to their subterranean "holes" and lower their basal metabolic rate considerably. If they are unable to deal with prolonged hot spells, they'll do the same thing—enter their holes and become as inactive as possible. While no one has measured the temperatures inside crocodile or alligator holes at various times of the year, it is reasonable to conclude that during cold weather they are warmer than surface conditions whereas in hot weather they're relatively cooler. They are ideal thermo-insulated sanctuaries for crocodilians when climatic conditions at the surface become too severe.

Captive crocodilians should have a range of temperatures available to them (25°–35°C) as they will select the temperature best suited to their needs at any particular time. Thermoregulatory behaviors are well developed almost from the moment hatching occurs. Newly hatched juveniles, those that are feeding, and juveniles with infections all seek higher temperatures (90°F to 93°F) whereas nonfeeding, older juveniles prefer somewhat cooler locales. Exposure to constant temperatures in the 90°'sF results in weight loss unless the animal is able to feed almost constantly. Thermal stress will ultimately kill crocodilians. On the other hand cooler temperatures inhibit feeding and decrease immunity to infectious disease.

Baby crocodilians are gregarious creatures that like to rest piled atop each other. By so doing they may create a somewhat amorphous mass that mimics the heat-conserving abilities of larger single individuals.

Nervous System and the Senses

The crocodilian nervous system, as in all vertebrates, relies primarily on specialized nerve cells or neurons which orchestrate a wide variety of activities including metabolism, senses, locomotion, heart and respiratory function, and complex biochemical reactions and interactions.

The nervous system is divided into two parts: the central nervous system consisting of the brain and spinal chord and the peripheral nervous system consisting of all nerve pathways leading to and from the central nervous system. The autonomic or peripheral nervous system is further divided into sympathetic and parasympathetic branches which serve to oppose each other. If one part causes specific muscles to contract, the other causes them to relax. If one speeds up heart rate, the other slows it down, and so forth.

The main organ of the central nervous system is the brain. It is located within and is protected by a sturdy bony cranial cavity atop the head. In crocodilians the brain weighs not more than 0.8% of the total body weight which compared to higher mammals and man makes it a relatively small brain. The crocodilian brain is divided into five principal parts:

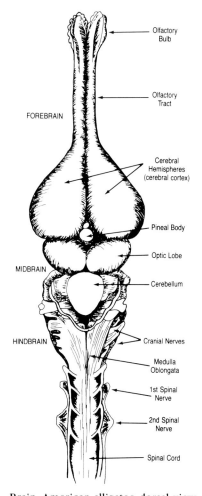

Brain, American alligator, dorsal view.

1. The **forebrain** which consists of the olfactory bulbs—centers for receiving stimuli involved in sensing smell.
2. The **cerebrum** or **cerebral cortex**. Crocodilians are the first animals on the evolutionary tree to have a true cerebral cortex, implying they are capable of conscious thought processes and learning.
3. The **midbrain** which is the site for receptors from the optic nerve responsible for conveying visual stimuli.
4 and 5. The **hindbrain** which consists of the **cerebellum** and **medulla oblongata**. These two areas control vital motor centers and contain nerve endings responsible for hearing senses and equilibrium or balance.

The brain stem leads to a spinal cord which, as in other terrestrial vertebrates, possesses twelve pairs of cranial nerves.

The eyes of crocodilians are suited for both day and night vision. At night they have a large dilated pupil capable of visual acuity in "available" light. In the daytime the pupil constricts to a narrow, vertical slit which modulates or restricts the entry of light. Crocodilians possess yellow, yellowish-green, and in several species, brown irises. Crocodilians demonstrate a sense of vision that enables them to recognize prey on land and in the water, their mates, their young, their nest, their environment, and their enemies. They can see both near and far, and have color vision, but they

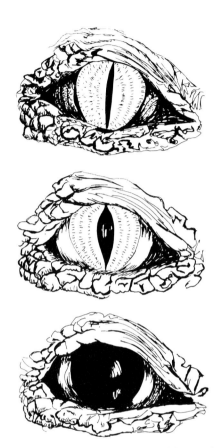

Crocodilians have a vertical slit-like pupil that dilates laterally in darkness. *Top:* Bright light. *Middle:* Moderate light. *Bottom:* Low light.

Crocodilian eye pupils remain vertical with the horizon regardless of head tilt; vision is distorted only when the animal is upside down on its back.

53

have limited depth perception. In air their far vision is better than near; underwater their vision is limited.

At night crocodilian eyes reflect any bright light that is shone at them, including moonlight. This ability is due to presence of a reflective layer in the eye called the *tapetum lucidum*. It lies directly behind the retina and acts as a mirror, causing the eyes to light up at night. The same property can be observed in the eyes of other animals, including domestic dogs and cats. Unfortunately for the crocodilian, it enables poachers to spot them at night by "eye-shine," and in the United States, at least, this method of hunting is generally prohibited except during open seasons. By counting the pairs of eyes, however, wildlife specialists use "eye-shine" to make population counts.

The narrow, vertical pupil of crocodilians is always held at 90° to the horizon, even when the head is tilted. However, should the animal be turned over on its back, the pupil would "see" upside down, and would cause a momentary loss of orientation and confusion probably similar to the sensation known as vertigo.

Thanks to a third transparent eyelid called the nictitating membrane, crocodilians can partially or fully cover their eyes when partially or fully submerged. This membrane acts like built-in diving goggles and enables them to have limited underwater vision.

Many crocodilians are not capable of complete binocular vision (viewing an object with both eyes focusing on it at the same time) because their eyes are set on opposite sides of the head but in some species such as the American alligator the eyes are oriented to permit a slight degree of binocular vision. According to Bellairs (1971), there is at least a 25° binocular overlap in alligators.

Crocodilians have inconspicuous external ears and ear drums which are located just posterior to the eyes on each side of the head. When submerged crocodilians close their ears with special muscles, thus preventing entry of water. Crocodilians do not rely on ear transmitted sound while under water but have the ability to detect sounds primarily in tones of low or even subsonic frequencies on the surface. Crocodilian vocalizations, which are deep, throaty sounds (bellows, roars, moans, grunts) are well within this range.

A single bone, the stapes, conducts sound waves received by the tympanum or ear drum to the inner ear. Underwater sounds and vibrations may be detected by integumentary sense organs located beneath the scales. Such sounds may also be transmitted, though muffled, via the ears.

Orientation toward home is a "sixth sense" that has been documented in a variety of amphibians, reptiles, and higher animals. Tales of dogs and cats that have traveled hundreds—even thousands—of miles from release

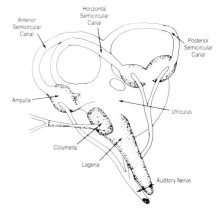

Internal and middle ear (*after Chiasson*)

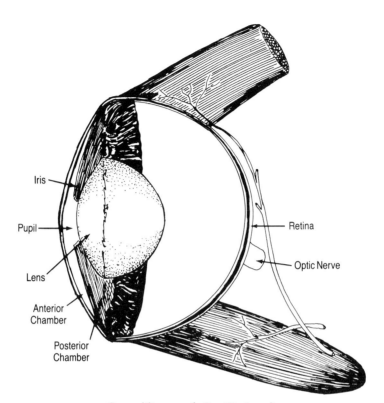

Iris

Pupil

Lens

Anterior
Chamber

Posterior
Chamber

Retina

Optic Nerve

Crocodilian eye (*after Chaisson*).

or loss sites to "back home" have been well documented. Sea turtles, fish and migratory birds travel thousands of miles, returning to the same nesting grounds every year with remarkable precision. Crocodilians also possess this ability although not for as long a distance as birds, fish or sea turtles. Homing has been studied in the American alligator, the Saltwater crocodile, the Spectacled caiman and in the Australian freshwater crocodile. Webb et al. (1983) documented that *C. johnstoni* was capable of homing after being translocated nearly 19 miles upstream. After 15 months, out of a group of 17 translocated animals, 7 were recaptured at the original capture site. One was halfway between the capture and release site. None was found at or near the release site.

Crocodilians may home using solar-compass orientation, navigating by gauging or analyzing the angle of the sun in the sky. Translocations that take place close to the winter dormancy period support this view. As the days grow shorter, animals trying to make their way home will stop and den until sunnier days return. A number of other factors have been documented by Murphy and Coker (1983) with respect to homing:

1. *Distance between capture and release sites*. Longer distances lessen the possibility of successful homing.

2. *Accessibility to capture site.* Open water routes back to capture sites increase the chance of homing success. If routes between the capture and release sites are either nonexistent or have physical or habitat barriers, then the chances of homing success decrease. However, even with such barriers, studies of American alligators show they continue to move toward home (capture site) even a year after being translocated.

3. *Sex.* Adult females return to their homes or capture sites more often and with greater speed and accuracy than males. Subadult males are least likely to return home after translocation.

4. *Size and/or age.* The smaller and younger the animals, the less likely they will try to home and the less likely they will home successfully if they do try.

Human-Crocodilian Relationships

Humans and crocodilians have been interacting since the dawn of civilization. The arena for this early interaction was probably Africa, and Asia. It can be presumed that crocodilians preyed upon humans for food, but as man became a hunter, he stalked the crocodilians and was much more successful.

Descriptions of the Nile crocodile were recorded by the ancient Greeks, and the Romans captured live specimens 50 to 100 years B.C. to exhibit in their menageries in Rome. Nile crocodiles figure prominently in the Bible. Women and children washing clothes in the Nile have been attacked, killed, and eaten by crocodiles dating back thousands of years up to the present day. Wherever and whenever humans meet crocodilians, there is bound to be fear, revulsion, and on occasion injury or death for either the person or the animal. Strangely, there is rarely any "hatred."

Crocodilians, however, have recently been the losers in this interspecies battle. While surviving for tens of millions of years, it has just been within the last hundred years that the few species remaining on earth have been so severely threatened with extinction. The discovery that their hides make prized leather has been the chief cause of this demise. Secondary causes include hunting of the animal for sport and for food (including eggs) and loss of habitat due to human encroachment.

In this century government agencies began keeping records of crocodilian confrontations, attacks, and fatalities. As would be expected, the largest number of such reports involve confrontations which result in no injury, followed by attacks that caused injury including serious injuries such as the loss of a limb, and thirdly by attack which result in human

Miccosukee Indian alligator wrestler, shown here in the difficult job of holding open the jaws of an alligator at a popular Florida tourist attraction (*Courtesy of Florida Department of Commerce, Division of Tourism*).

deaths. Since 1948 there have been a total of 95 recorded unprovoked alligator attacks on people in Florida. Of these, there were only five fatalities. There have been tens of thousands of reported confrontations. In 1988, during a six-month period (January–June) there were three serious attacks by alligators on humans in Florida, one of which resulted in the death of a four-year-old girl in Englewood. According to Hughes (1989) in Northern Australia, Western Australia, and Queensland, between 1975 and 1987 there were 12 fatal attacks by crocodiles on humans.

There are measures people can take to prevent such gruesome confrontations and deaths. These measures have been collected from a variety of wildlife agencies and field experts and represent a consensus. Professional herpetologists called upon to counsel the general public may find the following advice useful.

PART 1   GENERAL INFORMATION

Whether you reside in or are just visiting areas known to be inhabited by crocodilians, the following rules can help keep you safe:

1. Always stay alert, don't use intoxicants, think ahead, try to stay calm, and never panic.
2. If you see a crocodilian, never charge or bluff it.
3. If you're in the water and you see a crocodilian, swim as quietly as possible to shore. If that's not possible, keep calm and stay as motionless and as quiet as possible.
4. Know where small children are AT ALL TIMES; teach them to respect crocodilians. Use pictures or take them to the zoo if necessary to reinforce this teaching. It's reasonable to tell them that the animals they're looking at can hurt them.
5. Keep dogs and cats under close supervision and control. If necessary, leash or cage them on outings or when you reside in areas with crocodilian-occupied waters nearby.
6. Fisherman should keep their bait or strings of fish-catch in covered buckets or chests of ice. Never store fish on a string trailing from the side of your boat, or you may attract an unwanted crocodilian. In Florida most canal fishing occurs from shorelines or off bridges. This is the safest way to fish in such waters. Clean fish well away from the water and dispose of the remains in a covered receptacle.
7. NEVER swim in waters you even suspect may be occupied by crocodilians. Especially don't let children in or even near such waters.
8. If you're out to snap a picture of a crocodilian in the wild, do it from at least 20 feet away. Use a telephoto lens for best results and for close-ups.
9. Never throw anything at a crocodilian unless you're in imminent danger and are using projectiles as weapons. Never hit or prod an alligator with a stick. If you can do this, you're TOO CLOSE. Use a stick only as a weapon, if necessary, to fight off an attack. Don't go looking for a fight.
10. NEVER FEED wild crocodilians. They learn quickly to associate humans with food. They may also come to think of humans as food although this has never been proven. They have been trained to perform in stage acts using a food-based reward system.
11. If confronted by a crocodilian, yield the right of way with as wide a detour as possible. DON'T PROVOKE IT. Back away slowly if the animal is moving toward you. Always keep your eyes firmly fixed

on it. Crocodilians are good sprinters and you may have difficulty outrunning one on land—so always keep a respectable distance.

12. If contact occurs, you can avoid injury or even save your life by holding the animal's jaw shut. Although they can snap their jaws shut with amazing force, crocodilians can't open them with the same degree of power. This is a trick that Florida's Indian tribes must have learned a long time ago and today enables them to wrestle with alligators to the delight of tourists. There are other tricks involved such as turning the animal over on its back to disorient it by distorting its vision—but this is difficult in the field—especially with larger animals (>3 feet).

13. Crocodilians may use their powerful tails as weapons and can knock large prey right off their feet with them, so stay away from this end of the animal. Always try to jump clear from any land confrontation.

14. Although this should be obvious, never chase a crocodilian that's retreating from you even if you feel you have the upper hand. The situation can turn around without warning. That especially includes the admonition NEVER to follow a crocodilian into the water. Your chance of surviving a contact confrontation in the water is far less than on land. Many crocodilians are shy and retiring, but animals develop different personalities under varying circumstances. A female alligator almost never attacks on land except if she perceives a threat to her nest. Exceptionally well-fed animals will never go out of their way to endanger themselves in a confrontation just to get a meal. If they're hungry, that is a different matter. Field workers netting juveniles for tagging experiments have learned that the distress calls emitted by the babies mobilize adults in the area toward their source. Often they have to quickly release the young in order to avoid the risk of attack.

There is no way to reliably predict the results of confrontations in the wild between humans and crocodilians, so the best thing to do is to avoid them.

Commercial alligator farm and tourist attraction at the Everglades Wonder Garders near Clewiston, Florida (*Courtesy of Florida Department of Commerce, Division of Tourism*).

PART TWO

THE SUBFAMILY ALLIGATORINAE
(Cuvier, 1807)

American alligator showing rows of nuchal scales. (*Courtesy Audubon Zoological Gardens, New Orleans*)

Alligators

Alligatorinae is a subfamily of the Class Reptilia, Order Crocodylia (Gmelin, 1789), Family Crocodylidae, consisting of 10 species and sub-species in 4 genera.

Special features: With the mouth closed, only the teeth of the upper jaw are clearly visible. The lower jaw, in the anterior part of the snout, is positioned behind and within the upper jaw teeth relative to the jaw. The fourth lower jaw tooth fits into a depression in the upper jaw and cannot be seen when the mouth is closed.

Two species in genus *Alligator*; six species and subspecies in genus *Caiman*,[1] one species in genus *Melanosuchus*, and two species in genus *Paleosuchus*.

There are only two species in the genus *Alligator*: *Alligator mississippiensis*[2] or the American alligator and *Alligator sinensis* or the Chinese alligator. Alligators differ from caimans and crocodiles because of a flat, broad snout. Alligators have a bony nasal septum whereas caimans do not. In addition there are at most six large cone-shaped nuchal scales on the nape of the neck.

Outside of the breeding season, the sexes occupy different habitats. Males prefer large, open, deep waters whereas females live in smaller, shallow, still waters. Males form breeding territories that are marked by bellowing and head slapping as well as by active physical defense against intruders. The strongest males control the largest territories. A more detailed description of mating is included in the commentary for the American alligator.

Mortality of the juveniles may be as high as 80% to 90% during the first two years. The main predators of juvenile alligators are raccoons,

---

[1]Includes *Caiman crocodilus chiapasius.*
[2]"*Mississippiensis*" was originally spelled by Daudin with only one "p." The American spelling has been approved by the Intl. Comm. Zool. Nomenclature (1985).

Alligator hauling out. (Courtesy of the U.S. Fish and Wildlife Service/by Luther C. Goldman)

otters turtles, birds, and large predatory fish. Such losses occur in spite of maternal protection of the young which usually ends by the second year.

The alligators, both in the United States and China, range quite far north, and freezing winter weather poses special problems. Since crocodilians, including alligators, do not technically hibernate, alligators stay warm in winter by remaining in the water or in burrows deep in the embankments of lakes and rivers they inhabit. By dropping their metabolic rates alligators are able to survive cold weather with little or no food and

Southeast United States—range of the American alligator.

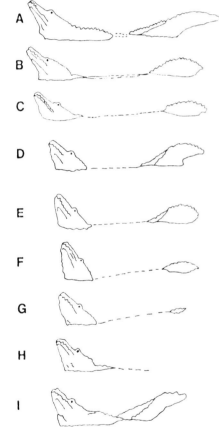

A bellowing cycle of a female alligator. *A, B*: Inhalation with gulp. *C, D*: Pre-exhalation. *E, F*: Exhalation and vocalization. *G*: Post-vocalization. *H, I*: The next inhalation with gulp. Time between events (in seconds): A–B = 1.25, B–C = 1.0, C–D = 2.99, D–E = 0.33, E–F = 1.33, F–G = 1.13, G–H = 0.50, H–I = 2.25; A–I = 10.08. (*Courtesy of the American Museum of Natural History [Garrick, Lang, and Herzog, 1978]*).

with a markedly reduced requirement for oxygen. While this tactic resembles hibernation, it differs from it in one important aspect. Alligators are unable to survive for prolonged periods without any oxygen, so they must surface to obtain air from time to time during their dormant states, and on cold but sunny days they can be observed basking in the sun.

In the wintry freezing cold reaches of its range, American alligators may "overwinter" in the water with their bodies suspended in the water below the ice but with their nostrils protruding through the ice in order to breathe.

The genus Alligator arose 38–26 million years ago in the Oligocene in North America.

American Alligator

SCIENTIFIC NAME: *Alligator mississippiensis* (DAUDIN, 1801–1802)

STATUS: Not threatened, CITES II.

GEOGRAPHIC RANGE: Within the confines of the United States of America as far south as the tip of Florida; northward throughout the coastal plains of Georgia, South and North Carolina; westward to Alabama, Louisiana, Texas; northward to Mississippi, Arkansas, and Oklahoma.

HABITAT: Wetlands including lakes, rivers, streams, canals, swamps, and brackish coastal marshlands.

DIET: A wide variety of aquatic and terrestrial vertebrates and invertebrates are eaten. Juveniles eat large insects and small fish. Adults and subadults will consume any aquatic organism including turtles and snakes as well as terrestrial mammals which forage near water and drink from or swim in alligator inhabited bodies of water. Bird bands that once belonged to nonaquatic birds that probably died and fell into the water are found inside the stomachs of alligators. Such findings indicate that alligators also consume dead animals or carrion.

Comments

The Seminole Indian name for the alligator is "al-a-paw-taw" and the early Spanish explorers first called it "el lagarto" meaning lizard and through usage by English speakers the term was first corrupted to "aligarto" and later to "alligator."

In 1979, through its range in Florida and Louisiana, the alligator was determined to be out of danger as populations began to resume historically high levels. However, they still remain scarce in other states. A state-by-state discussion follows.

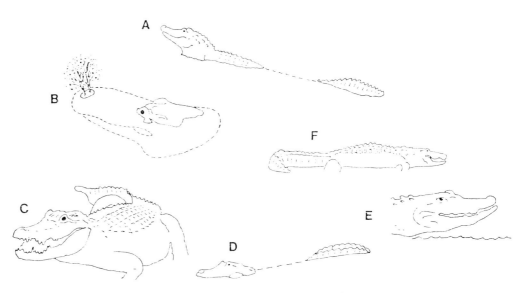

Postures and behaviors of adult alligators. *A*: Bellow growl posture (female). *B*: Narial geysering. *C*: Hiss posture (female at next). *D*: Head emergent tail arches posture. *E*: Snout lifting (female). *F*: Inflated posture (male). (*Courtesy of the American Museum of Natural History [Garrick, Lang, and Herzog, 1978]*).

The record size for the alligator is 19 feet 2 inches but animals over 14 feet are exceedingly rare with average full-grown adult males reaching maximum lengths between 7 and 10 feet. A 14 foot 1 1/16 inch, 714 pound alligator was killed in the Apalachiola River in June, 1989. The heaviest alligator in recent times was taken in April, 1989, near Gainesville. It weighed 1,043 pounds. During the September, 1989 open season, an 800 pound animal was caught near Clewiston, Florida.

The start of the breeding season coincides with the onset of warmer weather; therefore, the time of the year when mating, nest building, and egg laying takes place will vary with geographic location and prevailing climate.

Since the American alligator is found as far north as Arkansas, Oklahoma, northern Mississippi and North Carolina, it will breed later, if at all, in these locales compared to cohorts living in more southern areas. In southernmost Florida the breeding season begins as early as February whereas in the more northern reaches, breeding does not begin until April or May.

Alligator mating and courtship comprise a series of complex ritualistic behaviors which last for hours and are constantly repeated. It is believed that these behaviors help to synchronize spermatogenesis and ovulation.

The first phase of the courtship ritual involves pair formation. For this phase, potential mates of both sexes emit loud bellows and slap their

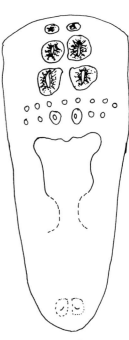

American alligator.

66

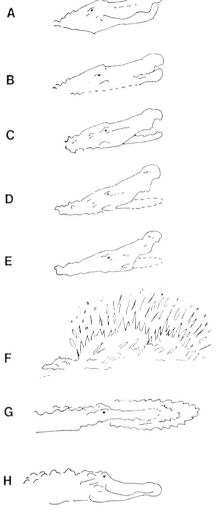

heads on the surface of the water creating a loud clapping sound. After pairs are formed, they fondle each other by rubbing snouts and swimming side-by-side almost touching. They also make cough-like sounds at this point, and either partner may decide not to pursue the other. Breaking off contact is accompanied by a series of loud growls and bellows. The uninterested partner then swims away.

Other mating behaviors include continual making of sounds, snout touching, back-rubbing, blowing of bubbles through nostrils, and circling. Courtship culminates in sexual intercourse, which takes place in the water. A single act of intercourse can last 15 minutes and may be repeated four to five times over a period of two to three days. The male then swims off, leaving the female to prepare the nest, lay her eggs, and protect the clutch.

Female alligators demonstrate elaborate behaviors with respect to nest site selection, construction, maintenance, and protection. Female

Headslap from the resting posture. Time between events (in seconds): A–B = 0.37, B–C = 0.04, C–D = 0.09, D–E = 0.04, E–F = 0.16, F–G = 0.75, G–H = 1.54; A–H = 2.99. (*Courtesy of the American Museum of Natural History [Garrick, Lang, and Herzog, 1978]*).

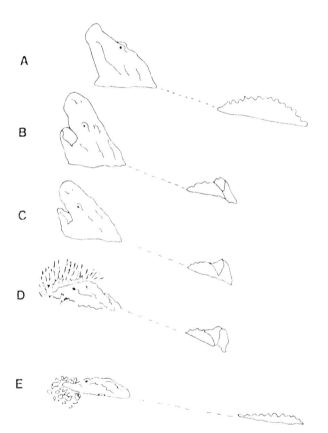

Alligator headslap from head oblique tail arched posture. Time between events (in seconds): A–B = 2.45, B–C = 0.09, C–D = 0.04, D–E = 2.21; A–E = 4.79. Bubbling through the mouth in shown in E. (*Courtesy of the American Museum of Natural History [Garrick, Lang, and Herzog, 1978]*).

crocodilians of other species, and occasionally males in some species, actively defend their nests against predators including man.

Female alligators carefully situate their nests on raised banks or high ground to assure that the eggs are not endangered by subterranean flooding. In laboratory simulations of flooding, alligator eggs were unable to survive immersion in water for more than twelve hours. The female alligator uses water levels to calculate the height of the spot where she builds her nest as well as to determine the elevation of the egg chamber within the nest. Nests are located anywhere from 3 to 18 feet from the water's edge. Occasionally nests are located atop elevated mounds of vegetation and other detritus or debris right in the middle of shallow streams or marshes.

Alligators obtain their nest-building material by crushing vegetation with their bodies or in their jaws. They pick up stalks and leaves in their mouths and carry this material to the nest mound site. After the mound is completed, the female digs a depression into the top of the mound which becomes the egg chamber. It is lined with mud and leaves. The egg chamber is conical. After it is ready, the female lays her clutch at a rate of approximately one egg every 45 seconds. She catches each egg with her hind legs and gradually and carefully lowers it into the egg chamber. She then covers the chamber with a layer of mud and vegetation which she brings to the nest, making six or more trips to gather the covering matter. She then compacts the material with the weight of her body, and it turns out as smooth and as slick as plaster, and nearly as impregnable as well.

The same nests may be used year after year by the same female, and occasionally a female will use the nest of another whether it has been abandoned or not. If not abandoned by the original owner, then two clutches may find their way into one nest.

Female alligators have been observed abandoning a nest in the middle of construction and building another one somewhere else. Whether this is done out of sheer whimsy or some new piece of scientific information regarding flood levels or sun exposure is unknown.

Alligators can complete their nests within a few days, or the process can go on for weeks. As many as a dozen or more trips are made by the female to bring nest-building material to the construction site. Alligator nest mounds measure up to 7 feet in diameter and 3.5 feet high.

The decomposition of the nesting material produces heat, making the nest a self-sustaining incubator which holds the temperature of the developing eggs relatively constant. Even precipitous drops in environmental temperature, especially at night, result in only small changes inside the chamber.

When the number of the eggs per clutch are mathematically averaged,

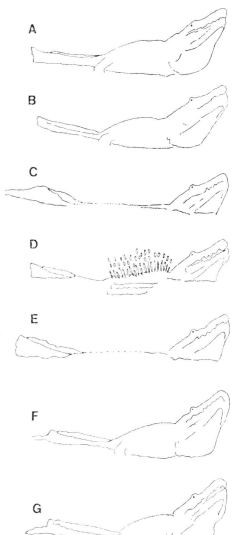

A bellowing cycle of a male alligator. *A, B*: Inhalation with gulp. *C*: Pre-exhalation. *D* Exhalation and vocalization. *E*: Post-vocalization. *F, G*: The next inhalation with gulp. Time between events (in seconds): A–B = 0.62, B–C = 1.71, C–D = 0.79, D–E = 1.50, E–F = 3.71, F–G = 1.33; A–G = 9.66. (*Courtesy of the American Museum of Natural History [Garrick, Lang, and Herzog, 1978]*).

American alligator nest mound.

wildlife surveyors obtain means between 40 and 45 eggs. Averages may vary from season to season with cooler temperatures associated with lower egg counts.

Juvenile alligators resemble their parents with the exception of color pattern, size, and sexual development. After hatching they remain together in a cohesive social group called a pod or creche. One pod may contain the offspring from different nests or may be made up exclusively by nest-mates. No other reptiles remain together for as long after hatching as crocodilians. Schooling, flocking, or running in packs has a significant effect on growth, development, and survival. Crocodilian pods may remain together for as long as three years. The advantage of staying together may be one of mutual protection. If one animal is attacked, the others will begin to emit distress calls, attracting adults to the defense.

Alligators measure between 8 and 10 inches at birth, and once they reach a length of over 2 feet, they have no enemies except for man, habitat destruction caused by man, or natural disaster and disease. Natural disasters such as prolonged drought may lead to death by starvation and dehydration, although well-nourished alligators can go without food for up to a year. Juveniles are also sensitive to increased salt concentrations in their aquatic environment which leads to a lack of suitable drinking water.

Animals that prey upon juvenile alligators include large turtles, raccoons, skunks, wolves, dogs, feral hogs, bears, larger predatory fish, and predatory birds. Just about any carnivore that can catch, subdue, and eat baby alligators will feed on them. In addition alligators will occasionally cannibalize juveniles of their own species. The most common theory is that

American alligator in its hole at Savannah National Wildlife Refuge. (*Courtesy U.S. Fish and Wildlife Service/by Luther C. Goldman*)

cannibalism occurs when normal foods are nonexistent. Whether this cause is valid among alligators is not clear, but it is plausible. Another theory for cannibalism when other foods are not an issue is that it represents an act of dominance by a larger member of the group.

Studies in the world of juvenile alligators are hampered by the elusiveness of these creatures. Even when a creche is located, it may be difficult to observe on a long-term basis.

Because of their relatively indiscriminate feeding habits, alligators help serve their environment in a number of ways. They consume slow-moving nongame fish such as gar and bowfin, which compete with and prey upon game fish. They also consume carrion which helps to prevent pollution in the waters they inhabit.

Alligators also serve their ecosystems in a variety of other ways. For example, it can be reasonably assumed that prior to the colonization of Florida by Europeans, most of the land in the southern half of the state that was above water had been put there by alligators, thanks to their earth moving, dredging, and nesting activities. Adult alligators move over the landscape like living bulldozers, and their propensity for gathering debris to construct huge nest mounds over millions of years has added considerably to the nonsubmerged real estate in much of the southeastern United States.

The nests built by alligators break down over time to form an organic substrate known as peat. This peat provides a fertile soil conducive to green plant growth. An added benefit of peat is that if ignited, it burns slowly. This substance serves to retard the spread of brush-fires which occur periodically by spontaneous combustion or lightning strikes during very hot, dry weather. In some parts of the world it is used in lieu of firewood as a fuel for this very reason.

(1) Leg scales in an American alligator. (*Courtesy Helen Longest-Slaughter/Nature's Images, Inc.*)
(2) Verticils and subcaudal scales in American alligator. (*Courtesy Helen Longest-Salughter/Nature's Images, Inc.*)
(3) Head (dorsal view) of American alligator in Everglades. (*Courtesy Helen Longest-Slaughter/Nature's Images, Inc.*)
(4) Head (dorsal view) of American alligator at Loxahatchee. (*Courtesy U.S. Fish and Wildlife Service; photo by Luther C. Goldman*)
(5) Tourists viewing alligators at the Alligator Farm, St. Augustine, Florida. (*Courtesy Florida Department of Commerce*)
(6) Captive American alligators on public display in Florida. (*Courtesy Florida Department of Commerce*)

PLATE 1

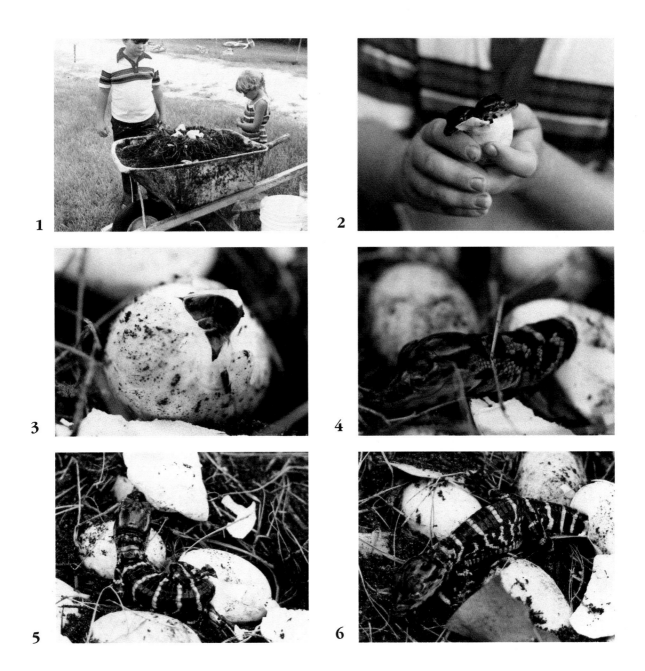

(1) Alligator nest removed nearly intact and relocated to wheelbarrow for hatching. This was necessary because of a construction project. Palm Beach County, Florida. (*Courtesy F. Grunwald*)

(2) American alligator twins hatching from single egg from wheelbarrow nest. (*Courtesy F. Grunwald*)

(3–6) American alligator hatching sequence. (*Courtesy F. Grunwald*)

PLATE 2

(1–2) *Alligator mississippiensis.* (*Courtesy Florida Department of Commerce*)

(3) *Alligator mississippiensis.* Everglades National Park. (*Courtesy Helen Longest-Slaughter/Nature's Images, Inc.*)

(4) American alligator female guarding her nest. (*Courtesy U.S. Fish and Wildlife Service; photo by A. W. Palmisano*)

(5) Characteristic wide V-shaped wake made by American alligator patrolling just below the surface. Palm Beach County, Florida. (*Photo by S. Grenard*)

(6) American alligator seen patrolling hauls out of water seeking food hand-out. It is illegal to feed wild alligators in Florida. This one is in a captive pond with seven others. (*Photo by S. Grenard*)

PLATE 3

1

2

3

(1–2) *Alligator sinensis.* (*Courtesy Atagawa Tropical and Alligator Garden, Shizuoka, Japan*)
(3) Although most crocodilians are solitary, captive American alligators endure crowding without much difficulty. (*Courtesy Atagawa Tropical and Alligator Garden, Shizuoka, Japan*)

PLATE 4

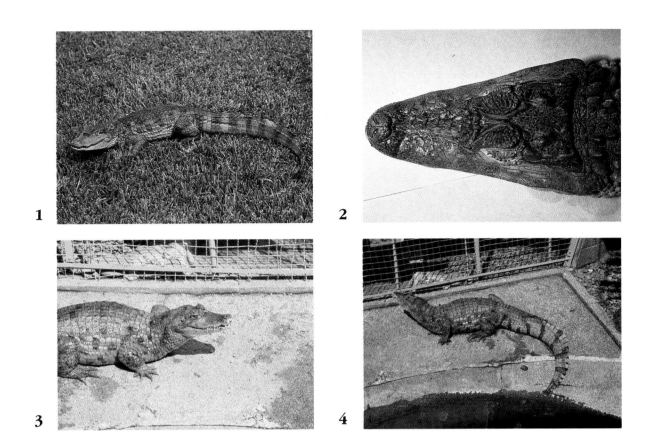

(1) Captive *Caiman crocodilus crocodilus*. (*Courtesy San Diego Zoological Society*)

(2) *Caiman crocodilus:* top of head showing bony ridge between eyes, giving a "spectacled" appearance. (*Courtesy Robert T. Zappalorti/Nature's Images*)

(3–4) *Caiman crocodilus apaporiensis.* (*Courtesy Atagawa Tropical and Alligator Garden, Shizuoka, Japan*)

(5) *Caiman crocodilus chiapasius* at Chiapas, Mexico. (*Courtesy Instituto de Historia Natural/Antonio V. Ramirez*)

PLATE 5

(1) Captive *Caiman yacare* showing nuchal scalation. (*Photo by S. Grenard/F. Grunwald*)

(2–3) *Caiman yacare*. (*Photo by S. Grenard*)

(4) Paraguayan caiman (*Caiman yacare*) with hatchling coloration. (*Photo by Jeff Wines*)

(5–6) Juvenile *Caiman c. fuscus*. (*Photo by S. Grenard*)

PLATE 6

(1) *Paleosuchus palpebrosus*. (*Photo by Jeff Wines*)

(2) *Paleosuchus palpebrosus* in aquatic bipedal stance. (*Photo by Jeff Wines*)

(3–4) *Paleosuchus trigonatus*. (*Courtesy Atagawa Tropical and Alligator Garden, Shizuoka, Japan*)

(5) *Melanosuchus niger*. (*Courtesy Robert T. Zappalorti/Nature's Images*)

(6) Juvenile *Melanosuchus niger*. (*Courtesy Robert T. Zappalorti/Nature's Images*)

PLATE 7

(1) *Crocodylus acutus*. (*Courtesy Florida Department of Commerce*)
(2) Juvenile *Crocodylus acutus*. (*Courtesy Robert T. Zappalorti/Nature's Images*)
(3–5) *Crocodylus acutus* at Chiapas, Mexico. (*Courtesy Instituto de Historia Natural/Antonio V. Ramirez*)

PLATE 8

Many terrestrial animals which live on the fringes of wetlands have been saved from certain death during floods thanks to the alligators' activities, finding salvation from rising waters on the mounds, levees, and embankments forged by alligators. In addition, the alligator nest mound also serves as a home for a variety of small mammals both when it's in use by the alligator as well as after it has been abandoned. The Florida Red Bellied turtle (*Chrysemys nelsoni*) routinely uses the base of alligator nests to deposit and incubate its own eggs.

Not only do alligators provide refuge for land animals during flooding but they do the same for aquatic species during drought. Their natural instinct to excavate holes or tunnels called "alligator holes" conserve or impound water, even when riverbeds, lakes, ponds, and canals dry up. Birds and terrestrial animals find drinking water, and aquatic species find a new, albeit temporary, home during dry periods. Fish, frogs, turtles, and crabs are among the guests of alligator holes during a drought. It is a convenient and wet place for them to wait until conditions return to normal.

The primary purpose of the alligator hole, however, is to provide a warm place in winter and a cool place in summer for alligators to find respite from the climate. It also provides shelter for juveniles regardless of weather conditions.

Stuzenbaker (1973) wrote that alligator holes in the J. D. Murphee Wildlife Management Area (Jefferson County, Texas) are found along the edges of man-made ditch banks and adjacent levees. Nest mounds were often found in proximity to holes, and when the young hatch, they begin life in or near the mother's alligator hole. At least three consecutive age groups have been observed occupying the niche in or near a single hole.

The Texas report goes on to say that alligator holes have their entrances located below the water's surface during times of normal water level. The entrance is between two and three feet in diameter, and its length may extend to the bottom level of the pond, marsh, or canal where it is located. The tunnel usually proceeds at a slight downward angle and terminates in a large cavern or so-called "turning basin." Field observations of frightened alligators dashing into their holes indicate that after the perceived danger has passed the animal reemerges, sometimes within a few minutes, head first.

The Texas report also confirms that during the dry season, the water impounded by alligator holes may be the only source of water enabling survival of fish, amphibians and other aquatic organisms. Terrestrial animals have been observed drinking from them during severe drought as well. Stuzenbaker points out that game fishing is particularly good near alligator holes because of the deeper water present at the inlet to the hole.

American alligator hauling out of water with belly close to ground. (*Courtesy of Florida Department of Commerce, Division of Tourism*)

Older, often used holes become wallowed out in time, and the report indicates that this results in the creation of productive duck blinds.

The holes are created through vigorous activity of both the tail and the mouth. The mouth is used to tear out vegetation and dig, the tail to sweep the debris toward the edge of the hole.

Alabama

The American alligator once existed throughout the southern half of Alabama with occasional sightings made farther north. Males tend to spend most of their time in larger bodies of open water whereas females tend to inhabit shallows in and around marshes and swamps with heavy vegetative cover.

Current population estimates indicate there are about 35,000 alligators in the state. More than half of Alabama's alligators are found in the

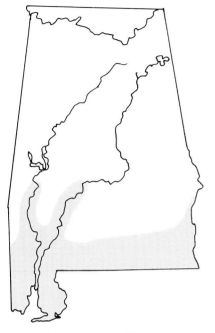

Range of the American alligator in Alabama.

Mobile Delta and connecting tributaries in Mobile and Baldwin counties. Landowners in several southern and central areas have stocked alligators in their larger farm ponds to help control turtles, beavers, and muskrats.

In spite of heavy concentrations of alligators in the Mobile Delta (one animal every 200 feet or 26 every mile), the Alabama Department of Conservation and Natural Resources says there has never been an alligator attack on man reported from the area.

In all of Alabama there have been only five recorded alligator attacks on people with no fatalities.

At one time the alligator was distributed throughout the lower coastal plain and occurred along the major streams and some of their larger branches northward nearly to the fall line (the "line" connecting the first major series of falls or rapids encountered going inland on any major waterway). In addition to the Mobile Delta, alligators are also concentrated in the Eufaula National Wildlife Refuge (Junction of Cowikee Creek and the Chattahochee River) in Barbour County with occasional sightings on the Tombigbee River as far north as Pickens County, on the Cahaba up to Marion in Perry County, and on the Alabama River up to Selma in Dallas County. There has been at least one report of a large alligator basking along the banks of the Coosa or Tennessee River in northern Alabama. Some 50 alligators were introduced into Wheeler Refuge between Decatur and Huntsville but public outcry against the restocking program caused these animals to later be recaptured and returned to the Mobile Delta.

Range of the American alligator in Arkansas.

Arkansas

According to the Arkansas Game and Fish Commission, the alligator is found in 45 southern and southeastern counties in that state. It frequents rivers, estuaries, swamps, marshes, oxbows, and lakes. Nesting females and juveniles require shallow, vegetation-choked fresh water whereas males use large, open bodies of water.

The cold weather in Arkansas drives alligators into their "winter dens," which are holes dug under a bank with underwater entrances. Here alligators go into an inactive state referred to as "winter dormancy."

The Game and Fish Commission says alligator populations are on the rise again in Arkansas due, in large measure, to increased protection and a vigorous restocking program. From 1972 through 1984, 2,800 subadult alligators were released into suitable habitat within what was considered the historical range of the species. Eighty percent were released on private lands by request. Successful reproduction has been documented in six counties previously devoid of alligators.

Florida

The alligator suffered a major population decline in Florida which became obvious in the 1960s. Together with the American crocodile, it was listed as endangered by the U.S. Fish and Wildlife Service in 1966 and eventually came under the protection of the Endangered Species Act of 1973.

Range of the American alligator in Florida.

In Florida alligators were always considered commercially valuable and have been exploited as a "cash crop" since the late 1800s. They were an important source of income for many early pioneer Florida families during the first half of this century. Because of widespread population losses, Florida closed the season on legal alligator hunting in 1962. Without effective federal legislation it was difficult for Florida to enforce its state laws, and illegal poaching continued almost unabated until 1970. From 1965 to 1970 alone, some 140,000 hides which originated in Florida were believed to have been sold. In 1969, the Lacey Act was amended to prohibit interstate commerce in illegal alligator and crocodile hides. It provided the first legal means by which Federal wildlife officers could control the movement of illegally obtained hides. As a result poaching ground to a halt and recovery of alligator populations began to occur rapidly.

Resurging populations at this point indicated that alligators were never endangered by natural disasters (flooding and drought), starvation, or other reasons such as saltwater incursion. Up to 1973, at least, loss of habitat or encroachment by human inhabitants was not a problem either. Population decline in Florida was laid squarely at the feet of hunters who took unlimited tens of thousands of hides annually that once belonged to reproductively mature animals. If allowed to continue, this situation would have resulted in the extinction of alligators and crocodiles in Florida.

After 1973, the Florida Game and Freshwater Fish Commission says alligator populations grew by as much as 30% annually. However, at the same time, human populations were also increasing. As a result, in 1976 alone, Commission field agents received move than 10,000 calls requesting that live alligators be removed from areas of human habitation.

Beset by a growing human population and more and more complaints, the Commission instituted its first alligator management program in 1977. The program received and logged complaints, mostly of animals in urban areas, and then notified licensed hunters who were permitted to hunt, capture, and either kill or relocate the alligator involved. In 1980, the Commission began its first of seven controlled experimental harvests on three bodies of water near Gainesville and Orlando. By 1987, the number of sites expanded to nine, and in 1988 the hunts were opened to 230 members of the general public who were selected by a random drawing.

Night light hunting of alligators is now illegal, as is the use of a gun. This extraordinary photo, capturing the muzzle flash of a rifle, was taken by Julian A. Dimock. (*Photo courtesy of the American Museum of Natural History*)

Each winner of a license was entitled to bag up to 15 alligators over a 30-day period in September. An additional 209 "agent" permits were issued to qualified professional alligator hunters who could hire themselves as guides to any novice wanting to pay the price—a price which usually included a split of the take. Over 20,000 people applied for permits in the 1989 alligator-license lottery, which was more than triple the 1988 total. It seems that many people realized that here was a new once-a-year lottery which, if they won, was worth at least $15,000 in prizes because an average 'gator is worth $1,000. Add to this a new kind of recreational excitement money can't buy anywhere, and you suddenly have a lot of "bettors" plunking down applications. Some 250 licenses were issued, each worth 15 alligators to be hunted within the 30 days of September in a choice of 32 selected bodies of water including parts of Lake Okeechobee and canals in Palm Beach and Broward counties. A total of 3,115 animals were taken in 1989, 635 less than the bag limit. In 1990, 189 permits were issued.

An accurate measure of the amount of wetlands in Florida has never been easy to determine. The alligator is found in every county of the state. In 1850 it was estimated that there were 8,321,680 hectares of wetlands in Florida. By 1965 this estimate had shrunk by 32%. Water-management projects that destroy habitat by either drainage or flooding and landfills have cut into alligator habitat.

There are 21 government protected wildlife refuges in Florida covering 1,194,364 hectares. In addition there are 11,000 square kilometers of inland waterways which also provide suitable alligator habitat.

While loss of habitat has not seemed to make a difference to alligators that have regained sufficiently high populations, they will continue to be threatened by human encroachment, and this, invariably, will mean that people will continue to be threatened by them. Wildlife officials feel that education is their best tool in fostering coexistence between people and alligators.

In July, 1989, Florida wildlife officials announced that tests of alligators in two Dade and western Broward County areas of the Everglades showed unusually high amounts of mercury. The average concentration of mercury found in 10 alligators sampled in June, 1989, was almost twice as high as the amount found in 8 alligators tested in February, 1989, from the same locations.

Concentrations of mercury in the latest group tested averaged 2.9 parts per million, with 6 of the animals having levels exceeding 3 parts per million. Frequent consumption of food containing more than 1 ppm is considered hazardous. The animals sampled were taken from the Miami Canal in Dade and the L-35B canal near the Sawgrass Fish Camp in western Broward County.

Florida Wetland Habitats

Salt Marshes are found coastally where freshwater streams or rivers empty into the ocean and blend with seawater to form wetlands of various, intermediate salinity levels.

Mangrove swamps are named for the presence, at water's edge, of Mangrove plants (*Rhizophora*). They are found in the southern part of the state extending as far north as the Suwanee River on the Gulf coast and-

Alligator making a belly-run-dive into water. (*Photo courtesy of the U.S. Fish and Wildlife Service/by R. G. Schmidt*)

Alligator basking with jaws agape, a maneuver which enables eavporative cooling across the palate. (*Photo courtesy of the Florida Department of Commerce/by Karen Aldhizer, Gatorland, Kissimmee, Florida*)

northern Brevard County on the Atlantic coast. Like salt marshes, mangrove swamps often consist of waters of intermediate salinity. The mangrove is characterized by its distinctive arched roots which help it find a firm anchor in the presence of the shifting sands associated with tidal flooding. It forms a dense vegetative cover and is an important habitat for a wide variety of Florida wildlife in addition to alligators and crocodiles. Unrestrained development and building in and around prime coastal areas has placed this habitat in grave danger.

Freshwater marshes occur throughout the state. They're typified by slow drainage with mostly standing or stagnant waters that disappear during droughts and fill up during rainy periods. The Everglades consists mostly of freshwater marsh and is a good example of this habitat. Water management projects, drought, and fires which occur as a result of drought are the primary threats to this habitat.

Temporary ponds and roadside ditches are a common sight in Florida and it is not unusual to find such bodies of water suddenly colonized by an alligator. Roadside ditches are man-made trenches dug alongside Florida highways and secondary roads to provide run-off and drainage. Without such ditches roads in Florida rapidly but temporarily flood during even limited periods of heavy rainfall. Temporary ponds occur in low areas such as in pine woods and at the bottom of shallow "sink-holes." They are dry during much of the year but become full during rainy periods. Temporary, man-made ponds are frequently dug near residences set at low elevations for the purpose of providing runoff and limiting flood damage during heavy rains. They are seen throughout the state but are most frequently observed in the more highly developed southern counties.

Permanent ponds and natural lakes are common in northern and central Florida. Permanent ponds may be man-made or natural, receive regular drainage, and remain filled year-round. The largest permanent lake in Florida is Lake Okeechobee which is situated in south-central Florida.

Cypress swamp and domes are freshwater areas containing cypress trees, the roots of which may be submerged during times of high water levels. They may dry up during part of the year or, depending on the water source, remain flooded most of the year with dark, tea-colored waters.

Gum swamps are situated in low lying river flood plains and contain concentrations of gum or tupelo trees.

Florida is also served by a number of medium to large rivers, the largest and longest of which is the St. Johns in the northeast part of the state. Other large Florida rivers include the Suwanee, Kissimmee, Caloosahatchee, Loxahatchee and the Apalachicola. The state is also criss-crossed by an interconnecting lattice of canals, streams and small waterways which are part of the state's water management system. In addition a high salinity waterway extends north to south for much of the length of the state along its Eastern coast. It is known as the intracoastal waterway and is separated from the ocean in many places by barrier islands which front on the Atlantic. Various channels and bays provide access between the intracoastal and the ocean. Because of its high salt content the intracoastal waterway is not a prime crocodilian habitat but, from time to time, crocodilians have been observed traveling it. American crocodiles that have ranged as far north as Vero Beach on the east coast of Florida probably migrated by using this body of water.

Georgia

The Georgia Department of Natural Resources estimates there are about 100,000 alligators in the state as of 1987–88. The majority of the population is found south of the fall line (Columbus to Macon to Augusta). There are approximately two million acres of suitable alligator habitats in the state.

The alligators in Georgia fall under two classifications depending on location: Classified as *endangered* are those found north of a line running from the South Carolina border south along U.S. 95 to the junction with

Range of the American alligator in Georgia.

U.S. 82 in Liberty County, then southwest along U.S. 82 to the junction with U.S. 84 at Waycross, then west to the Alabama-Georgia border. Those animals found south of these limits are classified as *threatened*.

The geographic range of the alligator in Georgia, historically, is confined mainly to the coastal plain region. A 1986 survey indicated alligators present in 103 counties with breeding populations evidenced by nests in 66 counties. Alligators found north of the Columbus-Macon-Augusta fall line do not appear to be breeding. In fact sightings in this region are believed to be of animals which have been relocated as a result of human intervention.

Georgia offers the following habitats suitable for alligators: inland deep marshes, coastal deep and freshwater marshes, farm ponds, man-made reservoirs and lakes. The Okefenokee Swamp and southeastern Georgia provides 0.4 million acres of habitat and contains the densest population of alligators in Georgia.

The Department of Natural Resources says it receives a steadily increasing number of complaints about alligators. In 1980 they received 88; in 1986 the number rose to 239. However, there have been no verified attacks on people by alligators.

Louisiana

The alligator is found throughout Louisiana and is present in virtually every river system, swamp, or bayou in the state. It has also been observed on at least one of the Chandeleur Islands off the Gulf coast of Louisiana.

The densest populations are in the state's 4 million acres of coastal marshlands. It is commonly found in fresh to slightly brackish waters, and occasional animals are found swimming in saltwater for short periods.

Alligator populations in Louisiana reached all-time lows during the late 1950s, but by the 1960s, private individuals and state wildlife officials acted to reverse the trend by having the legislature close the season on alligator hunting. Thanks to a rigorous federal and state enforcement effort, poaching was also eliminated. By the late 1960s, population levels were increasing. At the present time it is estimated that there are one million alligators in the state.

According to the Louisiana Department of Wildlife and Fisheries, the state's coastal marshlands extend from the Pearl River on the Mississippi line westward to the Sabine River on the Texas border and then northward in some areas 75 miles or more inland from the Gulf of Mexico to the timbered swamps, agricultural areas, and wooded uplands of the coast. This area consists of approximately 4 million acres of marshland and is the primary habitat of the American alligator in Louisiana.

Range of the American alligator in Louisiana.

These marshes are divided into three zones. At the mouth of the Mississippi River a 250,000 acre area is called the active delta. The inactive or subdelta consists of 2.55 million acres and extends from the Mississippi line to Vermillion Bay in the center of the state's coast line. The prairie marsh zone, also called the Chenier plain, extends from Vermilion Bay westward to the Texas state line and consists of 1.25 million acres.

These three zones are further divided into four marsh types based on salinity and vegetation. They include salt marsh, brackish marsh, intermediate marsh, and freshwater marsh. Approximately 700,000 acres of this coastal marsh is under federal or state control. The remaining 3.3 million acres are privately owned.

In Louisiana it's been determined that water level and salinity manipulation can be used to improve marsh conditions leading to improved animal populations. One form of water level control is called the weir, a barrier or small dam built across a drainage outlet slightly below the level of the marsh. These are usually used where water levels are affected by tides. Weirs permit tidal drainage while holding in a fair amount of permanent water. They provide improved habitat for alligators, and Tarver et al. (1987) say recent studies indicate that a greater number of alligator nests per unit area occur behind weirs compared to marshes without these structures in place. Another form of water management that benefits alligators is called impoundment. Under this system an area of the marsh is completely surrounded with levees, and the water level is controlled by gravity flow, tidal flow, or pumping stations, permitting better water level and salinity regulation. Weirs and bulkheads are less expensive than impoundments, which can only be built where soil is suitable for the purpose.

Since 1972 there has been limited harvesting of alligators every year except 1974. In 1975 the federal government delisted alligators in Cameron, Calcasieu, and Vermillion parishes although the season was not expanded statewide until 1981. Since 1981, the average annual "harvest" has been about 17,000 animals. Hunting remains forbidden on government refuges and on private sanctuaries such as the Rockefeller Wildlife Refuge. It is illegal to take alligators measuring less than 4 feet in length (1.2 meters) and to hunt between sunset and sunrise. All alligators taken in Louisiana must be by licensed alligator hunters, and all hides must be registered with the Louisiana Department of Wildlife and Fisheries under a special tagging procedure.

Mississippi

Historical records from the Civil War era indicate the presence of the American alligator in the South Delta region of Mississippi. Records of

Range of the American alligator in Mississippi.

General Ulysses S. Grant's campaign against Vicksburg in the spring of 1863 mention "numerous moccasins and alligators" in the creeks and bayous north of Vicksburg.

Personal communications with long-time residents of the Pascagoula River area in southeast Mississippi indicate that an abundant population existed in this region as late as the 1930s to early 1940s. Unrestricted harvest during the first half of this century for meat and hides eventually led to populations of very low numbers. The alligator was completely extirpated from much of its former range. However, small populations remained in the more remote and inaccessible areas. Passage of laws prohibiting the taking of alligators and especially the declaring of the alligator as a federally endangered species greatly reduced exploitation.

By the early 1970s alligator populations in Louisiana marshes had recovered to the point that surplus animals were available for restocking elsewhere. During this same time period, burgeoning beaver populations in Mississippi were creating severe economic losses to the timber industry and to private landowners. It was felt that a viable alligator population would help curtail problems caused by beavers. From 1972–1977 between three and four thousand alligators were captured on state and federal refuges in south Louisiana and released throughout Mississippi.

A statewide survey of conservation officers in 1977 indicated that 55 of 82 counties had alligators. Twenty-seven counties reported stable populations, and 28 counties indicated an increasing populations. Alligator populations have continued to increase over the past decade. The following figures from an annual census route in the Pascagoula River Marsh in Jackson County indicate how this population has increased despite evidence of some degree of illegal kill:

Year	Number of Alligators
1979	19
1980	15
1981	23
1982	44
1983	45
1984	47
1985	49
1986	60
1987	72
1988	71

Alligator numbers have increased sufficiently in Mississippi for the U.S. Fish and Wildlife Service to remove them from the Federal Endangered Species List in July of 1986 and place them in the less restrictive Threatened due to Similarity of Appearance classification. The 1987 session of the Mississippi Legislature removed the alligator from the State Endangered Species List and gave the Mississippi Department of Wildlife Conservation the authority to regulate and manage the species.

Beginning in the early 1980s, conservation officers began to receive calls complaining of alligators close to residences. These were predominantly from two areas of the state, the Gulf coast and the Ross Barnett Reservoir. Most of the nuisance complaints are directly the result of human residential development encroaching on alligator habitat. In the two areas mentioned, calls have reached the point where local conservation officers spend the majority of their time during the summer months checking these complaints and relocating alligators when warranted. The Mississippi Department of Wildlife Conservation is currently planning and preparing for a nuisance alligator program which will utilize trapper/agents to help operate it.

North Carolina

The alligators in northern North Carolina represent the current northernmost natural range of the species along the Atlantic seaboard. Most of the state's alligators occur in the southeastern coastal marshes as far north as the peninsula bordered on the east by Pamlico Sound. The northern limits include Washington, Terrel, and Dare counties.

Range of the American alligator in North Carolina.

Due to sparse human habitation in and around the coastal marshes, there have been no documented attacks by alligators on people, and the state receives less than 10 nuisance alligator reports annually.

The alligator remains scarce in North Carolina, and there are no plans to open even a limited season in the state at the present time.

Oklahoma

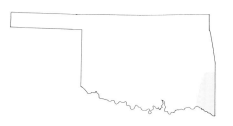

Sightings of alligators in Oklahoma are rare with many traceable to releases in McCurtain County. Because of subzero winters, alligators spend cold months in their holes. Breeding has not been documented in the state.

Alligators found in Oklahoma are restricted to the extreme southeast corner of the state. They may be part of contiguous populations in Texas, Arkansas, and Louisiana.

Range of the American alligator in Oklahoma.

Fossil evidence indicates that at one time the alligator ranged throughout the state, but because of its rarity it will remain classified as Endangered on an indefinite basis.

South Carolina

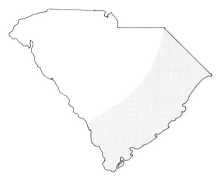

Range of the American alligator in South Carolina.

The South Carolina Wildlife and Marine Resources Department says 75% of all alligators in the state occur in some 170,000 acres of coastal marshlands. A 1983 population study estimated 41,163 animals, and in 1985 the figure was revised upward to 75,000 with an additional 25,000 occurring inland.

There are no plans for an open season, and attacks on humans by alligators are rare. In 1987–88 there were 400 nuisance reports involving alligators in Charleston and Berkeley counties. In 1987 a program team was established to deal with these complaints. All complaints, involving mostly confrontations and animals close to human habitation, are first investigated. The team will then, if necessary, arrange for a contract trapper or "control agent" to trap and kill offending animals. There will be no relocation of alligators because according to a study conducted in South Carolina by Murphy and Coker (1983), most return "home" to their capture site within a short time after relocation. One animal returned 8 miles to its capture site within a period of just 11 days. Some 391 alligators of all sizes were relocated to a site called Bear Island. Sometime later only 9 were still there and these were small males.

Texas

Range of the American alligator in Texas.

According to the Texas Parks and Wildlife Department, alligators in the state range as far north as the Red River, westward to the vicinity of Dallas, and southward through San Antonio and the Rio Grande on the Texas-Mexico border. Alligators don't venture into Mexico due to lack of suitable habitat south of the Rio Grande. Following heavy rains in late May, 1989, a solitary alligator measuring 5½ feet was reported in man-made Carolyn Lake west of Dallas in a heavily populated area called Las Colinas. Wildlife officials believe that the alligator, which was 100 miles farther west than its normal range, was introduced into a farm pond or stock tank in the area and then strayed when its habitat became flooded.

The alligator has been protected by law in Texas since 1969, and populations have increased substantially as a result. In heavily populated areas this increase has caused a corresponding rise in the number of nuisance complaints. The majority of such complaints come from persons residing near coastal marshes. These include Jefferson, Brazoria, Matagorda, Calhoun, and Arkansas counties as well as in work areas around refineries located in Port Arthur and Beaumont.

The historical distribution of the alligator in Texas conforms to the same land type as other states: available wetlands from the coast, throughout the coastal plains to the fall line. This line is defined as a line connecting the first major series of falls or rapids encountered going inland on any major waterway from the coast. In Texas, the fall line has as its western limit the line of the Balcones fault, extending eastward from a point near Del Rio to the northwestern part of Baxar county where it turns northeastward and then continues northward to the Red River. This fall line is regarded as the boundary between lowland and upland Texas. The largest number of alligators is found in the middle and upper coastal counties.

The habitats of alligators in Texas include all major river drainages in the Gulf coastal plain, their tributaries, wetlands, marshes, swamps, lakes, reservoirs, stock tanks, and farm ponds.

The northern limits of the alligator corresponds closely to the 35°F (0°C) isotherm of average minimum daily January temperatures. To the west and south, alligators are limited by lack of sufficient rainfall to maintain wetlands habitat, especially when high rates of evaporation further reduces water levels.

There are 550 square miles of coastal marshlands in Texas of which 63% is located in three southeastern counties: Orange, Jefferson, and Chambers. The marsh habitat then narrows along the remainder of the Gulf coast of Texas, decreasing to between 1 and 2 miles inland in some portions of the three lowermost coastal counties.

Three distinct alligator habitats occur in Texas: coastal marshes, inland freshwater rivers, swamps and marshlands, and natural as well as man-made ponds, lakes, and reservoirs.

There are four types of coastal marshlands found along the Texas coast. Saltwater marsh covers 100 square miles, brackish marsh covers 85 square miles, fresh-to-brackish marsh occupies 291 miles, and freshwater marsh covers 82 square miles. In addition there are coastal lakes and ponds which, while not actually marsh, make up an integral part of the ecosystem. Water in coastal lakes and ponds varies from fresh to salty depending on rainfall, runoff, and incursion by tidal washes. Inland alligator habitat consists of rivers, bayous, creeks, oxbows, stock tanks, ponds, lakes, and reservoirs.

A 1980 survey provided an estimate of 68,700 alligators in Texas, a 12.5% increase over a previous survey done in 1973 and 1974. In 1984, the number increased to 132,302 in the three-county southeastern coastal habitat and would have been more if inland animals were surveyed. As a result of increasing populations, the state opened a limited season on alligator hunting in 1984, but only 437 animals were captured that year. In 1988, however, a total of 1,600 animals were taken.

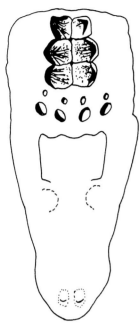

Chinese alligator.

Chinese Alligator

SCIENTIFIC NAME: *Alligator sinensis* FAUVEL, 1879
    STATUS: Endangered. CITES I. Endangered—U.S. Law.
    GEOGRAPHIC RANGE: Found only in the People's Republic of China and severely restricted to the lower Yangzi (Yangtze) or Chang Jiang Valley in the provinces of Jiangau, Zhejiang, and Anhui.
    HABITAT: Rivers and their tributaries forming lakes, ponds,

Range of the Chinese alligator.

and streams as well as in grassy swampland in the Yangtze Kiang Delta. Spends a great deal of time in holes or burrows excavated in river banks.

DIET: Aquatic invertebrates and vertebrates such as fish and snails.

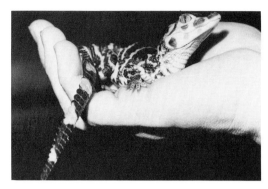

Chinese alligator hatchling (*Photo courtesy of the Bronx Zoo*).

Comments

The Chinese alligator, which together with the American alligator makes up the only known living species of the genus *Alligator*, is critically endangered. There are no current estimates of populations surviving in China, but some experts say there may be no more than 2000 animals left in the wild. It is threatened primarily by loss of habitat and competition with man. Occasionally it is the subject of illegal but willful capture and killing. In 1957 extensive flooding in the Yangtze Valley caused considerable destruction to nests. The Three-Gorges dam project projected to begin in the 1990s will destroy most of the remaining alligator habitat and displace an estimated 1 million people. It is being hotly contested by environmentalists worldwide and in China.

This species is rigidly protected under Chinese and U.S. law, which serves to prohibit its importation. A number of refuges have been established and captive breeding programs have been initiated at the Shanghai Zoo, the Rockefeller Wildlife Refuge in Louisiana, and the Xiadu Alligator Farm in Zhejiang Province. Specimens have also been bred at the Bronx Zoo in New York and at the Houston Zoo in Texas.

A state of dormancy is known to occur between October and April. The animal is seen abroad in the day during May but shifts to nighttime in June which coincides with the beginning of the mating season.

It is a mound-nesting species that lays between 10 and 40 eggs in July and August with hatching in about 70 days. Growth occurs rapidly, and sexual maturity is attained within five years. It reaches a maximum length of 2 meters.

The Chinese alligator is also known as the Yangzi alligator. Locally it is called the Yow-Lung or T'o which translates to "dragon." Some writers speculate the mythical and highly symbolic Chinese dragon was, in fact, the Chinese alligator.

Caimans

There are eight species and subspecies of caimans which are members of the subfamily Alligatorinae. Caimans include members of the genera, *Caiman*, *Paleosuchus*, and *Melansuchus*. They are confined to the north-

Jaw snap at water's edge. Black caimans feed on capybaras, large South American rodents that frequent the same waters.

ern parts of South America, mainly in the Amazon Basin. One species (*Caiman crocodilus fuscus*) extends northward into southern Mexico. Spectacled caimans (*Caiman crocodilus crocodilus*), which were extensively imported for the American pet trade, have established colonies in Broward County, Florida, and near Homestead in Dade County, which is south of Miami. These U.S. caimans were released by owners unable to care for them any longer and/or may be escapees from alligator farms or reptile exhibits elsewhere in Florida.

Caimans are closely related to alligators and are included in the alligator subfamily. Their snouts, while wider and flatter than those of crocodiles, are nonetheless not as wide as those of the alligator. Another important difference between crocodiles, alligators, and caimans is that the belly scales of caimans are reinforced by a bony plate or osteoderm which makes them almost useless for the skin trade. Juveniles are tanned, stuffed, and sold as curious, however. The smallest species is the Cuvier's dwarf caiman and the largest is the Black caiman.

Caimans kill their prey by drowning and crushing. Prey captured on land, usually near the water's edge, is dragged back into the water. To swallow, caimans stretch their heads and necks out of the water, thrusting them upward in almost a completely vertical line. Other habits peculiar to caimans include their frequent use of the hind legs to scratch themselves, rub their eyes, as well as adjuncts to the teeth for tearing apart food.

Caimans feed on a wide variety of aquatic animals including crustacea, amphibians, and fish when they're small. As they get larger they will tackle birds and larger mammals as well. However, the Yacare or Paraguayan and the Broad-nosed caiman may consume a diet mainly of snails. Where they coexist with the piranha, caimans also feed on this most vicious of all fish. It is unlikely, however, that caimans are a match for a rampaging school of these killer fish and are successful only in attacking and eating occasional strays.

Like other crocodilians, caimans have enemies only as juveniles. They have been found inside the stomachs of Anacondas and jaguars. As they get older, their chief enemy is man who kills them for sport, for food (including taking eggs from nests), for stuffed curios (juveniles), and low-grade hides since they are difficult to tan properly.

Caimans are a mound-nesting animal, and the female opens the nest in response to the vocalizations of the young from within. They usually hatch themselves with the aid of their so-called "egg-tooth" which sits on the front of the snout. In most caimans, the juveniles are colored similarly to the adults. Most species are dark to light brown and have black crossbands. Their sides are lighter brown, and their bellies are light yellowish-tan or "creamy" white. The Black caiman (*Melanosuchus niger*) is dark as an adult although the young are black with yellow bands, a color pattern reminiscent of the juvenile American alligator.

While it is assumed that crocodilians hunt their prey guided by their sense of smell, laboratory studies conducted with caimans support an entirely different point of view. While a malodorous piece of carrion would attract any crocodilian by its stench, studies on caimans and other crocodilians indicate they may be more discriminatory in their choice of foods. Tests reveal that caimans, at least, rely both on sight and taste in choosing their food.

All crocodilians, whether underwater or partially submerged near the surface, close their nostrils as well as their ears. This makes both sound and smell unavailable. However, they are still able to see somewhat because they protect their eyes with a semi-transparent nictitating membrane which they use to cover their eyes. They are capable of covering either all or part of their eyes with this structure which is like a semi-transparent third eyelid. Since caimans are known to attack moving prey underwater, it is evident that they do so guided first by sight and second by taste. Even more remarkable, according to Vogel (1964), is that caimans can also recognize colors, distinguish or discern the shape lines of large objects up to 10 meters away, and detect rapid motion of any kind at least 100 meters away.

Vogel placed dried blood in an aquarium where his subject caimans were swimming. This produced no reaction. When he hung meat in the water on a string or placed it on a rock, there was no move toward it either. The deliberately starved, hungry caimans ignored these treats until they were placed on their tongues. After tasting the food, they eagerly gobbled it down. A bitter paraffin solution placed in the water did not seem to annoy the caimans until they opened their mouths and the water came in contact with their tongues. Meat juices that tinged the water red did not excite them until they opened up and tasted it. Vogel concluded that in caimans, at least, the primary sense organ for identifying food was the taste buds on the tongue while in the water and that the eyes came into play when caimans were either out of the water or partially submerged near the surface.

Caimans first appeared in South America during the Paleocene epoch between 65 and 54 billion years ago. This epoch marks the end of the Mesozoic era, which was followed by the Cenozoic or present era.

The word "caiman" is Spanish and it is defined as "alligator." Its earlier origins may be traced to the name of the Cayman Islands, which were discovered by Columbus in 1503. Columbus called these islands the Tortugas, Spanish for turtles. At some point the islands were renamed "Cayman" Islands, an Indian word for a lizard found there. Prior to the late eighteenth century, crocodilians have frequently been mistaken for lizards.

Julius O. Boos kneeling next to three examples of the "dwarf spectacled caiman" discovered on the Island of Tobago near Hillsborough Dam by Medem and Boos. (*Photo courtesy of J. O. Boos/photo by F. Medem*)

A dwarf race which may be a subspecies of *C. crocodilus* has been reported on the island of Tobago but detailed work has not been done to date on this report according to Julius Boos (1989 pers. comm.), An old, adult female specimen identified by Medem and collected by Boos & Medem measured just 69 cm.

Rio Apaporis Caiman

SCIENTIFIC NAME: *Caiman crocodilus apaporiensis* MEDEM, 1955
    STATUS: Indeterminate, CITES I.
    GEOGRAPHIC RANGE: The Rio Apaporis caiman occurs along a 200 kilometer stretch of the upper Rio Apaporis in southeast Colombia.
    HABITAT: Isolated to a small stretch of river.
    DIET: Small aquatic organisms.

Range of the Rio Apaporis caiman.

Comments

It is believed this subspecies is severely depleted in all or parts of its narrow range due to hunting and lack of effective protection. It is also "biologically" endangered because of cross-breeding with the Spectacled caiman (*Caiman crocodilus crocodilus*). Live captive specimens are held by the Roberto Franco Institute in Colombia, the Atagawa Tropical Gardens in Japan and at the Atlanta Zoo.

Spectacled Caiman

SCIENTIFIC NAME: *Caiman crocodilus* (LINNAEUS, 1758)
STATUS: Vulnerable, CITES II.
GEOGRAPHIC RANGE: From Mexico to Paraguay, east of the Andes. Northern South America including the Amazon River, Brazil, Colombia,

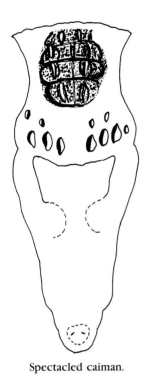

Spectacled caiman.

Range of the Spectacled caiman.

Ecuador, French Guiana, Guyana, Bolivia, Peru, Suriname, Trinidad, Tobago, and inland Venezuela.

HABITAT: Wetlands, lakes, and rivers, including the Pantanal of Mato Grasso.

Near the border of the Mato Grosso with Bolivia and Paraguay, the Paraguay River flows into an immense flood plain dating to the Holocene. In Brazil alone this plain measures some 770 kilometers north to south and has an area of 139,000 square kilometers. The western side of this plain is crossed by the Paraguay River and is called the Pantanal of Mato Grasso or simply the Pantanal. It extends from Brazil into Bolivia, Paraguay and just slightly into Argentina. The rainy season over the Pantanal occurs between October and March. The rains cover the Pantanal with a veritable sheet of water 2 to 4 meters deep, providing a prime habitat for the caiman.

DIET: Young feed on aquatic invertebrates including insect larva, snails, and crustaceans. Adults consume a variety of aquatic vertebrates including fish, amphibians, turtles and aquatic birds. They also consume terrestrial insects including ants.

Comments

Caiman crocodilus was formerly known as *Caiman sclerops*. Disputes over whether some caimans are a species in themselves or a subspecies of the Spectacled caiman remain unresolved. Protective legislation in Brazil has caused a resurgence in the population which was heavily depleted by trade in skins, stuffed juveniles sold as curios, and live juveniles exported as "pets." Recent increases in the pet trade have placed renewed pressure on populations of this crocodilian in some areas where it is not adequately protected by legislation. It is one of the most commonly exported (alive and hides) reptiles in South America (1988, CITES II).

The Spectacled caiman takes its common name from a bony infraorbital bridge in front of the eyes which gives it the appearance of wearing "spectacles." It has numerous common local names including Baba, Babilla, Tinga and Tulisio. It reaches a maximum length of 2.5 meters. A record specimen was measured at 2.7 meters.

Excrement from this species may help provide a nutrient base in some of the aquatic ecosystems that it occupies.

Breeding occurs at the end of the dry season, and nesting takes place from mid-August to early November. Between 14 and 40 eggs are produced, and hatching takes place in about 90 days.

This species is highly adaptable and is easily able to occupy any suitable niche or habitat, including man-made bodies of water. Specimens obtained through the pet trade or which have been released or escaped from owners in Florida have established colonies there in at least two locations. From time to time juvenile caimans have been "captured" in lakes, canals, and sewers in northern U.S. cities. These are isolated cases, however, and are attributed solely to releases of unwanted pets. However, caimans do not tolerate cold weather (<35°F) and will usually die if free living in such locales.

One of the most extensive studies done on young Spectacled caiman behaviors was made by Lewis (1985) at Northwestern University between May, 1979, and November, 1983. The study lasted 55 months and involved 1,635 man-hours of direct observation from behind a makeshift blind set up in the laboratory.

Lewis's objective was to determine the characteristic behaviors of captive juvenile caimans with respect to predation and feeding, growth, development, and sociality. Lewis painstakingly identified, documented, and catalogued 187 separate and distinct behaviors that he classified as follows:

1. Locomotion: 24 behaviors
2. Foraging: 6 behaviors
3. Prey capture: 25 behaviors
4. Feeding: 18 behaviors
5. Resting: 33 behaviors
6. Interactional/social reactions:
   14 nonaggressive behaviors
   8 different vocalizations
   31 antagonistic or aggressive behaviors
7. Defense and Attack: 22 behaviors
8. Care, comfort, and thermoregulation: 6 behaviors

Employing three pairs of Spectacled caimans, Lewis came to the following conclusions:

1. Social dynamics, namely the formation of a true hierarchy, influences the timing and regulation of behavior.
2. Social rank directly conditions the onset and continuation of growth.
3. The determination of dominance is first established within the "micro-habitats" of juveniles.

In each of Lewis's pair-sets, he was able to note that one member became dominant and the other became subordinate. This behavior had a profound effect on their growth and development. The dominant member grew normally whereas the subordinate member lagged far behind. In order to determine what, if any, role the level of food intake had on growth,

Lewis used pair-set #3 as a control and made sure each consumed identical amounts and types of food.

In spite of equal levels of nutrition, one animal in each pair-set always grew faster than the other. The food consumed by each animal could not account for the size differences between them. This lead Lewis to conclude that the effects of stress suffered by the subordinate members of each pair-set as a result of social interaction with the dominant members retarded their growth and development.

The time of the most rapid growth and development in all crocodilians is between the first and second year. After they leave the pod for a more solitary, less socially active, and presumably less stressful life, subordinate caimans may still lag behind their more dominant brothers and sisters.

Size, not age, determines the onset of sexual maturity in crocodilians. Subordinates, therefore, have less chance to breed and for many seasons may have no opportunity to breed at all.

Lewis's study indicates that assignment of rank during the first two years of life ultimately determines which caimans will have greater success in reproduction, predation, and territoriality.

A subspecies, *Caiman crocodilus crocodilus* is defined by its range, which is limited to: Colombia to Peru and the Brazilian Amazon drainage north and east of Bolivia.

Brown Caiman

SCIENTIFIC NAME: *Caiman crocodilus fuscus* (COPE, 1868)
STATUS: Vulnerable, CITES II.
GEOGRAPHIC RANGE: Southern Mexico and Nicaragua southward through Central America to Colombia, Ecuador and coastal Venezuela. Costa Rica, Cuba (introduced), El Salvador, Guatemala, Honduras, Panama, and Puerto Rico (introduced).
HABITAT: Brackish, freshwater, and saltwater wetlands including lakes, streams, marshes, and rivers.
DIET: Snails, crustaceans, fish, and other aquatic organisms.

Comments

The Brown caiman is rare in Venezuela, and populations are uncertain in most of Central America. While protected by law in Mexico, Venezuela, and Ecuador, legislation is inadequately enforced. Panama and Colombia have laws which specify size limits taken by hunters.

Populations in Mexico, ranging southward to the Pacific coast of

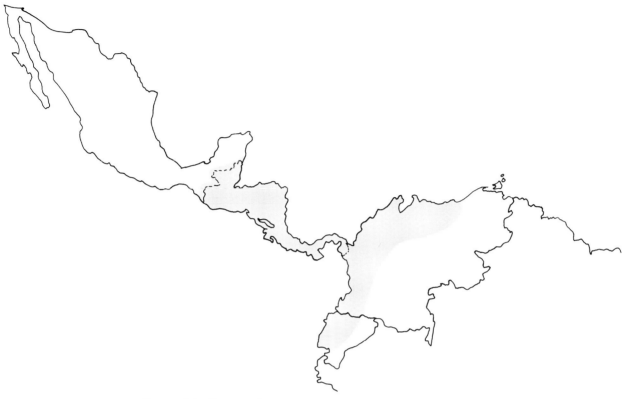

Range of the Brown caiman.

Colombia and Ecuador are considered by some experts as a separate subspecies, *Caiman crocodilus chiapasius*; *Caiman crocodilus fuscus* is believed restricted to those populations found exclusively in the Magada-lena and Sinu river systems of Colombia and coastal Venezuela.

The Brown caiman breeds throughout the year in most of its range. Some 15 to 30 eggs are deposited in a mound-type nest constructed of organic debris. Hatching occurs in about 80 days.

The maximum size reached by Brown caimans usually does not exceed 2 meters. It had been suggested by Brazaitis (as quoted in CITES II, 1988) that this subspecies be upgraded to CITES Appendix I, and this will be considered pending the outcome of ongoing population studies.

Broad-nosed Caiman

SCIENTIFIC NAME: *Caiman latirostris* (DAUDIN, 1801–1802)
STATUS: Endangered, CITES I.
GEOGRAPHIC RANGE: Parts of northern Argentina, Bolivia, southeast Brazil, Paraguay, and Uruguay.

95

Broad-nosed caiman (*Caiman latirostris*)—captive juvenile. (Photo courtesy of the American Museum of Natural History/by Raymond L. Ditmars)

HABITAT: Marshes, lagoons, streams, and rivers with dense aquatic and waterside vegetation.

DIET: Aquatic insects and their larva, snails, crustaceans, small fish, and amphibians.

Comments

This is an aquatic species that has been suffering serious declines throughout much of its range and has recently become extinct in areas where it was once common. Unlike most caimans, its skin yields a high grade leather and is therefore threatened by hunting as well as by loss of habitat. While it is protected by law, regulations are not adequately enforced.

The Broad-nosed caiman is a mound-nesting species that lays up to 40 eggs and has been bred in captivity. The female has been observed responding to vocalizations made by juveniles from within the nest by opening it and releasing her young. She has also been observed carrying her young into the water and continues to tend the offspring for an indeterminate period.

The Broad-nosed caiman reaches a maximum length of 3.5 meters. (Lamar, pers. comm. 1989)

This species is also known by a variety of different common names including: Jacare de papo Amerelo in Brazil and as Yacare Overo in Argentina.

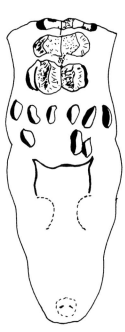

Broad-nosed caiman.

Range of the Paraguayan caiman.

Paraguayan Caiman

SCIENTIFIC NAME: *Caiman yacare* (DAUDIN, 1802)
   STATUS: Indeterminate, CITES II.
   GEOGRAPHIC RANGE: Central and South America including Brazil, Paraguay, Argentina, and Bolivia.
   HABITAT: The Paraguayan caiman is a freshwater species that prefers marshes, lagoons, lakes, and rivers.
   DIET: Snails and fish.

Comments

Hunting is the primary threat to this species, and import of skins or live animals into the United States is prohibited under the Endangered Species Act.

97

Young *Caiman yacare*. (*Photo courtesy of F. Grunwald*)

There is a limited open season on this species which includes minimum size limits. However, these laws are inadequately enforced.

Nesting occurs during the rainy season in Brazil with hatching in March. Between 21 and 38 eggs are laid. This species reportedly reaches a maximum length of 3 meters, but average maximums may be less.

Experts now believe the Paraguayan caiman is a separate and distinct species, *Caiman yacare* instead of a subspecies of *Caiman crocodilus*.

It is also known by the common name Yacare. Two other common names are the Red caiman for its reddish brown hue, and the Piranha caiman because of its showy dentition.

It has also been suggested that there are two other subspecies, *Caiman crocodilus matogrossiensis* and *Caiman crocodilus paraguauensis*, which are distinct from this species.

Black Caiman

SCIENTIFIC NAME: *Melanosuchus niger* (SPIX, 1825)
    STATUS: Endangered, CITES I.
    GEOGRAPHIC RANGE: French Guiana, eastern Ecuador, Peru, Colombia and Brazil.

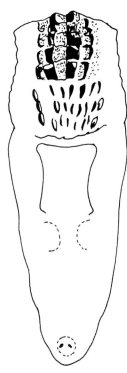

Black caiman.

98

Range of the Black caiman.

Range of the Broad-Nosed caiman.

HABITAT: The Black caiman prefers quiet river backwaters and forested and grassy wetlands. It also inhabits large rivers devoid of rocky banks.

DIET: Fish and other aquatic vertebrates. It also will attack and feed on the semiaquatic South American animal known as the Capybara which is the largest rodent in the world. The Capybara reaches weights in excess of 40 kg. and lengths up to 1.5 meters.

Comments

While once common throughout the Amazon, it is nearly extinct except for protected populations located in Kaw, French Guiana, at Limón Cocha in Ecuador, and in the Manu National Park in Peru. There are still a few in Colombia and other parts of Peru. It is inadequately protected even in refuges. It is a prize for hunters because of its fine hide which is devoid of bony plates or osteoderms and is used to produce a fine, shiny black leather.

The Black caiman is a mound-nesting species that lays between 35 and 50 eggs. The female is known to guard the nest and open it in response to vocalizations from hatchlings within. Juveniles are not uniformly black as adults but have yellow cross bands.

The Black caiman is one of the largest of all New World crocodilians and achieves a maximum length of 6 meters.

This species is also known by local names including Lagarto Negro in Ecuador and Jacare-Acu in Brazil.

Herron et al. (*J. Herpetol.* 24:314–16) report on a one-eyed 3 meter nesting female at Lake Cocha Cashu in Manu National Park, Peru in 1983–4. The animal built a nest of leafy debris with parts below the high water flood mark and laid 38 eggs on October 5, 1983. The eggs hatched about 3 months later on January 1, 1984 shortly before the rainy season. The female did not appear to actively lie on or defend the nest but remained in the vicinity. They attribute this to either human presence in the area (the observers) or shyness that may have occurred as a result of the incident in which the animal lost its eye. Of the 38 eggs laid, 28 successfully hatched. Two dead hatchlings, 2 infertile eggs and 2 eggs with dead embryos were found after the nest was abandoned. The four unaccounted for eggs may have been carried off by the mother or taken by a predator.

Cuvier's Dwarf Caiman

SCIENTIFIC NAME: *Paleosuchus palpebrosus* (CUVIER, 1807)
    STATUS: Not threatened, CITES II.
    GEOGRAPHIC RANGE: Widespread throughout the Orinoco and

Cuvier's dwarf caiman.

Range of Cuvier's dwarf caiman.

Amazon basins. Extends from Colombia, Venezuela and the Guianas south to São Paulo and the upper Rio Paraguay in southern Brazil and west to the Rio Pastaza in Ecuador.

HABITAT: This species prefers clean, clear, fast-moving streams or rivers in forested areas containing waterfalls and rapids. It likes cooler waters compared to other caimans.

DIET: A variety of smaller aquatic invertebrates and vertebrates including fish, amphibians, snails, and crustaceans.

Comments

This species is common throughout South America and travels either alone or in pairs. It is protected by law in Suriname. Since the belly scales are so strongly armored, it is difficult to tan its hide properly. This

101

fact alone has prevented it from being hunted and killed. New technology including a German machine that can shave down the osteoderms makes it more profitable to hunt, however. This species has a chocolate brown-colored iris.

This is a mound-nesting species that lays between 18 and 25 eggs. It may breed throughout the year.

A small species, its maximum length is only 1.5 meters and is probably the smallest crocodilian in the world according to Boos (1989 pers. comm.).

Also known as Cuvier's smooth-fronted caiman since both species of *Paleosuchus* lack the bony infraorbital bridge that occurs in *Caiman crocodilus*.

Schneider's Smooth-Fronted Caiman

SCIENTIFIC NAME: *Paleosuchus trigonatus* (SCHNEIDER, 1801)
    STATUS: Not threatened, CITES II.
    GEOGRAPHIC RANGE: Throughout the Orinoco and Amazon basins from Venezuela and the Guianas south to Bahia in southern Brazil.
    HABITAT: Cooler, clear forest streams with waterfalls and rapids.
    DIET: A variety of small aquatic vertebrates and invertebrates including snails and crustaceans.

Comments

Like Cuvier's dwarf caiman, this species has extremely thick belly scales backed by osteoderms or bony plates making skins difficult but not impossible to process. Eggs are occasionally eaten by native people, and both live and stuffed curios are sold to tourists. In the past it has also been hunted for food but not in very large numbers. It is protected legally in Suriname.

This is a mound-nesting species that lays between 15 and 20 eggs which hatch in 115 days. It has been bred occasionally in captivity.

Some observers report that this species has a greenish iris.

It reaches an average maximum length of 2 meters. Medem (1981) mentions a record specimen of 2 meters, 62 cm.

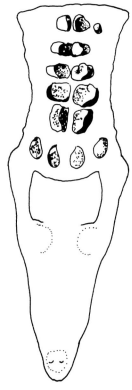

Schneider's smooth-fronted caiman.

Range of Schneider's smooth-fronted caiman.

PART THREE

THE SUBFAMILY CROCODYLINAE
(Cuvier, 1807)

Crocodiles

Crocodylinae is a subfamily of the Class Reptilia, Order Crocodylia, Family Crocodylidae, consisting of 13 species in 2 genera.

Special features: With the mouth closed, the fourth tooth of the lower jaw is clearly visible as opposed to alligators and caimans in which it is not. Crocodile snouts are generally narrower and more elongate than those of alligators and caimans. Compared to alligators and caimans, crocodile eyes are closer together, smaller, and less raised. Because of their oblique orientation, they often give the animal the appearance of being "cross-eyed."

The 13 species of crocodiles include 12 in the genus *Crocodylus* and 1 in genus *Osteolaemus*.

The name "crocodile" was used by ancient Greeks over 2,000 years ago while traveling in Egypt. The Nile crocodiles they saw there reminded them of a giant version of a small lizard in Greece that they called "kroko-delios" which translates to "pebble-worm."

The largest and only truly seagoing crocodilian is a crocodile—*Crocodilus porosus*, or the saltwater crocodile. Some crocodiles will venture into brackish waters but would not tolerate the salinity of open seas for as long a time as this species does.

Crocodiles include species which are both mound nesters and hole nesters, but most are likely to simply dig a hole in sandy embankments or beaches to lay their eggs. Many species exhibit a high level of parental care that includes guarding of nests, opening of nests and eggs, carrying young to the water after hatching, and guarding the pod for extended periods. In some species while the pod remains together, it does so without parental involvement because of the tendency for adults to cannibalize juveniles.

Crocodiles arose in the late Cretaceous era, either in North America or Eurasia. Before the end of the period they were present throughout Europe, Africa, northern and southern Asia as well as North and South America.

American Crocodile

SCIENTIFIC NAME: *Crocodylus acutus* (CUVIER, 1807)

STATUS: Endangered, CITES, I.

GEOGRAPHIC RANGE: Central Mexico south through portions of Central America to northern South America; Ecuador and northern Peru on the Pacific and Colombia and Venezuela on the Caribbean. Also present in Cuba, Martinique, Trinidad, Margarita, Jamaica, Haiti, and the Dominican Republic. Present in the United States at the southernmost tip of the Florida peninsula in Dade County and in isolated parts of the northern Florida Keys (Monroe County).

HABITAT: This species prefers coastal habitats, mangrove swamps, brackish waters, and canals, but in some areas outside the United States may extend inland to lakes and the tributaries of larger rivers.

DIET: Mainly fish and other aquatic organisms.

Range of the American crocodile.

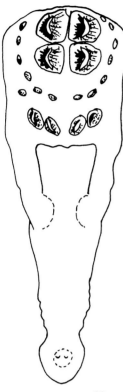

American crocodile.

Comments

Some researchers feel that the American crocodile once naturally extended coastally as far north as Vero Beach and Tampa in Florida. Others feel that this is not the case, at least in modern times, and that early sightings that far north were odd strays or artificially introduced. According to Kushlan and Mazzotti (1989a) they were once a common sight throughout the upper keys, westward to Florida Bay and in other intracoastal waterways bordering Miami and Fort Lauderdale including Biscayne Bay.

Today there are only three breeding populations in the United States—at the Turkey Point Nuclear Power Plant, in North Key Largo, and in the Everglades bordering Florida Bay.

According to Kushlan and Mazzotti (1989b), there are only 220 ± 78 adult and subadult crocodiles remaining in the United States. After annual hatching, this number would be no more than 500 animals if every hatchling was counted. There are only about 50 nesting females, but the number of viable eggs produced or eggs that escape predation is low—at best about 200 hatchlings per year. However, more than 90% of these may not survive their first year of life.

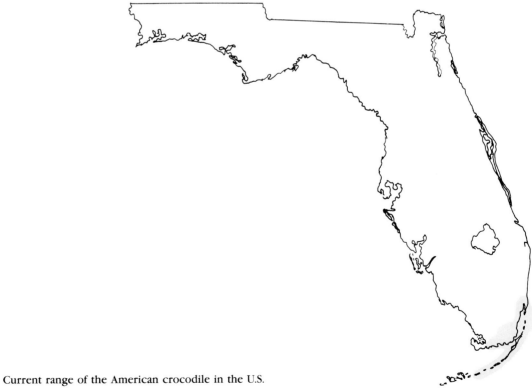

Current range of the American crocodile in the U.S.

Historical range of the American crocodile in Florida.

Outside the United States, the American crocodile was once widely distributed but now is seriously depleted as well, almost solely because of hunting for skins coupled with a loss of habitat. One of the last large populations outside the United States is an estimated 300 animals at Lago Enriquillo in the Dominican Republic.

The American crocodile is protected by U.S. and international laws. Outside the United States it is threatened because of similarity of appearance to other legally hunted species.

The American crocodile produces an average clutch of 38 eggs which it deposits in mound nests, holes, or excavations on sandy embankments. The female guards the nest, opens it at hatching, assists juveniles in escaping the egg, and may carry young to the water in her mouth. Both males and females protect their pods. In spite of this excellent parental behavior reproductive success has been disappointing when compared to the American alligator.

Breeding begins in the U.S. population as early as February with courtship and mating rituals that last six to eight weeks.

They site their nests on any suitable piece of land above the waterline or high tide mark. Nests have been found at the heads of beaches, along creek banks, and on canal levees. Occasionally females will dig a flask-shaped hole, not bothering to construct the traditional mound and egg chamber. In a remarkable example of adaptation, American crocodiles, which inhabit the cooling water canals at Florida Power and Light's Turkey Point Nuclear Power Plant south of Miami, build their nests on the man-made berms located between canals.

If material for the construction of a traditional nest is either not available or in short supply, this will not deter females from their reproductive imperative. They'll improvise. One way is to deposit their eggs in the nest of another female. Nests with as many as 80 eggs are believed to contain two families, not one. Recently workmen digging in the Everglades found a clutch of viable crocodile eggs ensconced in a gravel pit. The eggs were carefully removed, incubated, hatched in the lab, and then released near where they were found. In another case workers observed a female crocodile "stealing" mouthfuls of sand from a construction site to use in her own construction project.

Nest building begins in March, and eggs hatch in about 90 days, in late July or early August.

Crocodiles reach an average length of 4 meters. A maximum of 7 meters has been recorded but is exceedingly rare.

Mazzotti (1985) has studied the effects of increased water temperature and salinity levels on the growth and development of this species in an effort to determine what, if any role, these factors may have.

An important part of the American crocodile's range in the United States is the 12,700 acre site of the Turkey Point Nuclear Power Plant in Dade County, Florida, 25 miles south of Miami. To the northeast it is bordered by Biscayne Bay and to the southeast by Card Sound. The site outside the plant itself and its cooling water canals is composed of coastal marshland and mangrove swamps. Some 9,500 acres are occupied by the four generating units, support facilities, cooling water canals (brackish water) and buffer zones. The closed loop cooling system is 8.2 kilometers long, 2.4 kilometers wide, and has 32 discharge and 6 return canals with a total length of 270 kilometers. Each canal is about 60 meters wide and anywhere from 0.5 to 2 meters deep. Cooling water is discharged into the northeastern corner of the system where it flows westward, then south, and is collected at the southern end of the system where it's returned to the plant via intakes. About 64% of the system consists of brackish to very salty water. About 36% of the system consists of man-made berms or ridges which were created from dredged material during construction. The berms range from 1 to 5 meters high, have sloping banks, and average 27 meters in width. Mazzotti et al. (1985) estimate that the resident population of crocodiles at Turkey Point numbers 19 adult, subadult, and juvenile animals. Three nesting females build their nests on the berms between the canals. They reported that the long-term outlook for this small population is good, and they predict growth and expansion. Mazzotti and Dunson (1984) say that juvenile American crocodiles do not grow in full-strength seawater in captivity. In the field, however, animals inhabiting extremely salty waters were tracked and found to grow rapidly. This was attributed to the observation that wild juvenile crocodiles selectively drank from non-salty, low-salt or brackish waters that pooled during rainfalls. Crocodiles hatch during the rainy season, and they apparently manage this way for three to four months when they reach a size where they're more able to tolerate higher levels of salinity.

The water at Turkey Point is constantly recirculated in the plant and cools the generators by absorbing excess heat; the heat is then dissipated in the miles of canals through which the water flows. The average temperature of this water should, theoretically, be much warmer than nearby natural waters. Mazzotti et al. (1986) determined that the average maximum water temperature in the southwestern part of the system where nests and hatchlings occur ranged from 34° to 42°C during the summer, and during the summer of 1980, the mean maximum water temperatures in the system were between 1.9° and 7.4°C warmer than nearby natural water. The overall absolute temperatures inside and outside the system did not differ significantly. In the laboratory, hatchlings exhibit thermal stress at a water temperature of 40°C. At this temperature, hatchlings remain out of the water, cease to feed, and begin to lose weight. At Turkey Point it is noted that the hatchlings avoid warmer portions of the system. In 48 captures of three-month-old hatchlings, the water temperature ranged from 32° to 35°C.

In 1984 the U.S. Fish and Wildlife Service issued its "Crocodile Recovery Plan," which was prepared by a six-member team of experts dubbed the "American Crocodile Recovery Team." Team members included Paul Moler (leader), Tommy Hines, Richard Klukas, James A. Kushlan, John C. Ogden, and William B. Robertson. The plan makes many excellent recommendations in order to save a species which, in the U.S. as well as elsewhere, is very close to extinction. On the subject of captive hatching and/or rearing programs, which have been successful elsewhere, the plan does not think such a program is necessary but holds in reserve the possibility for action on this it if becomes necessary. The criteria to initiate such a program are vague. The placement of culverts or tunnels under roadways near where crocs have been killed by cars in the past may help cull some of this mortality. However, several factors mitigate against crocodiles using them in preference to going over the roadway. One factor is the croco-

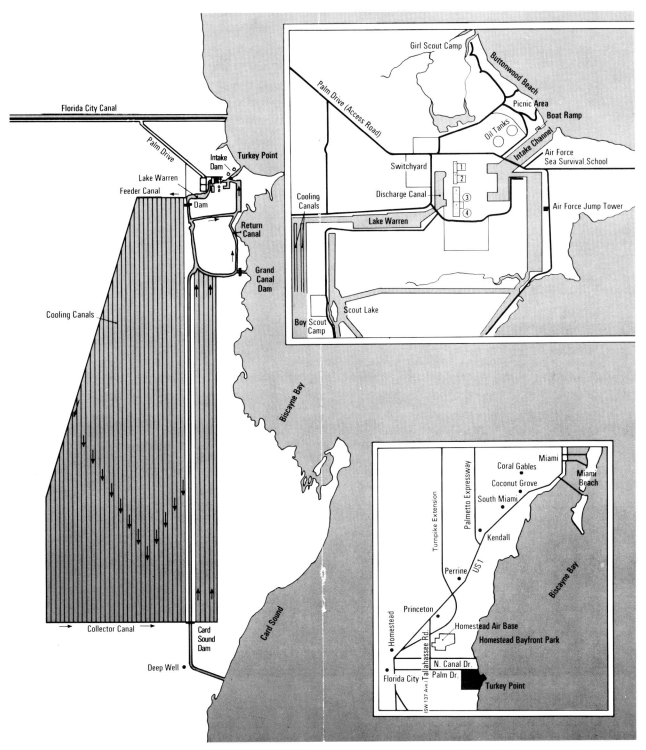

Turkey Point Nuclear Power Plant. The cooling canals are home to some 19 American crocodiles, including nesting females. (*From "Welcome to Turkey Point," Florida Power and Light*)

dilians' use of roadways to thermoregulate. The heat absorbed and then radiated by roads, especially at night, may continue to attract these animals over the top. In addition many workers seem to feel that crocodilians navigate using celestial cues. If this is true then they would be reluctant to enter a darkened tunnel and lose sight of such cues, even momentarily.

U.S. Fish and Wildlife Recovery Plan

The American crocodile (*Crocodylus acutus*) is a tropical, estuarine species that reaches its northern range limit in southern Florida. Elsewhere, this species occurs in Cuba, Jamaica, Hispaniola, and both coasts of Mexico from Sinaloa and Tamaulipas south through Central America to Peru and Colombia. The American crocodile is listed as "endangered" throughout its total range by the United States Fish and Wildlife Service (Fed. Reg. 44: 75074–75076) and the International Union for Conservation of Nature and Natural Resources (Honegger, 1975). In Florida, the crocodile has only infrequently been the subject of surveys or studies, thus its status and distribution have generally been poorly known. Surveys and some assessment of nesting success, primarily by National Park Service personnel since the early 1950's (Moore, 1953; Ogden, 1978), revealed continued declines by the Florida population. The Florida population of the American crocodile was placed on the U.S. Department of the Interior's List of Endangered and Threatened Wildlife on 25 September 1975 (Fed. Reg. 40: (44)149), and critical habitat was designated 24 September 1976 (Fed. Reg. 41:(419)1415).

The American crocodile in south Florida is generally associated with mangrove-lined creeks and bays, isolated from frequent human intrusion. Crocodiles often are detected in small ponds or creeks with two to five feet of water, which are protected from winds or strong currents and which are adjacent to larger bodies of water. Crocodiles readily move into abandoned or little-used canals or flooded quarries in mangroves or coastal hardwoods where similar conditions exist. This species appears to be shy and may not often be seen even where a few live in close proximity to human dwellings. Crocodiles are generally inactive during the day and rest on secluded creek or canal banks, in dens, or hidden in thickets at the edge of water. They appear to be more active at night, moving into creeks, canals, or open bays, primarily to feed. Adult crocodiles are known to feed on fish, crabs, birds, and turtles. Juveniles have been observed feeding on small fish (*Poecilia latipinna*) and arthropods.

Crocodiles often construct low nest mounds in sand, marl, or peat soil, at the heads of small beaches, along high creek banks, or on abandoned canal levees through mangrove swamps, although they occasionally

114

Crocodilian in a field jumping up with jaws agape in an obvious threat/attack display. (*Photo courtesy of the American Museum of Natural History/by Julian A. Dimock*)

dig nest holes without first constructing a mound. A female may return to re-use the same site for several years. Eggs are laid during late April or early May and hatch during July or August. Reported clutch size in Florida ranges from 19 to 81 eggs (Ogden, 1978), but there is some evidence suggesting that the larger reported egg complements may represent the combined clutches from more than one animal. Adult females are not known to defend nests, but females do open nests to release young and may carry hatching eggs or young from the nest to the nearby water (Ogden and Singletary, 1973). Ogden (1978) reported that adults and newly hatched young apparently move away from the more exposed nesting sites in Florida Bay within a few days after the hatch, possibly going to places that are better for salinity, food, and cover. Little is known of American crocodile behavior patterns or daily and seasonal activity patterns and movements of each age-class, although Garrick and Lang (1977) reported that courtship in captive American crocodiles (of Jamaican origin) is complex and occurs over a six-week period during February and March.

Crocodiles are approximately 26 cm. long at hatching, while the smallest breeding females seen in Florida Bay during the early 1970's were about 2.5 m. long and of unknown age. The largest crocodiles reported from Florida have been about 4.6 m. in length.

Historical Florida Range and Numbers

The first certain record of an American crocodile in Florida was in 1869, based on a specimen from the Miami River (Barbour, 1923). Succeeding visits to southeastern Florida by naturalists and biologists revealed that crocodiles occurred on the Atlantic coast at Lake Worth, Palm Beach County, in proper habitat along the entire length of Biscayne Bay, Dade County, and south in Florida Bay and the Florida Keys to the Matecumbe Keys (Smith, 1896; Hornaday, 1904; Dimock, 1918; G. Voss, pers. comm.). The occurrence of crocodiles in the lower Florida Keys, including Key West (Neill, 1971), is poorly documented, and it remains uncertain if the two populations were once contiguous. Crocodiles have been occasionally reported, both historically and recently, along the southwest and western coast of Florida (LeBuff, 1957), including a 1953 report of a crocodile hatch in the Ten Thousand Islands region (H. Campbell, pers. comm.). Within this historical range, verified crocodile nesting was observed along the shoreline and on islands of eastern and central Florida Bay (Dimock and Dimock, 1908), along the shoreline of Biscayne Bay (Smith, 1896), and at Lake Worth (G. Voss, pers. comm.).

The number of crocodiles in south Florida during the late nineteenth century is unknown, although it seems likely that it was not a common animal. Crocodiles were regularly seen along the mainland shore between northern Biscayne Bay and central Florida Bay, and were most numerous in a region ten miles long and three miles wide lying west from Card Sound into northeastern Florida Bay (Dimock, 1918). A close reading of the accounts of the exploration of this region suggests that no more than 5 to 10 crocodiles were seen in a day in prime habitat. Based on this information, Ogden (1978) estimated that the number of crocodiles in southern Florida near the end of the nineteenth century probably was no greater than five times the present number, or roughly 1,000 to 2,000 animals. Crocodiles may have been more numerous prior to the late nineteenth century, as there is evidence that crocodiles were already fairly extensively hunted by the 1890's (Dimock and Dimock, 1908; Hornaday, 1904).

Several American crocodiles from Florida are known to be in captivity. Behler (1978) provided a list of these animals and their locations.

Recent Florida Range and Numbers

The range of crocodiles in Florida during the early 1970's is based on Ogden (1978) and more recent observation by members of the recovery team. Crocodiles are regularly seen in Everglades National Park along the mainland shoreline of Florida Bay from Terrapin Bay east to Long Sound and on some adjacent islands in northeastern Florida Bay, and less frequently west to the Cape Sable peninsula. Crocodiles are also on the upper Florida Keys from lower Plantation Key north to the upper end of Key Largo, and along Cross Key to the mainland shoreline of Barnes Sound, Card Sound, and southern Biscayne Bay north to Turkey and Black Points. Crocodiles may also occur in the lower Florida Keys, primarily within the boundaries of the Key Deer and Great White Heron National Wildlife Refuges, on Big Pine, Little Pine, Howe, Johnston, and upper Sugarloaf Keys (J. Watson, pers. comm.), but recent field work has failed to verify the continued presence of crocodiles in this area (H. Campbell, pers. comm.; T. Jacobsen, 1983). Within this range, nesting is known from the mainland shore of Florida Bay, on one island in north-central Florida Bay, on Key Largo at Lake Surprise, and in mangrove swamps on the Barnes Sound side of upper Key Largo, and on the mainland inland from Mangrove Point. Nesting was reported in the early 1970's on Little Pine Key (J. Watson, pers. comm.), but there are no recent records of nesting in the lower Florida Keys. Comparison of this nesting range with the historical records shows that crocodiles have ceased to nest at Lake Worth in Palm Beach County, along the full length of Biscayne Bay, Dade Country, and in most of Florida Bay, Monroe County. Ogden (1978) estimated the number of crocodiles in this region during the 1970's at 100 to 400 animals, including no more than 20 breeding females.

Reasons for Decline

The decline in the south Florida population of the American crocodile has been due to two types of human activities: (1) habitat alterations and (2)

117

direct human disturbance to crocodiles and their nests. Considering the scarcity of supporting data, the relative importance of the two factors, both historically and presently, is difficult to assess.

Mangrove estuaries have been considerably reduced outside of Everglades National Park, thus crocodiles have been displaced by urbanization at Lake Worth, central and northern Biscayne Bay, and along most of the upper Florida Keys. Conversely, crocodiles remain in the few regions where habitats are relatively undeveloped—Florida Bay, upper Key Largo, spots along the mainland shore between southern Biscayne Bay and Barnes Sound, and possibly in the National Wildlife Refuges in the lower Florida Keys. No management action that will benefit crocodiles can be taken where habitats are already lost, thus this plan is directed towards protection of remaining crocodile habitat, and control of human activities therein.

We have learned of direct, human-related mortality involving 24 crocodiles between 1971 and 1983: 8 by shooting, 13 as highway road kills, and 3 from unknown causes. Six of these animals died on northern Key Largo, and 8 were reported from the Lake Surprise-Blackwater Sound region of central Key Largo. At least 8 were adults: although there are no available data on recruitment of young adults, this rate of human-caused mortality to adult crocodiles on Key Largo may exceed the recruitment of young adults into that segment of the Florida population.

Vandalism to active nests does not appear to occur frequently, although the combined effect of vandalism and direct killing may be adversely affecting crocodile numbers, especially in the Key Largo region.

Indirect disturbance to crocodiles by people is less measurable but may also be an important factor in the human regulation of crocodile numbers and distribution. Crocodiles may have abandoned some otherwise suitable habitats because of the presence of apparently innocuous human activities such as camping, fishing, and boating. Observations made in Florida Bay during the early 1970's (Ogden, pers. comm.) suggest that adult female crocodiles may become disturbed by repeated close human presence during the weeks that nests are being built or reworked and may relocate nests. On northern Key Largo, nests near the Old Card Sound Road in 1971 and at Basin Hills in 1976 were abandoned following increased human activity at these two sites. The opening of nests by adult crocodiles to release newly hatched young means that the females must make repeated trips to nests during late summer, again creating a situation where human presence near nests can adversely affect crocodile reproductive success. Additionally, disturbance during courtship may be disruptive, as has been suggested for the Nile crocodile (Cott, 1968). Crocodile nesting sites on creeks along the north shore of Florida Bay have been seasonally closed to human activities by the National Park Service since the early 1970's, an action that appears to have resulted in increased nesting activity at these sites. Effective in 1980 the National Park Service expanded the sanctuary areas to provide for the year-round closure of Little Madeira Bay, Taylor River, East Creek, Mud Creek, Davis Creek, and Joe Bay and further prohibited landing along the shoreline of northeast Florida Bay (Fed. Reg. 45(33):10350–10355).

The impact that recent levels of raccoon predation on crocodile nests have had on the decline remains unknown. Between 1970 and 1974, six of forty nesting attempts in Florida Bay and the upper Keys were destroyed by raccoons. This 15% rate of nest predation appears relatively low compared to other crocodilian populations. Radio-tracking of juvenile crocodiles in 1973 (Land, pers. comm.) revealed that newly hatched animals are eaten by raccoons, although the extent of this predation remains unknown.

The effects of commercial and sport fishing on crocodiles are unknown, although mullet fishermen working at night in Florida Bay use gill nets in the same "lakes" and bays where crocodiles are active. Crocodiles have occasionally been caught in the gill nets and, at least in the past, sometimes killed. Gill netting is considered an important factor in declines of the Indian gharial, *Gavialus gangeticus* (R. Whitaker, pers. comm.) and the Australian saltwater crocodile, *Crocodylus porosus* (Messel et al., 1981; Jenkins, 1980). Within Everglades National Park, all commercial and net fishing is now prohibited within areas of major crocodile activity (Fed. Reg. 45 (33):10350–10355).

Recovery Objective

Due to the nature and extent of threats to the crocodile, complete delisting may never be possible. Reclassification to a threatened status, however, does appear to be an attainable although long-term objective. Reclassification would be predicated upon an increase in the number of breeding females to a minimum of 60. Censusing would be done by nest counts since this is the simplest method and is approximately equivalent to the number of breeding females. The population increase could be accommodated within currently available habitat. Sixty breeding females translates into an estimated total population size of 1,500 individuals, assuming that, as determined for other crocodilians, breeding females comprise 4–5 percent of the total. Because crocodilians require up to 10–15 years to reach sexual maturity, it would take a minimum of 10–15 years to see any significant recovery, and about 30 years to reach the reclassification objective.

PART 3 THE SUBFAMILY CROCODYLINAE

Step-down Outline

1. Establish secure habitat for all phases of the life cycle.
    1.1. Determine habitat needs throughout life cycle.
        1.1.1. Courtship; seclusion, water depth, temperature, etc.
        1.1.2. Nesting; seclusion, slope, vegetative cover, salinity, temperature relationships, soil type, etc.
        1.1.3. Hatchling; vegetation and cover, water depth, salinity, seclusion, food, etc.
        1.1.4. Sub-adult; food resources, vegetation and cover, home range, water depth, salinity, etc.
        1.1.5. Adult; home range, territory size, space, water depths, vegetation and cover, food resources, etc.
    1.2. Determine habitat distribution and status.
        1.2.1. Conduct surveys to locate areas meeting known needs of crocodiles.
            1.2.1.1. Upper Keys
            1.2.1.2. Lower Keys
            1.2.1.3. Whitewater Bay north to Sanibel Island
            1.2.1.4. Other areas as identified
        1.2.2. Identify ownership and availability of private land containing adequate crocodile habitat.
        1.2.3. Determine historical distribution of the crocodile in Florida.
    1.3. Acquire and/or otherwise protect areas for crocodiles.
        1.3.1. Assign priority values to privately owned crocodile habitat areas.
        1.3.2. Designate new or delete established Critical Habitat areas as indicated.
        1.3.3. Protect identified habitats by acquisition, lease, easement, etc.
    1.4. Manage habitat for specific crocodile needs.
        1.4.1. Determine impacts of ongoing habitat use and modifications on crocodiles.
            1.4.1.1. Evaluate impacts of habitat modifications, dredging, filling, road construction, etc., on Key Largo and elsewhere as needed.
            1.4.1.2. Evaluate impact of habitat use by humans, commercial and sport fishing, camping, boating, etc.
            1.4.1.3. Evaluate impact of drainage alterations on habitat suitability for crocodiles.
            1.4.1.4. Evaluate impact of exotic species on crocodile habitat (*Caiman*, *Casuarina*, e.g.).

1.4.1.5. Determine levels of pesticide residue in crocodile eggs.

1.4.1.6. Other impacts as identified.

1.4.2. Regulate habitat modification and use where necessary.

1.4.2.1. Regulate sport fishing, camping, boating, and other public use of nesting areas during nesting season.

1.4.2.2. Regulate commercial fishing in high mortality areas.

1.4.3. Assure coordinated management authority by interagency agreements or other means.

1.4.4. Review and comment on impacts of proposed habitat modifications.

2. Provide the maintenance of self-sustaining populations at natural carrying capacity in appropriate habitats.

2.1. Determine present population characteristics.

2.1.1. Evaluate, develop, and apply population census techniques.

2.1.2. Develop marking criteria for identification of crocodiles (ACCOMPLISHED).

2.1.3. Determine present demographic profile.

2.1.3.1. Florida Bay

2.1.3.2. Whitewater Bay north to Sanibel Island (selected areas)

2.1.3.3. Key Largo-Card Sound

2.1.3.4. Lower Keys

2.2. Control man-related mortality and disturbance.

2.2.1. Conduct intensive public education program.

2.2.2. Post St. Rd. 905 and U.S. 1 with warning signs.

2.2.3. Provide box culverts under U.S. 1 and St. Road 905.

2.2.4. Conduct program to minimize conflicts by public education and relocation.

2.2.4.1. Move nuisance animals into protected habitat areas identified during habitat surveys.

2.2.4.2. Develop public education programs.

2.3. Determine feasibility of and need for captive propagation.

2.3.1. Evaluate captive propagation for production of young (ACCOMPLISHED. Behler, 1978)

2.3.2. Monitor need for implementation of captive propagation.

2.4. Monitor natural mortality in nesting and nursery areas and evaluate need for predator control program.

2.5. Examine past releases-relocations (ACCOMPLISHED).

2.6. Monitor demographic, numerical, and distribution trends for five years; then reevaluate needs.

2.7. Evaluate carrying capacity of habitat.

2.8. Determine demographic characteristics of natural self-sustaining crocodile population.

2.9. Develop criteria for distinguishing Florida from other crocodiles.

Narrative

1. *Establish secure habitat for all phases of the life cycle.* Loss of the habitat to human use has been an important factor in the decline of the crocodile. If the species is to be maintained, adequate habitat for all of its needs must be provided.

  1.1. *Determine habitat needs throughout life cycle.* The variety of habitats required for successful courtship and nesting and the specific needs of each age-class must be determined. Both abiotic (temperature, salinity, e.g.) and biotic requirements (food resources, territorial requirements, e.g.) need to be analyzed.

  1.2. *Determine habitat distribution and status.* The location and legal availability of areas of habitat utilized by crocodiles in the past and the present must be determined.

    1.2.1. *Conduct surveys to locate areas meeting known needs of crocodiles.* The Florida Keys from Key Largo south, especially Big Pine, and adjacent Keys and the southwest coast of Florida from Whitewater Bay north to Marco Island should be surveyed to determine the location of suitable habitats. Other areas outside these boundaries should also be surveyed if information indicating past or present crocodile use is obtained.

    1.2.2. *Identify ownership and availability of the crocodile in Florida.* Historical and archaeological records should be searched to develop a more precise documentation of the past ownership and availability of crocodiles.

    1.2.3. *Determine historical distribution of the crocodile in Florida.* Historical and archaeological records should be searched to develop a more precise documentation of the past distribution of crocodiles.

  1.3. *Acquire and/or otherwise protect areas for crocodiles.* Once the habitat requirements are documented and distribution of adequate habitat known, the Critical Habitat designation should be reviewed and altered if found inadequate. Immediate action is needed to acquire areas of principal crocodile activity on Key Largo. The establishment of Crocodile Lake National Wildlife Refuge by the U.S. Fish and Wildlife Service was a major step toward implementation of this recommendation. We reiterate the urgent need for prompt action to acquire the Basin Hills and Chastain tracts as early as possible so that human disturbance in these critical areas can be reduced and appropriate management actions initiated. The Refuge should be staffed as soon as possible. Staffing would provide increased opportunity for population monitoring and habitat management. Service presence would also aid in reducing human disturbance, vandalism, and shooting of crocodiles.

1.4. *Manage habitat for specific crocodile needs.* All activities affecting areas of crocodile habitat should be evaluated for impacts on the crocodile and appropriate steps taken to insure that the habitat is maintained in a condition of optimum suitability for crocodiles.

    1.4.1. *Determine impacts of ongoing habitat use and modification on crocodiles.* Specific review of the impacts of drainage alteration in the Everglades National Park and adjoining areas, of road construction, of dredging and other habitat modifications, and of human use, especially commercial and sport fishing with nets, is urgently needed. The impact of exotic species, both plant and animal, on habitat quality also needs review. Studies on pesticide (and possibly heavy metal) levels in crocodile eggs (Ogden et al., 1973, Hall et al., 1979) should be repeated at five year intervals.

    1.4.2. *Regulate habitat modifications and use where necessary.* If detrimental factors are identified, corrective regulations should be imposed.

    1.4.3. *Assure coordinated management authority by interagency agreements or other means.* Responsibility for the management of the American crocodile is currently divided between the State of Florida (Florida Game and Fresh Water Fish Commission), the U.S. National Park Service, and the U.S. Fish and Wildlife Service. Steps should be taken to insure that the actions of these agencies are coordinated and non-conflicting.

    1.4.4. *Review and comment on proposed habitat modifications.* Steps are needed to insure that all actions which alter the habitats utilized by crocodiles are fully evaluated. Many projects of importance are currently unevaluated.

2. *Provide for the maintenance of self-sustaining populations at natural carrying capacity in appropriate habitats.*

2.1. *Determine present population characteristics.* An overview of the present population, both in and out of the Everglades National Park, is needed.

    2.1.1. *Evaluate, develop, and apply population census techniques.* Available techniques should be evaluated, new ones designed, if necessary, and a standardized census programs implemented to establish a baseline and monitor future population trends.

2.1.2. *Develop making criteria for identification of crocodiles.* Crocodiles relocated or handled in the course of other studies should be marked to allow for future recognition. The system used should be coordinated with all such programs (ACCOMPLISHED).

2.1.3. *Determine present demographic profile.* Age-class and sex distribution data within the population are needed in addition to basic population numbers and distribution data.

2.2. *Control man-related mortality and disturbance.* No data are available to indicate the severity of natural mortality on the crocodile population. Current human-related factors are clearly unnatural; however, and should be controlled. Some specific problems are already identified and others need evaluation.

2.2.1. *Conduct intensive public education program.* Public education through the public media in south Florida is needed to increase the public's awareness of the critical status of the crocodile. There has been some information and a fair amount of misinformation independently generated in the printed media in south Florida, but there has been no effort to institute a well-planned public education campaign. As a result, there remains a considerable popular misunderstanding of the biology and disposition of the American crocodile.

2.2.2. *Post State Road #905 and U.S. Hwy. #1 with warning signs.* Crocodiles are periodically hit by cars on these roads, and motorists should be alerted to watch for them. The signs could also serve an educational function.

2.2.3. *Provide box culverts under U.S. Hwy #1 and State Road #905.* Culverts placed in areas of significant historic crocodile highway mortality should eliminate the need for crocodiles to cross the roadway and thus minimize highway mortality.

2.2.4. *Conduct program to minimize conflicts by public education and relocation.* The public should be reassured that smaller crocodiles are no threat. Problem animals should be translocated to areas where conflicts can be avoided.

2.3. *Determine feasibility of and need for captive propagation.* Present data do not indicate a need for immediate implementation of a captive propagation effort. However, the feasibility of captive propagation should be determined and an implementation protocol developed so that captive propagation may be initiated as expeditiously as possible should the need arise.

    2.3.1. *Evaluate captive propagation for production of young.* Captive propagation versus rearing of eggs produced in the wild should be evaluated. The availability of wild-produced eggs, the economics of captive propagation versus simple rearing, the availability of a native south Florida breeding stock, all should be reviewed (ACCOMPLISHED, Behler, 1978).

    2.3.2. *Monitor need for implementation of captive propagation.* Status of wild populations should be frequently reviewed and captive propagation program implemented if it appears necessary to artificially increase recruitment.

2.4. *Monitor natural mortality in nesting and nursery areas and evaluate need for predator control program.* Predation on nests and hatchlings should be monitored and predator control programs initiated if and when the need becomes apparent.

2.5. *Examine past releases-relocations.* The genetic status of the present population may have been disturbed by indiscriminate release of American crocodiles from other parts of the species' range. The full extent of such releases needs to be evaluated (ACCOMPLISHED).

2.6. *Monitor demographic, numerical, and distribution trends for five years; then reevaluate needs.* The continuing status of the population should be regularly monitored through the techniques developed in 2.1.1. This program should be designed to provide a specific check on the effects of proposed management actions.

2.7. *Evaluate carrying capacity of habitat.* For the ultimate selection of quantitative goals for the recovery program, we will need data on the natural carrying capacity of crocodile habitats. This should be approached by reviewing historical information on the south Florida crocodiles and by reference to present and past crocodile populations in foreign areas as available.

2.8. *Determine demographic characteristics of natural self-sustaining crocodile populations.* Age-class and sex ratio distributions are possibly more important than sheer numbers in determining the stability of crocodile populations. Goals for the recovery program should be set using comparative data from foreign populations.

2.9. *Develop criteria for distinguishing Florida from other crocodiles.* Criteria to specifically identify native Florida crocodiles would facilitate an evaluation of the extent to which non-native crocodiles have contributed to the present wild populations.

Note: The references cited in the recovery plan have been incorporated in the general bibliography.

African Slender-Snouted Crocodile

SCIENTIFIC NAME: *Crocodylus cataphractus* CUVIER, 1825
   STATUS: Indeterminate, CITES I.
   GEOGRAPHIC RANGE: West and west-central Africa; has been collected in East Africa in Lake Tanganyika.
   HABITAT: Restricted to rain forests, rivers, and larger lakes. Depletion of known populations due to hunting for skins. It is protected by local laws which have been inadequately enforced since they went into effect.
   DIET: Usually fish and other small-to-medium aquatic vertebrates.

Comments

Maximum length is 4.2 meters but averages are much smaller. Little else is known of its habits or reproduction. This species is also known as the Long-snouted crocodile and as the Panzer crocodile.

   There is an unsubstantiated report that this species may occasionally venture into brackish coastal marshes.

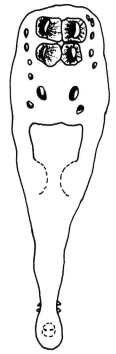

Slender-snouted crocodile.

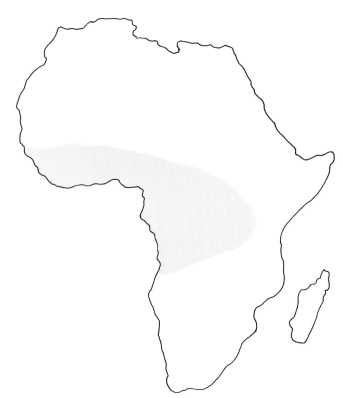

Range of the African Slender-Snouted crocodile.

Orinoco Crocodile

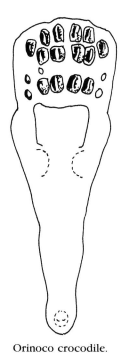

Orinoco crocodile.

SCIENTIFIC NAME: *Crocodylus intermedius* GRAVES 1819

STATUS: Endangered, CITES I.

GEOGRAPHIC RANGE: Restricted to the Orinoco drainage in Venezuela and eastern Colombia.

HABITAT: This is a freshwater species that prefers open waters and occupies an ecosystem known as the llanos, which is a form of savannah covering a wide area in eastern Colombia and Venezuela. The llanos is typified by completely dried out grasslands during the dry season, but during the rainy season it is covered in parts by shallow water. There are occasional patches of palms and deciduous trees.

DIET: Fish and other aquatic vertebrates as well as land mammals drinking at the water's edge or wading in waters inhabited by this species. Juveniles eat smaller fish and invertebrates such as snails.

Comments

This is a moderate (average to 4 meters, record to 7 meters) to very large species with a hide that is ideally suited for tanning. Because of its valuable hide, it has become severely depleted throughout much of its range, and it is protected by international and local laws. It is nearly extinct in Colombia with an estimated 500 surviving animals. Venezuelan populations have not fared much better, and only a thousand animals are believed to exist. However, these figures do not include a recently discovered population on the Rio Caura in the State of Bolivar in Venezuela. This population is threatened, however, by a hydroelectric power plant in the area.

The Orinoco crocodile has also become severely depleted because of intensive hunting for its hide, for food (eggs and meat), and for its teeth, which are ground into a powder and used as a folk medicine. Although it is protected, local laws are inadequately enforced, and smuggling occurs.

This species lays its eggs in holes that the female digs in sandy embankments. It lays anywhere from 15 to 70 eggs in January and February with hatchlings emerging in March. This species is highly protective of its young, and juveniles of up to three seasons have been observed in a single parentally-protected pod.

Medem (1981) describes three color phases: "mariposo" or grey to grey-green with black patches along the back; "amarillo" or light brown or sand-colored back and sides with a few darker patches; and "negro" or dark grey. A "negro" color-phase specimen has been observed changing to "amarillo" during a two-year stint in captivity.

Range of the Orinoco crocodile.

Gorzula (1987) writes that there are numerous myths concerning crocodile lore in Venezuela including the following:

1. *C. intermedius* is strictly a fish-eater, implying it is not a man-eater.
2. This species is important in maintaining river courses in the llanos because their movements cause sediments to move. The implication is that by over-killing this species, flash floods occur as a result.
3. The Orinoco crocodile, as well as the caiman, eats the deadly piranha fish and therefore benefits man by getting rid of this dangerous predator. These crocodiles are of no consequence in ridding their local waters of piranha even though they will eat them.
4. The Orinoco crocodile maintains the ecological balance of fishes, birds, and mammals in the llanos. While holing species may preserve other animals by providing drinking water and a reservoir (for fish and other aquatic species), it is not known to what extent the Orinoco contributes to this process.

5. The Orinoco crocodile's excrement is very important for its value in fertilizing the primary productivity of the llanos. While the excreta of any animal provides an important nutrient base for vegetative growth, in or out of the water, the extent of the Orinoco's contribution to this use is not known. Falling leaves and dead grasses probably provide greater sustenance to successive plant growth than crocodile excrement.

Australian Freshwater Crocodile

SCIENTIFIC NAME: *Crocodylus johnstoni* KREFFT, 1873
STATUS: Vulnerable, CITES II.
GEOGRAPHIC RANGE: Northern Territory, western Australia, and in the Kimberly Region of Queensland, Australia.
HABITAT: Found throughout northern Australia in freshwater rivers, streams, and billabongs or ponds. Occasionally found in coastal marshes and tidal waters with the saltwater crocodile (*C. porosus*).
DIET: Freshwater invertebrates and vertebrates. Larger animals, given the opportunity, feed on terrestrial species.

Comments

Although considered a sacred animal by some tribes, this species has been hunted for food—meat and eggs—by aboriginal peoples some 40,000 years before the first Europeans arrived.

Hunting for hides was largely ignored up to 1958 in favor of the saltwater crocodile, whose hide made a better leather given the technology of the period. However, in 1959 tanning technologies advanced to a point where it was feasible to process *C. johnstoni* hides as well. According to Webb et al. (1987), these technological advances created a market for hides beginning in 1959, causing widespread population depletion as nonaborigines and natives using modern weapons hunted the species. As a result it became protected by law in 1962 in western Australia, in 1964 in the Northern Territory, and in 1974 in Queensland. It is still hunted and killed illegally both by aborigines and by Australians of foreign descent.

This species nests in holes excavated in embankments where it deposits relatively small clutches averaging 13 to 20 eggs. Eggs are laid during the dry season, August to September, and hatch in about 65 to 95 days. Mating occurs six weeks prior to nesting. In addition to being a hole nester, it has also been described as a "pulse nester," because all females in a given population nest within a contracted period of three weeks each season.

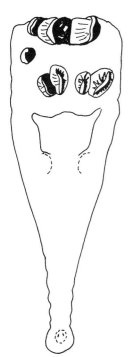

Australian Freshwater crocodile.

Range of the Australian Freshwater crocodile.

Females do not appear to guard their nests, which are heavily preyed upon by feral pigs and monitor lizards. Egg laying usually occurs at night, according to Webb and Manolis (1988). High and low temperatures (33–34°/29–31°C) produce females, intermediate temperatures (32°C) give males.

In late October females reappear at their nesting sites in anticipation of hatching. They will open the nest and have been observed carrying the young in their mouths to the water. They also protect young for indeterminate periods. The species has been bred in zoos and commercial crocodile farms.

The role played by the crocodile as a sacred totem in primitive aboriginal religion is described in an article translated from the German magazine *Stern* by Hans Conrad Zander (1988). The fact that the aborigines hunt and kill as well as worship the crocodile has created a considerable amount of confusion for wildlife authorities charged with protecting these animals.

Zander's essay relates one of the aboriginal legends surrounding Australia's crocodiles. The native peoples believe that all of Australia was a single crocodile. They believe the animal is a true reflection of God's righteousness. The legend goes on to say that it is not their parents to whom children owe their lives—it is the Great Crocodile. It seems that two mothers were fighting over a child, and they beat the child. This caused the

Great Crocodile to become angry. The crocodile god transformed the abused child into a mighty crocodile who devoured the two bad mothers. Since then the crocodile has only been eating bad people.

Aborigines justify the hunting, killing, and eating of crocodiles and their eggs by pointing out that not all animals are sacred animals. Some tribes prefer to think it is only the largest and most mighty of the beasts that is the god whereas some small clans treat all crocodiles with deference. While this legend has no doubt done much good in preventing child abuse, it has had little impact on saving crocodilians from aborigines who crave a meal of the animal. In addition, many aborigines have been converted to Christianity and are prohibited from worshipping idols or totems such as crocodiles and other animal, earth, wind, water, or fire spirits.

This species is also known as Johnstone's River Crocodile. The scientific name has also mistakenly been written as *Crocodylus johsoni*. The original type specimen described by Krefft was collected by a man named "Johstone" in the Herbert River. The Australians refer to this species as "freshies."

Philippine Crocodile

SCIENTIFIC NAME: *Crocodylus mindorensis* SCHMIDT, 1935
    STATUS: Endangered, CITES I.
    GEOGRAPHIC RANGE: Restricted to the Philippine Islands of Luzon, Mindoro, Busuanga, Masbate, Negros, Samar, Mindanao, Jolo, and the Sulu Archipelago.
    HABITAT: Prefers freshwater ponds, smaller tributaries or streams of large rivers.
    DIET: Small aquatic vertebrates and invertebrates including crustaceans and snails.

Comments

This is a small species (record maximum 3 meters) that is critically endangered with small numbers in existence on Mindoro, Negros, and Mindanao. Total population estimates range from 100 to 300 animals. Decline is due to hunting for skins, but the primary threat now appears to be loss or alteration of habitat because of agricultural and aquaculture projects. There is a captive breeding program at Silliman University in Damaguete, Negros. Juveniles are raised and then released in wildlife sanctuaries. It was once suggested that this species was a subspecies of *C. niloticus* and a subspecies of *C. novaeguineae*.

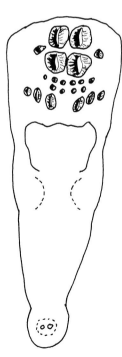

Philippine crocodile.

131

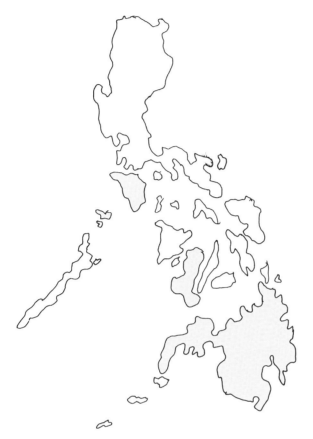

Range of the Philippine crocodile.

Philippine crocodile. (*Courtesy of Bronx Zoo*)

132

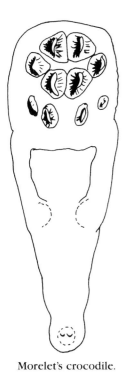

Morelet's crocodile.

Morelet's Crocodile

SCIENTIFIC NAME: *Crocodylus moreletii* BIBRON & DUMERIL, 1851
STATUS: Endangered, CITES II.
GEOGRAPHIC RANGE: Atlantic regions of Central America from Tamaulipas, Mexico south to Belize and northern Guatemala.
HABITAT: Prefers freshwater lagoons, streams, and backwaters in heavily forested regions with floating plant life.
DIET: Small aquatic vertebrates, invertebrates; small mammals, birds, fishes, reptiles, crabs and domestic animals including dogs and goats. According to Pérez-Higareda et al. (1989), a significant percentage of the wild living Morelet's crocodiles at a lake near southern Veracruz regularly sequester killed prey and will consume it 24 or more hours later, after decomposition has set in.

Comments

Because of its fine belly skin, which makes a high quality leather, this species has been severely exploited. While it is protected by law in Mexico, Belize, and Guatemala, these laws are not effectively enforced, and the species remains threatened. Its similarity to other crocodilians makes identification by unsophisticated law enforcement officers difficult. This problem, along with official corruption, threaten the future of the species.

It is a relatively small species, the record length being 3.5 meters. It has been bred in captivity, and there is a captive breeding program at the Tuxtla Gutierrez Zoo in Chiapas, Mexico. It is a mound-nesting species that lays between 20 and 45 eggs. The female guards the nest and the pod after hatching. In one extraordinary observation, a female guarding her pod literally "scolded" juveniles from another pod who decided to intrude

Old capitve Morelet's crocodile. (*Photo courtesy of the American Museum of Natural History*)

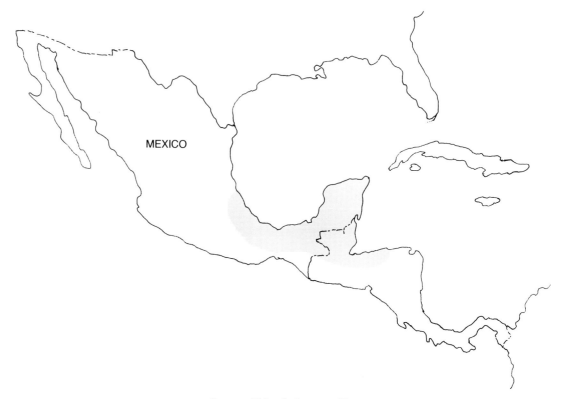

MEXICO

Range of Morelet's crocodile.

upon her brood. She picked up the offending juveniles, shook them in her jaws as a warning, and then released them. They scampered off quickly and did not return. Both males and females have been observed protecting their offspring from potential predators.

Nile Crocodile

SCIENTIFIC NAME: *Crocodylus niloticus* LAURENTI, 1768
STATUS: Vulnerable, CITES I & II.
GEOGRAPHIC RANGE: Widespread throughout Africa south of the Sahara. On the east extends northward as far as Lake Nasser in Egypt. Absent from the extreme southern and southwestern portions of South Africa. Also found on Madagascar. Exterminated in Palestine (Israel) in the early 1900s and no longer found in Egypt below the second cataract of the Nile.
HABITAT: Present in a variety of freshwater wetland habitats including lakes, rivers, swamps, and coastal or brackish swamps. Its presence in

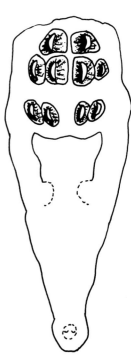

Nile crocodile.

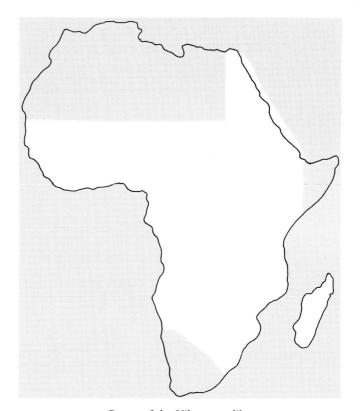

Range of the Nile crocodile.

Madagascar indicates that it may also swim the seas off the southeast coast of Africa.

DIET: Where Nile crocodiles live in large numbers, they compete with humans for food fish sought by indigenous peoples. Full-grown animals in Kruger National Park (South Africa) kill antelopes like impala, bushbuck, and water buck. They also attack, kill, and eat giraffes, buffalo, young hippos, hyenas, wild dogs, porcupines, and lions. According to park officials, the Nile crocodile has killed more humans in Kruger than all other predatory animals combined, including poisonous snakes. Along the Luangue River in Zambia, crocodiles have been observed tracking animal corpses for miles. This population consumes water buffalo that drown in floods, male hippos, and elephants that either die naturally or in fights with rivals, and similar carrion.

Feeding parties on dead animals or carrion are not only attended by crocodiles but by a variety of birds, fish, and other predators. Their presence is tolerated by the crocodiles even though some of these species at other times end up as prey for them. Up to 120 crocodiles have been observed feeding on the cadaver of a hippo, and no other crocodilians were observed at the time for a distance of two miles downstream of the feeding party. Crocodiles less than 2.5 meters in length are never observed together with larger crocodiles at such forays.

The Nile crocodile also tolerates the presence of several species of birds which seem to enjoy a symbiotic relationship with this predator. These birds have been observed feeding on pieces of flesh adhering to the Nile crocodile's teeth. The crocodile gets its teeth cleaned and the bird gets a meal.

Since the teeth of crocodiles are not suited for tearing apart or chewing large prey with heavy hides, they are initially content with biting off ears and tails. This may be one reason other animals are tolerated by crocodiles because the razor-sharp beaks of some birds and the teeth of some fish tear away at large chunks of meat which the crocodile can then eat. In the absence of such assistance, crocodiles have been observed pushing cadavers into underwater hollows where they are stored until softened by decay. A ranger at Kruger reported that a dead native boy was discovered after being missing for a week. His body was firmly lodged among the roots of a tree overhanging an embankment, and it was believed he was put into storage there by the crocodile that killed him.

Nile crocodiles tear the flesh from a cadaver by placing their teeth firmly into it and then quickly rolling over in the water, revolving around the long axis of their bodies.

The tail is flung out of the water during this movement, and the light belly becomes visible in the process. This roll may be repeated several times. Once it has torn off a mouthful, the animal will raise its head above the surface, gulping down the food by so doing. Using a series of jerky movements, the food moves deeper and deeper into the esophagus. Hungry crocodiles will eat until they are full, and when the first part of their two-compartment stomach becomes engorged, they'll continue to feed, stor ng the excess in their esophagus.

A study by Graham and Beard (1973) in Kenya's Lake Rudolf (now Lake Turkana) revealed the probable consequences of social hierarchy among the Nile crocodiles living there. This lake is totally landlocked, occupies 2,473 square miles, and at its longest point extends for some 154 miles. There are no aquatic means by which Nile crocodiles can migrate to other bodies of water so that in spite of reaching adulthood, Lake Rudolf's crocodiles must endure sociality throughout their lives.

One thousand animals were captured and their stomach contents were examined. In 48% of the crocodiles examined, the stomach was empty revealing that nearly one-half of the animals in the lake practiced self-starvation, most likely in favor of the other half. Presumably the 52% with food in the stomach were the more socially dominant members of the population. Crocodilians can live for long periods, perhaps a year or more, without eating, but if hungry and could eat, most healthy active animals clearly would prefer to do so.

Comments

The Nile crocodile has been hunted for food since biblical times but has been severely depleted in modern times for its hide. Substantial populations remain in Botswana (Okavango), Ethiopia (Omo River), northern Kenya (Lake Turkana), Malawi (Lake Malawi), parts of north and northeastern South Africa (Natal), Zambia, and Zimbabwe. It was originally included in CITES I in Zimbabwe but was transferred to CITES II in 1983. Populations in the Cameroons, Zaire, Kenya, Madagascar, Malawi, Mozambique, Sudan, Tanzania, and Zambia were placed in CITES II in 1985 (CITES II allows for legal hunting but with restrictions including size limits, bag limits, and short open seasons).

During mating, the males usually emit a low bellow while lifting up their heads and opening the jaws wide as if yawning. They will also emit a strong musky odor that comes from paired glands located in the cloaca. Courtship and copulation occur in the water usually in the morning. If a male patrolling his territory notices a female intruding, he arches his tail out of the water and lifts his head out of the water while the jaw appears to be resting on the surface. He bellows and vibrates his flanks so vigorously that it causes a fine spray of droplets. He also slaps his head against the water, slaps his jaws open and closed, and makes other noises by beating his tail against the water. He follows the female, overtakes her, and pens her, forcing the potential mate to swim in a circular motion. She acknowledges the advances by emitting low, throaty sounds and then either may flee or allow the male to mount. While the ritual can last for hours, copulation is completed in a few minutes.

The breeding season for the Nile crocodile occurs at different times of the year depending on geographic location. Crocodiles in the Victoria Nile (Uganda) lay eggs in December and January during the dry season. Further south, in Lake Rudolf (Kenya) the eggs are laid after the first rainy season at the end of December. In the Natal portion of South Africa they are laid in November. The Nile crocodile is a hole-nesting species that prefers sandy beaches or embankments. They excavate their nest holes about 2 meters above the water line and between 5 and 10 meters from the water's edge. Occasionally nests may be sited as far as 30 meters from the shoreline in spots selected for only short periods of direct exposure to the sun. Nests are often sited close together, and one study on the shores of Lake Albert counted 24 nests in a 62m² area (Cott, 1961). Nile crocodiles dig their nests with the forefeet and use the hind legs to sweep away the excavated material. Grass is torn away using the teeth and feet. The hole may be anywhere from 20 cm. to 50 cm. in depth, deeper holes dug in areas with the least shade. The entrance to the hole is round, narrowing as it approaches the egg chamber. After the nest is readied, the female deposits about 40 eggs laid in several sessions and piled as high as three layers deep. She covers the eggs with some of the nearby excavated material or grass. The distance between the top layer of eggs and the top of the nest's covering layer may be no more than 10 cm. Modha (1967) measured incubation temperatures in Nile crocodile nests near Murchison Falls and found averages of 30°C. Over a 24-hour period the temperature varied by not more than 3°C.

Incubation requires between 10 and 14 weeks, and during this entire period the female watches over her nest. Pooley (1973) studied the nests of the Nile crocodile at the southern limits of its range in South Africa (Zululand) and found that 22 out of 65 nests were plundered by Nile monitors. The nests have many other predators including mongoose, hyenas, insects, and, of course, man. When the sun becomes too hot, the female guardian may retreat to a shady spot and oversee her nest from there. If the heat becomes excessive, she'll enter the water for a short time, leaving the nest unguarded. This is the time when predators are most likely to do their work. When she returns, she checks the nest by lying over it and at the same time moistens the ground cover with water dripping from her body.

When the young crocodiles are ready to hatch, they start emitting distress vocalizations from within the nest. The female opens the nest and allows the hatchlings to escape. She is so protective during this process that she will attack human observers, something Nile crocodiles rarely do on land.

The female crocodile leads her pack of juveniles around like a mother hen and reportedly watches over them for up to two years. After this period, the juveniles studiously avoid larger crocodiles, probably because they are likely to be attacked by them.

The Nile crocodile is known to dig holes under the embankments of various bodies of water it inhabits. Even youngsters are likely to dig such holes or dens, using them for protection against predators as well as abiotic factors such as drought, heat waves, or cold spells. They dig these burrows by excavating quantities of earth using their mouths as shovels.

Nile crocodiles grow rapidly their first 7 years. Growth rate has been averaged at 26.5 cm. per year and slows as the animal ages. For example, 22-year-old animals grow at a rate of only 3.6 cm. per annum. Males become sexually mature at 2.5 meters, and 8 to 12 years of age. The

Captive Nile crocodile (*Crocodylus niloticus*). *Photo by S. Grenard*

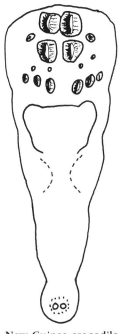

New Guinea crocodile
Southern form (*after Hall*)

maximum length is around 5 meters, but a 1903 report boasts of a 7.6 meter specimen that was taken in the Mbaka River (Tanzania). Today, however, specimens reaching even 5 meters are exceedingly rare.

At one time, the Nile crocodile found in Madagascar was considered a separate species, *Crocodylus madagascariensis*.

New Guinea Crocodile

SCIENTIFIC NAME: *Crocodylus novaeguineae* SCHMIDT, 1928
    STATUS: Vulnerable, CITES II.
    GEOGRAPHIC RANGE: Restricted to the islands in the New Guinea archipelago including Papua New Guinea, Irian Jaya (Indonesia), and the Aru Islands.
    HABITAT: This species occurs primarily in whatever freshwater habitats are available but prefers areas inaccessible to man such as remote, grassy swamplands. These animals are secretive and rarely emerge from cover, even to bask.
    DIET: Emerges at night to feed on fish, water fowl, and other aquatic or semiaquatic vertebrates. Hatchlings eat insects and other invertebrates.

Comments

This species has been extensively hunted for its skin, which produces a high grade leather. Its hide is so highly valued that an early missionary nun even hunted them and used her proceeds to build a mission with church and school, on New Guinea. There are few protected sanctuaries for this species on New Guinea, and laws are inadequately enforced. Exploitation peaked in the 1960s when populations became severely depleted.

Hall (1989) confirms that it is a mound-nesting species that nests during the first rains in Papua in the south, and in the north they nest during the dry season. Between 22 and 35 eggs are laid. Females guard their nests, and both males and females have been observed opening the nest and carrying their hatchlings into the water.

Sexual maturity occurs between 1.8 and 2 meters in females, 2.5 in males. Males may reach a length of 3 to 3.3 meters, but animals this size are scarce.

Using scale counts, skull structure, and varying reproductive strategies, Hall (1989) has determined that there are two distinct races of the New Guinea crocodile, one occupying the north and the other the south. Hall also claims his study has resolved a dispute that has been raging for decades regarding this species.

European scientists said Schmidt's New Guinea crocodile was a form of the Philippine crocodile or vice-versa because they are so structurally similar. After examining the scale counts, patterns, and skull structures of hundreds of specimens of both species, Hall vindicates Schmidt (1928, 1935) who did his original work on the basis of just two skulls of the New Guinea crocodile and four skulls of the Philippine crocodile. This species was also once suggested as a subspecies of *C. niloticus*.

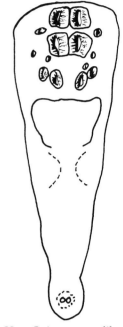

New Guinea crocodile
Northern form (*after Hall*).

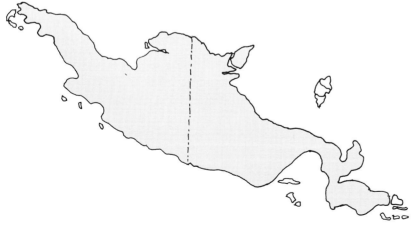

Range of the New Guinea crocodile.

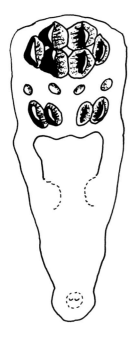

Mugger crocodile.

Mugger Crocodile

SCIENTIFIC NAME: *Crocodylus palustris* LESSON, 1831
STATUS: Vulnerable, CITES II.
GEOGRAPHIC RANGE: Indian subcontinent, extending into Pakistan, Iran, Sri Lanka, and possibly Bangladesh. Isolated populations have been observed in the Sunda Archipelago and possibly in Indochina (Vietnam, Thailand, and Cambodia). Extends northward into Nepal where it is protected by law.
HABITAT: Inhabits any freshwater wetlands including rivers, lakes, drainages, reservoirs, marsh, or swamplands. With over 800 million people in India, loss of habitat and competition with humans is a real threat for this species.
DIET: Fish, frogs, crustaceans, and occasionally birds and mammals.

Comments

This species has been exploited for its hide and has been threatened by habitat loss due to human encroachment. Indigenous peoples collect eggs for food. In spite of these problems, substantial populations have been maintained in Sri Lanka, Nepal, and at the Gir Sanctuary in the State of Gujarat and in the Amaravathi Reservoir in the Anamallais Sanctuary in the State of Tamil Nadu. Good populations are also sustained at the Yala and Wilpattu National Parks. Like a number of other species, the Mugger

Captive adult Mugger crocodile (*C. palustris*). (*Photo courtesy of the American Museum of Natural History/by Raymond L. Ditmars*)

141

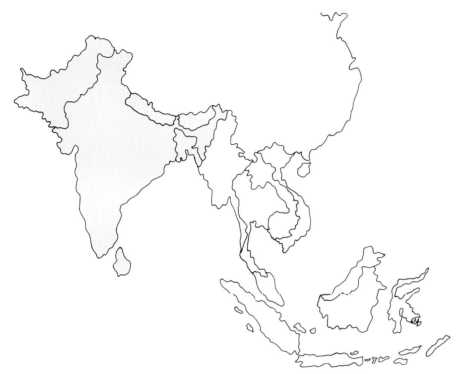

Range of the Mugger crocodile.

excavates holes or tunnels in which to den during excessively cold, hot, or dry weather conditions. This species can migrate overland for great distances during both the dry and rainy (monsoon) seasons.

A clutch of 10 to 48 eggs (average 28) is laid between December and February and hatches in May. Hatching may occur later—in June, in the more northerly reaches of the Mugger's range. It is a hole-nesting species that constructs or excavates a pitcher-shaped nest situated on high, sloping banks. Incubation takes between 55 and 75 days. Lang et al. (1989) report incubation temperatures of 28°C to 31°C produce all females. At 32.5°C only males occur. Both sexes in various proportions hatch at 31.5°C, 32.0°C, and 33.0°C.

Sexual maturity is attained in females at 1.7 to 2 meters in length at about 6 years of age, but occurs later in males. The record size for a Mugger is 5.8 meters.

In a captive group of Muggers, an adult male was noted to have engaged in an unusual case of "role-reversal"—taking on the job of the female, including opening the nest and transporting the hatchlings to the water while the female stood by and watched.

The Mugger has been protected by law in India and neighboring

142

countries since 1972. Many states, with the assistance of the United Nations Development Program and the Food and Agriculture Organization, have started farming programs and captive rearing/releasing programs.

The Mugger is also known as the Marsh or Swamp Crocodile. According to Whitaker (1987), it is called the "magar machh" in Hindi.

A subspecies of the Mugger in Sri Lanka (Ceylon) was once suggested: *Crocodylus palustris kimbula* by Deraniyagala.

Saltwater crocodile.

Saltwater Crocodile

SCIENTIFIC NAME: *Crocodylus porosus* SCHNEIDER, 1801

STATUS: Endangered, CITES II (in Australia, parts of New Guinea, and Indonesia), CITES I (elsewhere).

GEOGRAPHIC RANGE: Covers a widespread area, extending from Sri Lanka, eastern India, Andaman and Nicobar Islands, Bangladesh, through coastal southeast Asia to the Philippines, Western Carolines (Palau), and south through Indonesia to Papua New Guinea, northern Australia, east to Vanuatu, and the Solomon Islands.

Animals driven out to sea by the tides and wind make amazingly long voyages. One crocodile arrived at the Cocos Islands in the Indian Ocean after having traveled at least 1,100 km. from its point of origin.

HABITAT: This species has been found in the Irrawaddy Delta in Burma, coastal Brunei, Malaysia, Philippines, Thailand (possibly extinct), Vietnam (possibly extinct), and Cambodia (no recent information available, possibly extinct). This species is home both at sea, in fresh water, and in coastal (brackish) marshlands.

DIET: Juveniles eat crustaceans, insects, and smaller fish. Adults feed on larger fish, aquatic vertebrates.

Comments

The high commercial value of this large species' hide is due to the small belly scales and large area devoid of blemish-causing osteoderms. Although protected by legislation throughout most of its range, laws are not adequately enforced, and poaching occurs regularly. Adequate populations remain in northern Australia and parts of New Guinea.

This is a mound-nesting species that lays from 25 to 90 eggs. Average clutch size is 50. Mounds are constructed of grassy plant matter, and after the nest is sealed, the female keeps it moist by regularly spraying water on it from an adjacent water pit she digs for the purpose. This activity keeps

Range of the Saltwater crocodile.

the female near the nest most of the time, and she will defend it against predators. She opens the nest on hearing cries from within and has been observed carrying newborns to the water in her mouth. According to Webb and Manolis (1988) average nest temperatures of 31.6°C produce mainly males, but temperatures a little lower (31°C) or higher (33°C) produce all females. At temperatures of 29°C, eggs hatch in about 106 days; at 33°C they hatch in 75 days.

Under commercial farm conditions, this species has been successfully bred. However, there is a poor record of captive breeding in zoos.

This species is the largest of all living crocodilians and reportedly can reach a length of 8 meters but this is doubtful. Maximum lengths are around 6 meters. Arthur M. Jones (pers. comm. 1990) has a 17.5 foot specimen in his collection. According to the *Guinness Book of World Records* (1989), a *C. porosus* measuring 8.05 meters and weighing 2,000 kg. was killed in Australia's Normal River in 1957. *Guinness* also says that the largest living captive crocodilian is a hybrid Siamese/Saltwater (*C. siamensis* × *C. porosus*) named "Yai" that was born on June 10, 1972, in a Thai zoo. At the present time it is 5.9 meters long and weighs 1,100 kgs. A Ceylonese subspecies, *C. porosus minikanna* has been suggested by Deraniyagala but never has been accepted.

This species is also known as the Estuarine and as the Indo-Pacific crocodile. Australians refer to this species as "salties."

The Saga of Sweetheart

Sweetheart was not named for his disposition but rather for the billabong he inhabited which was a part of the Finniss River system, in a portion of the Finniss lagoon called Sweet's Lookout, south of Darwin, Northern Territory, Australia. He was a massive, 5.1 meter (16 foot 9 inch) male, weighing 780 kgs. His girth was 2.3 meters (7 feet 6 inches) in diameter. It was estimated he was anywhere from 40 to 80 years old. At the time of his capture newspapers reported he was 23 feet long and over 300 years old. According to Colin Stringer, a local fisherman who wrote a book about the croc, Sweetheart was a totem animal of the Matngala-Weret tribe of aborigines. They called him "Ngirrwak" which means "old man" and they believed they were related to him. Although the tribe were crocodile hunters they never bothered Sweetheart and he never bothered them.

But in 1971 something happened—Sweetheart set out on a vendetta against motorboat engines and motorboats in general. Although he attacked and upset many a power boat and played endlessly with the engine cowlings (one is shown here in his mouth) he never killed a human being. But the amount of damage he was doing to power boats started to mount so David Lindner, a Northern Territory parks ranger and croc expert set out to capture Sweetheart alive with the intention of retiring him to a captive farm. Unfortunately the stress of the capture coupled with the anesthetic used (Flaxadil) rendered Old Sweetheart unconscious and he drowned before anyone realized it. He was preserved by the Darwin Museum which took 14 months to prepare the exhibit and he is displayed there today together with the full story of his defensive battle against the power boats which invaded his lagoon. (Edwards, 1989)

Record-breaking Saltwater crocodile (*C. porosus*) named Sweetheart with the motor cowling he liked to play with while alive.

Cuban crocodile.

Cuban Crocodile

SCIENTIFIC NAME: *Crocodylus rhombifer* CUVIER, 1807
    STATUS: Endangered, CITES I.
    GEOGRAPHIC RANGE: Zapata and Lanier Swamps on the Island of Cuba. Also known from Cuba's Isle of Pines.
    HABITAT: Freshwater marshes or swamps, ponds, and other small, still bodies of water.
    DIET: Fish, frogs, crustaceans.

Comments

This species is severely depleted and endangered. Remaining populations in Cuba are outnumbered by hybrids of *C. rhombifer* × *C. acutus*. Most of the remaining Cuban crocodiles are kept in outdoor enclosures and are isolated from *C. acutus*. The population in the Lanier swamp is also

146

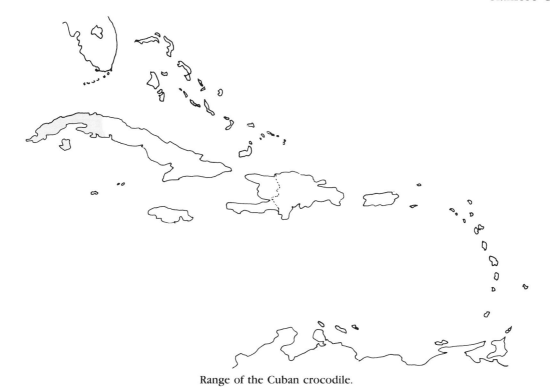

Range of the Cuban crocodile.

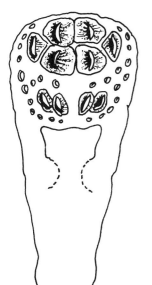

Siamese crocodile.

reportedly threatened by *Caiman crocodilus fuscus*, which has been introduced, since young may be preyed upon by caimans—furthering the threat to this species. This species is stocky and unusually patterned earning it the name Pearly crocodile.

It is a hole- and mound-nesting animal, adopting whatever type of nest is most convenient at the time and place egg laying occurs.

Size: maximum of 4 meters.

Siamese Crocodile

SCIENTIFIC NAME: *Crocodylus siamensis* SCHNEIDER, 1801
STATUS: Endangered, CITES I.
GEOGRAPHIC RANGE: Vietnam, Cambodia, Thailand, Laos, Kalimantan in Java, and possibly Sumatra (Borneo).
HABITAT: Formerly inhabited lowland, freshwater lakes, and swamps but is extinct or nearly extinct throughout much of its historical range. Many areas have been inaccessible to naturalists for decades because of political unrest, war and organized drug smuggling operations.
DIET: Fish, amphibians, and other small aquatic vertebrates.

Siamese crocodile emerging from egg at the Miami Metrozoo. (*Photo courtesy of Metrozoo, Dade County, Florida*)

Comments

The last known significant population (200 animals) was at Bung Boraphet in Thailand, but it has been depleted by unregulated hunting for skins and habitat loss.

Captive specimens become sexually mature in 10 to 12 years. They lay 20 to 48 eggs, which are deposited in a mound nest.

This species is protected by law in Indonesia and hunting is banned at Bung Boraphet. A breeding stock is also maintained at the Samutprakan crocodile farm near Bangkok where it has cross-bred with the Saltwater crocodile producing hybrids.

In August, 1989, a 6.5 foot Siamese crocodile was captured in a canal in Davie, a suburb west of Fort Lauderdale, Florida. It was taken to the Metrozoo in Miami where it was pronounced in good condition. This animal obviously escaped or was released.

It has a maximum recorded length of 3.8 meters although *C. porosus* hybrids are much larger (see *C. porosus*).

Range of the Siamese crocodile.

African Dwarf Crocodile

SCIENTIFIC NAME: *Osteolaemus tetraspis* COPE, 1861
    STATUS: Indeterminate, CITES I.
    GEOGRAPHIC RANGE: West and west-central Africa including Sierra Leone, Guinea, Ghana, Togo, Nigeria, Cameroons, Gabon, Liberia, and Angola. A subspecies, *Osteolaemus tetraspis osborni* (Schmidt) or Osborn's Dwarf crocodile inhabits Zaire (the Congo) and *Osteolaemus tetraspis tetraspis* comprises a more west African form.
    HABITAT: Prefers swamps and slow-moving streams in tropical rain forests.
    DIET: Fish, frogs, and crustaceans.

149

Comments

This species has been exploited for its hide, as food (including eggs) and for the live animal trade.

It is a mound-nesting species that lays between 16 and 30 eggs that hatch in 85 to 105 days. It has bred in captivity.

It is a timid, slow-moving nocturnal species that is rarely seen abroad in the day. It travels alone as an adult and little else is known about its habits. Field work has been difficult to accomplish because it is so shy and retiring. It has been observed considerable distances from the nearest body of water, but the reason has not been explained.

It is one of the shortest known crocodilians with a maximum recorded length of 1.9 meters. It has a short snout, and its upper eyelid is almost entirely ossified. Unlike other crocodilians its hide is uniformly dark both dorsally and ventrally.

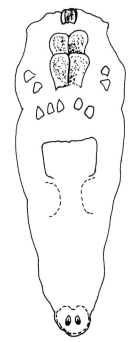

West African dwarf crocodile.

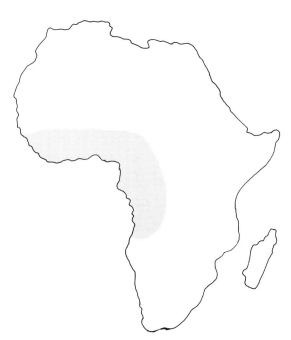

Range of the African dwarf crocodile.

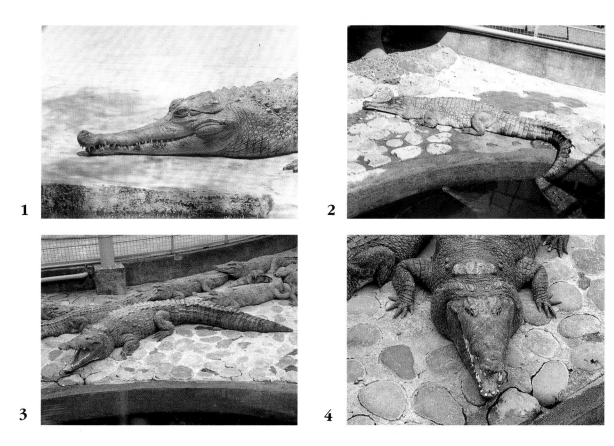

(1) Captive *Crocodylus cataphractus*. (*Courtesy Robert T. Zappalorti/Nature's Images*)
(2–4) *Crocodylus intermedius*. (*Courtesy Atagawa Tropical and Alligator Garden, Shizuoka, Japan*)
(5) *Crocodylus johnstoni*. (*Courtesy Atagawa Tropical and Alligator Garden, Shizuoka, Japan*)

PLATE 9

(1–2) *Crocodylus mindoriensis. (Courtesy Atagawa Tropical and Alligator Garden, Shizuoka, Japan)*
 (3) *Crocodylus niloticus. (Courtesy Robert T. Zappalorti/Nature's Images)*
 (4) *Crocodylus niloticus. (Courtesy Atagawa Tropical and Alligator Garden, Shizuoka, Japan)*
(5–6) *Crocodylus novaeguineae. (Courtesy Atagawa Tropical and Alligator Garden, Shizuoka, Japan)*

PLATE 10

(1) *Crocodylus moreletii* (female). (*Courtesy Instituto de Historia Natural/Antonio V. Ramirez*)
(2) Female *Crocodylus moreletii* guarding her nest. (*Courtesy Instituto de Historia Natural/Miguel A. del Toro*)
(3) Male *Crocodylus moreletii* tending juvenile. (*Courtesy Instituto de Historia Natural/Antonio V. Ramirez*)
(4) Juvenile *Crocodylus moreletii* A-6 Swamp, Chiapas, Mexico. (*Courtesy Instituto de Historia Natural/Miguel A. del Toro*)
(5) *Crocodylus moreletii*. (*Courtesy Instituto de Historia Natural/Antonio V. Ramirez*)
(6) Skulls of *Crocodylus acutus* (*lower*) and *Crocodylus moreletii* on display in Belize, Central America. (*Courtesy F. Grunwald*)

PLATE 11

(1–2) *Crocodylus palustris.* (*Courtesy Atagawa Tropical and Alligator Garden, Shizuoka, Japan*)
(3) *Crocodylus palustris.* (*Courtesy Robert T. Zappalorti/Nature's Images*)
(4) *Crocodylus porosus.* (*Courtesy Atagawa Tropical and Alligator Garden, Shizuoka, Japan*)
(5) *Crocodylus porosus.* (*Photo by M. J. Cox*)

PLATE 12

(1) *Crocodylus rhombifer.* (*Courtesy Robert T. Zappalorti/Nature's Images*)
(2) *Crocodylus siamensis.* (*Courtesy Atagawa Tropical and Alligator Garden, Shizuoka, Japan*)
(3) *Crocodylus rhombifer.* (*Photo by Jeff Wines*)
(4) *Crocodylus siamensis.* (*Courtesy Atagawa Tropical and Alligator Garden, Shizuoka, Japan*)
(5) *Crocodylus siamensis.* (*Photo by M. J. Cox*)

PLATE 13

(1) *Osteolaemus tetraspis*. Head of a 50+ year old acquired by Lincoln Park Zoo in 1940 and still alive in 1990. This animal, which measures about 5′ in length, was about the same length when acquired 50 years ago. Photo taken in 1978. (*Photo by James P. Rowan, Lincoln Park Zoo, Chicago, IL.*)

(2) *Osteolaemus tetraspis*. (*Courtesy Atagawa Tropical and Alligator Garden, Shizuoka, Japan*)

(3–5) Two year old Florida captive born *Osteolaemus tetraspis tetraspis*. This subspecies of the African dwarf crocodile is also known as the rough-backed dwarf crocodile because of the keels on its dorsal scales. (*Photo by S. Grenard*)

PLATE 14

(1) *Tomistoma schlegelii*. (*Courtesy Atagawa Tropical and Alligator Garden, Shizuoka, Japan*)

(2) Main entrance of Atagawa Tropical and Alligator Garden, Shizuoka, Japan, the largest captive collection of crocodilians with 27 species and subspecies represented.

(3) *Tomistoma schlegelii*. (*Photo by Jeff Wines*)

(4) *Tomistoma schlegelii*. (*Courtesy F. Grunwald*)

(5) *Gavialis gangeticus* photographed in Nepal. (*Courtesy Atagawa Tropical and Alligator Garden/Masahiro Iijima, Shizuoka, Japan*)

(6) *Gavialis gangeticus* in water (Nepal). (*Courtesy Atagawa Tropical and Alligator Garden/Masahiro Iijima, Shizuoka, Japan*)

PLATE 15

In the latest American taxonomic reference (King and Burke, 1989) reviewers for *Osteolaemus* do not mention two previously confirmed subspecies, *Osteolaemus tetraspis tetraspis* and *Osteolaemus tetraspis orborni*. The existence of at least one and possibly both subspecies is supported by the following cursory observations; work by taxonomists needs to be done not just perhaps to confirm their status but even possibly to raise these two additional forms to species status.

Each of these animals, save for their short stature and relative geographic proximity (coastal west Africa eastward to Zaire or the Congo) may differ sufficiently in both bone structure and external appearance to justify species status.

A living example of the so-called broad-nosed form resides at the Lincoln Park Zoo; an example of a much narrower up-turned snouted version resides with the author (S.G.). The Lincoln Park Zoo specimen, ostensibly *Osteolaemus tetraspis*, is extremely dark in color, almost black and has a snout that is broad enough to classify as alligatorine. Mertens (1943) published a description of a skull in the Senckenburg Museum in Frankfurt reportedly belonging to a subadult that, in shape and form, clearly belongs to the same species in the Lincoln Park collection. The

A freshly killed crocodilian lying on embankment in the Congo and identified by DeSola (1933) as photographed by Herbert Lang. The original caption called it the smooth-backed crocodile named for Osborn. (*Photograph courtesy of the American Museum of Natural History*).

living animal belonging to the author is brown, not nearly black as the Lincoln Park specimen, has flecks of yellowish or cream, a dark brown iris, boney elevations or keels on its dorsal scales and mottled (brown blotches on cream) maxillary and mandibular scales. As the color photos herein show, the snout is short, much narrower than the Lincoln Park animal and slightly upturned. It's also been called the "rough-backed" dwarf crocodile by other authors and its dorsal scalation clearly supports this appellation. This animal is obviously the subspecies known as *Osteolaemus tetraspis tetraspis*. The only evidence this author has for the third animal, *Osteolaemus tetraspis osborni* (var: *osbornii*) appears in an old black and white photograph of an animal dead on an embankment. The photograph is attributed, by the American Museum of Natural History, to the late, great Congo explorer Herbert Lang who spent six years in the Congo for the museum—his principal mission was to obtain an okapi. This photo shows a crocodilian with a narrow, down-turned snout and relatively smooth dorsal scales. Previous authors have called the Congo or Osborn's dwarf crocodile the "smooth-backed" dwarf crocodile for this reason.

PART FOUR

THE SUBFAMILY GAVIALINAE
Adams, 1854

AND

THE SUBFAMILY TOMISTOMINAE
Kälin, 1955

Gharial or Gavial

The subfamily Gavialinae is represented by one species, the Gharial (*Gavialis gangeticus*). A recent study by Densmore and Dessauer (1984) indicates that the False Gharial (*Tomistoma schlegelii*), subfamily Tomistominae, may be genetically closer to the Gharial than to the Crocodylinae based on similarities in blood proteins. Traditionally taxonomists group species in specific families on the basis of numerous external as well as internal anatomical traits. As more and more species are subjected to typing by the use of DNA probes and biochemical protein analysis, some reorganization may occur. In the case of the False Gharial, the absence of the bulbous structure that grows on the tip of the snout in adult male true Gharials has led some taxonomists to include the False Gharial in the Crocodylinae, the rationale being that it is an extremely slender-snouted crocodile.

In 1972, Hecht and Malone published an analysis of the skull similarities and dissemilarities between *Gavialis* and *Tomistoma* in addition to tracing their evolutionary lineage. They concluded that *Gavialis* has attained a more advanced level of organization compared to *Tomistoma* and other slender- or long-snouted (longirostrine) crocodilians and should remain as the sole living example of its subfamily. They also point out that several now extinct slender-snouted species should be removed from the genus *Tomistoma* and be reassigned to *Gavialis*.

The Gharial is named for the pot-like bulbous structure, known as a narial excrescence, that appears on the dorsal tip of the snout in adult males. It is from a Hindi word ("ghara") which describes a long-necked clay pot which superficially resembles the shape of this crocodilian's snout and head.

The Gharial is also referred to as the Gavial, which is believed to be a term that appeared in earlier literature as a result of a typographical error misspelling Gharial. All modern literature on this species correctly refers to it as the Gharial. Curiously, however, the subfamily and genus names "Gavialinae" and "Gavialis" have never been changed to "Gharialinae" or "Gharialis" to reflect the correct origin of its common name. According to

155

Lateral snout swing and grab. Neil (1971) noted that the slender-snouted gharials crawl along the bottom; reaching a school of fish, they freeze motionless until members of the school swim closely past at which point the crocodilian swings its snout laterally, then grabbing its prey.

Lamar, etymology has no relevance to systematic procedure (1989, pers. comm.).

Of all living crocodilians, this species is the most closely bound to its watery environment because its legs are weak and not well-suited to walking on land. It only hauls itself out of the water to bask, to build its nest, and to lay its eggs. On land it uses a clumsy, forward pushing motion known as the "belly slide." Its legs are too weak to support its great weight in the more rapid "high walk" of other crocodilians. On the other hand, its broad oar-like tail helps propel this species in the water, making it highly mobile in an aquatic milieu.

The Gharial has an extremely elongated, narrow snout that is 3½ to 4 times longer than it is broad at its widest point. Its teeth are almost identical with at least 54 in the upper jaw and 48 in the lower jaw. While gharial teeth are razor sharp and can inflict great damage, their narrow snouts make them most adept at catching fish and aquatic frogs to the exclusion of larger animals, including terrestrial species. In the water they capture their prey by a whip-like, sideways snatching motion. Its flat, narrow snout experiences little resistance moving through the water.

Gharials arose in the Cretaceous and members of the family were present in South America from the Oligocene to the Pliocene between 38 and 2 million years ago.

Gharial

SCIENTIFIC NAME: *Gavialis gangeticus* (GMELIN, 1789)

STATUS: Endangered, CITES I.

GEOGRAPHIC RANGE: The Himalayan-fed rivers of the north Indian subcontinent, in the Indus, Kolawadi, Irrawaddy, Ganges, and Brahmaputra drainages as well as in the Mahanadi River in the Indian State of Orissa. Range includes populations in Bangladesh, India, Nepal, Pakistan, and Bhutan.

HABITAT: The Gharial prefers clear, fast-moving sinuous rivers and deep pools with high sandy banks on which to bask and nest.

DIET: Almost exclusively fish and aquatic frogs.

Range of the Gharial.

Comments

The Gharial was near extinction throughout much of its range by 1970. Biswas (1970) reported on a Zoological Society of India study done in 1968 that reported there were about 250–300 Gharials extant in the three branches of the Ganges, the Chambal, Girwa, and Narayani. The survey estimated that no more than 100 animals remained in Nepal. In Bhutan, Bangladesh, and Pakistan, fewer than 20 adults were believed to exist. In 1972, the Wildlife Protection Act prohibited the capture and killing of all three species of crocodilians in India. However, it was ratified by the individual states slowly over a period of four or five years. In one state it wasn't ratified for ten years. This area became a conduit for trade in illegally taken hides as a result.

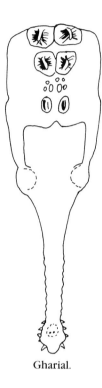

Gharial.

The depletion of the Gharial is attributed largely to habitat loss and encroachment by rapidly escalating human populations as well as to hunting for skins and accidental drowning deaths caused by ensnarement in seine nests used by fisherman. The Gharial is not hunted by orthodox Hindus who are dedicated to the Hindu god Vishnu. Indians of other religious sects and religions, as well as foreigners, are not under any constraint and will hunt and kill this animal.

An Indian gharial emerges from its approximately 9 centimeter long egg at a hatchery in the Saktosia Gorge, Orissa, India, where an Indian-United Nations (FAO) program seeks to re-establish this endangered species, which has been over-exploited for its magnificent hide. Some 71 of them have already been released in the natural habitat, Himalayan-fed rivers in northern India. (*Photo courtesy of the United Nations/U.N.D.P./FAO*).

A captive hatching/juvenile rearing "rehabilitation" program has been in effect in India and surrounding countries since the early to mid-1970s. Juveniles are released into protected sanctuaries. In 1975, a breeding and management program sponsored by the Indian government and the United Nations Development Program was inaugurated. A similar project was instituted in Nepal at the Royal Chitawan National Park in 1978 with the first batch of 50 juveniles released in 1981. These animals are difficult to breed in captivity, but breeding has occurred in the Nandan-kanan Biological Park in Orissa in 1980. A reestablishment program has also been put into effect in Madras through the Madras Crocodile Bank, which was established with help from the World Wildlife Fund in 1975. At the present time, egg collecting, followed by captive hatching and rearing of juveniles seems like the most effective way to reestablish wild populations. Thanks to a variety of such programs, an estimated three thousand animals were extant by 1986 compared to one tenth that number in 1968.

Females reach sexual maturity by their 11th year when they join a "harem" of 4 to 6 females to 1 adult male. Mating occurs in November to December, and nesting occurs between March and May depending on locale. The Gharial is a hole nester that excavates an egg chamber in mid-river sandbars or high, sandy embankments above the flood water line. Average clutch size is 37 eggs, and incubation requires 83 to 94 days. Females guard their nests and closely monitor juveniles for less than a year after hatching. The maximum size for Gharials is about 6 meters.

The Gharial is not a man-eater, but occasionally pieces of personal jewelry have been recovered from the stomachs of animals captured in the Ganges. Clearly these trinkets were swallowed by the animals after being liberated from human corpses that are cremated and committed to the Ganges in the traditional Hindu funeral ceremony. Rivers inhabited by the Gharial are also a receptacle for many uncremated human bodies which may be fed upon by this species. There is also a Hindu ritual wherein participants celebrate by actually throwing jewelry and coins into the river.

False Gharial

SCIENTIFIC NAME: *Tomistoma schlegelii* (MÜLLER, 1838)
STATUS: Endangered, CITES II.
GEOGRAPHIC RANGE: Malay Peninsula, possibly still extending into southern Thailand and the Islands of Sumatra and Borneo, Kalimantan and Java.
HABITAT: Freshwater rivers, swamps, and lakes.

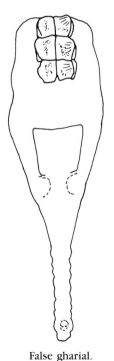
False gharial.

159

PART 4   THE SUBFAMILY TOMISTOMINAE

DIET: As an extremely slender-snouted species, its diet is mainly fish, but small primates and other animals may be taken.

Comments

This is a large species that is protected by law in Malaya and Indonesia. It is held in a number of reserves, and it is a popular attraction in zoos because of its odd appearance. It is threatened by hunting for its skin as well as by alteration or loss of habitat.

Its maximum size is about 4 meters.

It differs from the true gharial by differences in head shape and bone structure.

Range of the False Gharial.

PART FIVE
BIBLIOGRAPHY

Ackerman, D. 1988. A reporter at large: (Oct. 10, 1988) Crocodilians. *New Yorker* 64:42–80.

Adler, K. et al. 1989. "Contributions to the History of Herpetology." Soc. Study of Amphibians and Reptiles, St. Louis.

Allen, E. R., Neil, W. T. 1949. Increased abundance of the alligator in the eastern portion of its range. *Herpetologica* 4:109–12.

Allen, G. R. 1974. The marine crocodile, *Crocodylus porosus* from Ponape, Eastern Caroline Islands w/notes on the food habits of crocodiles from the Palau Archipelago. *Copeia* 1974:553.

Alvarez Del Toro, M. 1974. "Los Crocodylia de Mexico," Inst. Mexicano de Recursos Naturales Renovables, Mexico.

Alvarez, K. C. 1984. Sighting of an American crocodile at Collier-Seminole State Park. *Florida Field Naturalist* 13:104–5.

Anon. 1978. Plop, Plop, Fizz, Fizz: Bicarbonate regulator in crocodile blood. *Chemistry* 51:4.

Arthur, S. C. 1928. The fur animals of Louisiana: the alligator. *Louisiana Dept. Consv. Bull.* 18:165–86.

Ashford, R. M., Miller, R. 1978. *Paratrichosoma crocodilus* new genera, new species (Nematoda: Trichosomoididae) from the skin of the New Guinea crocodile. *J. Helminthol.* 52:215–20.

Ashley, D., David, D. N. 1987. Marketing crocodilian skins, in: "Wildlife Management—Crocodiles and Alligators," Webb, G. J. W., et al. (eds.), Surrey Beatty and Sons, Chipping Norton, NSW, Australia.

Ashton, R. E., Jr., Ashton, P. S. 1985. "Handbook of Reptiles and Amphibians of Florida—Pt. Two—Lizards, Turtles and Crocodilians," Windward Publishing, Miami.

Astheimer, L. B. et al. 1989. Egg formation in crocodiles: avian affinities in yolk deposition. *Copeia* 1989:221–224.

Audubon, J. J. 1827. Observations on the natural history of the alligator (letter to Sir Wm. Jardine). *Edinburgh New Phil. Jour.* 2:270–80.

Ayarzaguena, S. J. 1983. Ecologia del caiman de anteojos (*Caiman crocodilus*) en los Ilianos de Apure Venezuela. *Donana Acta Vertebrata—numero especial.* 10:1–136.

Bakker, R. T. 1986. "The Dinosaur Heresies," Zebra Books, Kensington Press, New York.

Bara, M. O. 1972. Alligator research project. Annual Progress Report of the South Carolina Wildlife and Marine Resources Department, Columbia, South Carolina.

BIBLIOGRAPHY

Barbour, J. 1976. Poachers at work, crocodiles at bay. *Intl. Wildl.* 6:4–11.

Barbour, T. 1923. The crocodile in Florida. *Occasional Papers, Museum of Zoology, Univ. of Michigan* Number 131, pp. 1–6.

Barbour, T. 1944. "The Vanishing Eden," Little, Brown & Co., Boston.

Basu, D. 1980. Baby crocs in a valley of death (gharials). *Intl. Wildl.* 10:3–11.

Bayliss, A. F. et al. 1986. Estimating the abundance of saltwater crocodiles, *Crocodylus porosus*, in tidal wetlands of the Northern Territory. *Austral. Wildlife Research* 13:309–20.

Bayliss, P. 1987. Survey methods and monitoring, in: "Wildlife Management—Crocodiles and Alligators," Webb, G. J. W., et al. (eds.), Surrey Beatty and Sons, Chipping Norton, NSW, Australia.

Behler, J. L. 1978. Feasibility of the establishment of a captive breeding population of the American crocodile. U.S. National Park Service, South Florida Research Center Report T-509. pp. 94.

Bellairs, [A.] d'A. 1969. "The Life of the Reptiles," Weidenfeld and Nicholson, London.

Bellairs, [A.] d'A. 1971. The senses of crocodilians, in: "Crocodiles," IUCN, Gland, Switzerland.

Bellairs, [A.] d'A., Cox, C. B. 1976. "Morphology and Biology of Reptiles," Academic Press, London.

Bellairs, [A.] d'A. 1987. The Crocodilia, in: "Wildlife Management—Crocodiles and Alligators," Webb, G. J. W., et al. (eds.), Surrey Beatty and Sons, Chipping Norton, NSW, Australia.

Benedict, F. G. 1932. The physiology of large reptiles with specific reference to the heat production of snakes, tortoises, lizards and alligators. *Carnegie Institute of Washington* Publication Number 425, Washington, D.C.

Ben-Moshe, G. 1987. An Alligator Farm in Israel, in: "Wildlife Management—Crocodiles and Alligators," Webb, G. J. W., et al. (eds.), Surrey Beatty and Sons, Chipping Norton, NSW, Australia.

Bennett, A. F. et al. 1985. Mass-dependance of anaerobic metabolism and acid-base disturbance during activity in the saltwater crocodile, *Crocodylus porosus*. *J. Exper. Biol.* 118:161–71

Biswas, S. 1970. A preliminary survey of Gharial in the Kisi River. *Indian Forester* 96:705–10.

Blair, J. 1978. A bad time to be a crocodile. *National Geographic* 153:90–114.

Blake, D. K., Loveridge, J. P. 1975. The role of commercial crocodile farming in crocodile conservation. *Biol. Conserv.* 8:261–72.

Blake, D. K., Loveridge, J. P. 1987. Observations on the behavior of Nile crocodiles, *Crocodylus niloticus*, in captivity, in: "Wildlife Management—Crocodiles and Alligators," Webb, G. J. W., et al. (eds.), Surrey Beatty and Sons, Chipping Norton, NSW, Australia.

Blake, N. M. 1980. "Land into Water—Water into Land—A History of water management in Florida," Florida State University, University Presses, Tallahassee.

Blohm, T. 1948. Observaciones sobre los caimans traidos del rio Orinoco en abril de 1946. *Mem. Soc. Cienc. Nat. LaSalle VII* 22:129–32.

Bolton, M. 1978. Crocodile farming in Papua, New Guinea. *Oryx* 14:365–9

Bothwell, D. 1962. "The Great Outdoors Book of Alligators and other crocodilia. Great Outdoors Publishing, St. Petersburg, Florida.

Bowman, D. 1983. Endangered and threatened wildlife and plants; final rule to change the status of the American alligator in the State of Texas. *Federal Register* 48:46332–46336.

Brander, A., Dunbar, A. 1972. Wild animals in central India, in: "Crocodiles," C. A. Guggisberg. Stackpole, Harrisburg, Pa.

Brazaitis, P. J. 1968. The determination of sex in living crocodilians. *Brit. J. Herpetol.* 4:54–58.

Brazaitis, P. J. 1971. *Crocodylus intermedius* Graves, a review of the recent literature. *Zoologica* 56:71–75.

Brazaitis, P. J. 1973. The identification of living crocodilians. *Zoologica* 58:59–101.

Brazaitis, P. J. 1987. Identification of crocodilian skins and products, in: "Wildlife Management—Crocodiles and Alligators," Webb, G. J. W., et al. (eds.), Surrey Beatty and Sons, Chipping Norton, NSW, Australia.

Breen, J. F. 1974. "Encyclopedia of Reptiles and Amphibians," TFH Publications, Neptune City (N.J.).

Brisbin, I. L. 1966. Reactions of the American alligator to several immobilizing drugs. *Copeia* 1966:129–30.

Brisbin, I. L. et al. 1982. Body temperatures and behavior of American alligators during cold winter weather. *American Midland Naturalist* 107:209–19.

Brooks, D. A., O'Grady, R. T. 1989. Crocodilians and their Helminth parasites: Microevolutionary considerations. *Am. Zool.* 29:873–893.

Brown, C. R., Loveridge, J. P. 1981. The effect of temperature on oxygen consumption and evaporative water loss in *Crocodylus niloticus. Comp. Biochem. Physiol.* 69A:51–7.

Bufferenil, V. de 1980. Mise en evidence de l'incidence des conditions de milieu sur la croissance de *Crocodylus siamensis* et valeur des marques de sequelettiques pour l'evaluation de l'age individuel. *Archives Zool Exp. Gen.* 121:63–76.

Bufferenil, V. de 1980. Donees preliminaires sur la structure des croissance sequelettiques ches les crocodilians actuels et fossiles. *Bulletin Zool. Soc. France* 105:355–61.

Buffetaut, E. 1979. The evolution of the crocodilians. *Scientific American* October, 1979:130–144.

Buffetaut, E. 1985. The place of *Gavialis* and *Tomistoma* in eusuchian evolution: a reconciliation of paleontological and biochemical data. *N. Jb. Geol. Paleont. Mh.* 12:707–16.

Burbridge, A. A. 1987. The management of crocodiles in Australia, in: "Wildlife Management—Crocodiles and Alligators," Webb, G. J. W., et al. (eds.), Surrey Beatty and Sons, Chipping Norton, NSW, Australia.

Burghardt, G. M., Herzog, H. A. 1977. Vocalization in juvenile crocodilians. *Z. Tierpsycol.* 44:294–304.

Burrage, B. R. 1965. Copulation in a pair of *Alligator mississippiens. Br. J. Herpetol.* 3:207–8.

Burton, M. 1973. "Snakes, Crocodiles and Lizards," Orbis Books, London.

Bustard, H. R. 1968. Rapid learning in wild crocodiles (*Crocodylus porosus*). *Herpetologica* 24:173–5.

Bustard, H. R. 1971. Temperature and water tolerance of incubating crocodile eggs. *Brit. J. Herpetol.* 4:198–200.

Bustard, H. R. 1974. India: A preliminary survey of the prospects for crocodile farming. FAO/IND Proj. No. 71/033. Rome.

BIBLIOGRAPHY

Bustard, H. R. 1980. A note on nesting behaviour in the Indian gharial, *Gavialis gangeticus. J. Bombay Nat. Hist. Soc.* 77:514–15.

Bustard, H. R., Choudhury, B. C. 1980. Long distance movement of a saltwater crocodile (*Crocodylus porosus*). *Brit. J. Herpetol.* 6:87.

Bustard, H. R., Kar, S. K. 1981. Defense of the nest against man by the saltwater crocodile, *Crocodylus porosus. J. Bombay Nat. Hist. Soc.* 77:514–15.

Bustard, H. R., Singh, L. A. K. 1981. Gharial attacks on man. *J. Bombay Nat. Hist. Soc.* 78:610–11.

Butler, W. H. 1987. Living with crocodiles in the Northern Territory of Australia, in: "Wildlife Management—Crocodiles and Alligators," Webb, G. J. W., et al. (eds.), Surrey Beatty and Sons, Chipping Norton, NSW, Australia.

Calderwood, H. W. 1971. Anesthesia for reptiles. *J. Am. Vet. Med. Assn.* 159:1618–25.

Campbell, G. 1980. Croc! *Island Reporter* 81:133.

Campbell, G. R. 1981. "Jaws, Too! The Story of Sanibel's Alligators and other Crocodilians," Sanibel-Captiva Conservation Foundation, Sanibel Island, Florida.

Campbell, H. W. 1972. Ecological of phylogenetic interpretations of crocodilian nesting habits. *Nature* 238:404–5.

Campbell, H. W. 1973. Observations on the acoustic behavior of crocodilians. *Zoologica* Spring, 1973:1–11.

Carr, A. 1967. Alligators, dragons in distress. *National Geographic* 131:133–48.

Chabreck, R. H. 1963. Methods of capturing, marking and selling alligators. in: *Proc. Ann. Conf. SE Assn. Game and Fish Comm.* 17:47–50.

Chabreck, R. H. 1965. The movement of alligators in Louisiana. *Proc. Ann. Conf. Assn. Game and Fish Comm.* 19:102–10.

Chabreck, R. H. 1966. "Methods of determining the size and composition of alligator populations in Louisiana," Louisiana Wildlife and Fisheries Commission, Grand Chenier, Louisiana.

Chabreck, R. H. 1967. "The American Alligator—Past, Present, and Future," Louisiana Wildlife and Fisheries Commission, Grand Chenier, Louisiana.

Chabreck, R. H. 1971. The foods and feeding habits of alligators from fresh and saline environments in Louisiana. *Proc. Ann. Conf. Assn. SE Game and Fish Comm.* 25:117–24.

Chabreck, R. H. 1975. Moisture variation in the nests of the American alligator (*Alligator mississippiensis*). *Herpetologica* 31:385–9.

Chabreck, R. H., Dupuie, H. H. 1976. Alligator predation on Canada goose eggs. *Copeia* 1976:404–5.

Chabreck, R. H., Joanan, T. 1979. Growth rates of American alligators in Louisiana. *Herpetologica* 35:51–7.

Chaisson, R. B. 1962. "Laboratory Anatomy of the Alligator," W. C. Brown Publishing Co., Dubuque, Iowa.

Chermock, R. L. 1952. "A key to the amphibians and reptiles of Alabama," Geol. Survey of Alabama, Museum Number 38, University, Alabama.

Child, G. 1987. The management of crocodiles in Zimbabwe, in: "Wildlife Management—Crocodiles and Alligators," Webb, G. J. W., et al. (eds.), Surrey Beatty and Sons, Chipping Norton, NSW, Australia.

Choquenot, D. P., Webb, G. J. W. 1987. A photographic technique for estimating the size of crocodilians seen in spotlight surveys and quantifying observer bias in estimating sizes. *Ibid.*

Choudhury, B. C., Bustard, H. R. 1980. Predation on natural nests of the saltwater crocodile (*Crocodylus porosus*) on North Andaman Island with notes on the crocodile population. *J. Bombay Nat. Hist. Soc.* 76:311–23.

Choudhury, B. C. 1981. Mugger releases. *Hamadryad* 6:9.

Cintra, R. 1989. Maternal care and daily pattern of behavior in a family of caimans, *Caiman Yacare*, in the Brazilian Pantanal. *J. Herpetol.* 23:320–22.

Clark, H. et al. 1957. Excretion of nitrogen by the alligator embryo. *J. Cell. Comp. Physiol.* 50:129–34.

Clarke, S. F. 1888. The nest of the alligator *Alligator lucius* Cuvier. *Ann. Nat. Hist.* 2:509–11 *Zool. Anz.* 11(290):568–70.

Clarke, S. F. 1891. The habits and embryology of the American alligator. *J. Morphol.* 5:181–205.

Cogger, H. F. 1979. "Reptiles and Amphibians of Australia" (2nd ed.), Reed Publishing, Sydney.

Cohen, M. M., Gans, C. 1970. The chromosomes of the Order Crocodilia. *Cyogenetics* 9:81–105.

Cohn, J. P. 1988. Exotic Meats. *FDA Consumer* U.S. Food & Drug Administration, Nov. 1988. Rockville, Maryland.

Colbert, E. H. et al. 1946. Temperature tolerances in the American alligator and their bearing on the habits, evolution and extinction of the dinosaurs. *Bull. Amer. Mus. Nat. Hist.* 86:327–74.

Compton, A. 1981. Courtship and nesting behavior of the freshwater crocodile, *Crocodylus johnstoni* under controlled conditions. *Austral. Wildl. Resrch.* 8:445–50.

Compton, G. H. 1979. Shrinking habitat: timid, nocturnal American marine crocodile. *Oceans* 12:42–8.

Conant, R. 1975. "Peterson Field Guide: Reptiles and Amphibians of Eastern/Central North America," Houghton Mifflin Co., Boston.

Congdon, J. D., Gibbon, J. W. 1989. Posthatching yolk reserves in hatchling American alligators. *Herpetologica* 43:305–9.

Coulson, R. A. 1950. Alkaline tide of the alligator. *Proc. Soc. Exper. Biol. Med.* 74:866–869.

Coulson, R. A., Hernandez, T. 1964. "Biochemistry of the Alligator—A study of Metabolism in Slow Motion," Louisiana State University Press, Baton Rouge.

Coulson, R. A., Hernandez, T. 1983. "Alligator Metabolism Studies on Chemical Reactions in Vivo," Pergamon Press, Oxford.

Coulson, R. A. et al. 1973. Some observations on the growth of captive alligators. *Zoologica* 58:47–52.

Coulson, R. A. et al. 1989. Biochemistry and physiology of alligator metabolism in vivo. *Am. Zool.* 29:921–34.

Cott, H. B. 1961. Scientific results of an inquiry into the ecology and economic status of the Nile crocodile (*Crocodylus niloticus*) in Uganda and Northern Rhodesia. *Trans. Zool. Soc. Lond.* 29:211–356.

Cott, H. B. 1968. The status of the Nile crocodile below Murchison Falls. *IUCN BULL.* N.S. 2(8):62–4.

Cott, H. B. 1971. Parental care in the crocodile with special reference to *Crocodylus niloticus*. *IUCN PUBL.* n.s. Paper No. 32:166–180.

BIBLIOGRAPHY

Craighead, F. C. 1968. The role of the alligator in shaping plant communities and maintaining wildlife in the southern Everglades. *Florida Naturalist* 41(1&2): January & April, 1968.

Cunningham, B., Horowitz, A. 1936. Water absorption by reptile eggs during incubation. *American Naturalist* 70:590–5.

Daniel, J. C., Hussain, S. A. 1974. The record saltwater crocodile (*C. porosus*). *J. Bombay Nat. Hist. Soc.* 71:309–12.

David, D. N. 1987. Effects of alligator skin storage techniques on "Red Head," in: "Wildlife Management—Crocodiles and Alligators," Webb, G. J. W., et al. (eds.), Surrey Beatty and Sons, Chipping Norton, NSW, Australia.

Davis, J. E. et al. 1980. Evaporative water loss from the American alligator (*Alligator mississippiensis*): the relative importance of respiration and cutaneous components and the regulatory role of the skin. *Comp. Biochem. Physiol.* 67A:439–46.

Deeming, D. C., Ferguson, M. W. J. 1989. The mechanism of temperature dependent sex determination in crocodilians: a hypothesis. *Am. Zool.* 29:973–85.

Delaney, M. F., Abercrombie, C. L. 1986. American alligator food habits in north-central Florida. *J. Wildl. Management* 50:348–53.

Delaney, M. F. 1987. What do alligators eat? *Florida Wildlife* November/December, 1987.

Delaney, M. F. 1987. Bird bands recovered from American alligator stomachs in Florida. *No. American Bird Bander* 11:92–4.

Densmore, L. D. 1983. Biochemical and immunological systematics of the Order Crocodilia in: "Evolutionary Biology," Hecht, M. K., et al. (eds.) Plenum, New York.

Densmore, L. D., Bessauer, H. C. 1984. Low levels of protein divergence detected between *Gavialis* and *Tomistoma*: evidence for crocodilian monophyly? *Comp. Biochem. Physiol.* 77B:715–20.

Densmore, L. D., Owen, R. D. 1989. Molecular systematics of the order Crocodilia. *Am. Zool.* 29:831–41.

Deraniyagala, P. E. P. 1934. Neoteny in *Crocodylus porosus. Ceylon J. Sci.* 19:97–100.

Deraniyagala, P. E. P. 1936. A new crocodile from Ceylon. *Ceylon J. Sci. Sec. B: Zool. & Geol.* 19:279–86.

Deraniyagala, P. E. P. 1939. "The Tetrapod Reptiles of Ceylon: Vol. I—Testudinates and Crocodilians. Colombo Museum, Colombo, Sri Lanka.

Dessauer, H. S. 1989. Roland Armstrong Coulson (tribute). *Am. Zool.* 29:823–9.

DeSola, C. R. 1933. The crocodilians of the world. *Bull. N.Y. Zool. Soc.* 36(1):3–24.

Dickinson, D. 1981. Marine crocodiles (*Crocodylus porosus*) in Vanuatu. *Naika* (Journal of the Vanuatu Natural Science Society), No. 3, p. 5.

Dickinson, W. E. 1953. In Quest of an Adult Crocodile. *Everglades Nat. Hist.* 1:151–6.

Dietz, D. C., Jackson, D. R. 1979. Use of American alligator nests by nesting turtles. *J. Herpetol.* 13:510–12.

Dietz, D. C., Hines, T. C. 1980. Alligator nesting in north-central Florida. *Copeia* 1980(2):249–258.

Diffenbach, C. O. 1975. Thermal perfusion and thermoregulation in *Caiman crocodilus. Copeia* 1975:530–40.

Diffenbach, C. O. 1975. Gastric function in *Caiman crocodilus* 1. rate of gastric digestion and gastric motility as a function of temperature. *Comp. Biochem. Physiol.* 51A: 259–65.

Diffenbach, C. O. 1981. Regurgitation is normal in Crocodylia. *Ciencia e Cultura (São Paulo)* 33:82–3.

Dimock, A. W. 1908. "Florida Enchantments," Outing Publishing Co., New York.

Dimoch, A. W. 1918. The Florida crocodile. *The Amer. Mus. Jour.* 18(6):447–452.

Dowling, H. G., Brazaitis, P. J. 1966. Size and growth in captive crocodilians. *Intl. Zoo. Yearbook* 6:265–70.

Drane, C. R. et al. 1977. Pattern of heating in the body, trunk and tail of *Crocodylus porosus. J. Therm. Biol.* 2:127–30.

Dugan, B. A. et al. 1981. Interactions between nesting crocodiles and iguanas. *J. Herpetol.* 15:409–14.

Dunson, W. A. 1969. Reptilian salt glands, in: "Exocrine Glands," Botelho, S. Y., et al. (eds.), University of Pennsylvania Press, Philadelphia.

Dunson, W. A. 1970. Some aspects of electrolyte and water balance in three estuarine reptiles, *Comp. Biochem. Physiol.* 32:161–74.

Dunson, W. A. 1982. Salinity relations of crocodiles in Florida Bay. *Coipeia* 1982:374–385.

Eaton, T., Cerabino, F. 1988. 10-foot Alligator kills girl, 4, in attack by Gulf Coast lake. *Miami Herald* June 6, 1988, page 1.

Edmund, A. G. 1962. Sequence and rate of tooth replacement in the crocodilia. *Life Sci. Div. Royal Ontario Museum* 56:1–42.

Edwards, H. 1989. "Crocodile Attack," Harper & Row, New York.

Evans, D. H., Ellis, T. M. 1977. Sodium balance in the hatchling American crocodile, *Crocodylus acutus. Comp. Biochem. Physiol.* 58:159–62.

Federal Register 1985. Endangered and threatened wildlife and plants; reclassification of the American alligator in Florida to threatened due to similarity of appearance. 50(119):25672–25678 (June 20).

Ferguson, M. W. J. 1981a. Increasing porosity of the incubating alligator eggshell caused by extrinsic microbial degredation. *Experientia* 37:252–4.

Ferguson, M. W. J. 1981b. Extrinsic microbial degradation of the alligator eggshell. *Science* 214:1135–7.

Ferguson, M. W. J. 1982. The structure and development of the palate in *Alligator mississippiensis*. PhD thesis Queens University, Belfast. University Microfilms International, Ann Arbor and London.

Ferguson, M. W. J. 1982. The structure and composition of the eggshell and embryonic membranes of *Alligator mississippiensis. Trans. Zool. Soc. Lond.* 36:99–153.

Ferguson, M. W. J., Joanen, T. 1982. Temperature of egg incubation determines sex in *Alligator mississippiensis. Nature* 296:850–3.

Ferguson, M. W. J., Joanen, T. 1983. Temperature dependent sex determination in *Alligator mississippiensis. J. Zool. Soc. Lond.* 200:143–7.

Ferguson, M. W. J. 1984. Craniofascial development in *Alligator mississippiensis*, in: Ferguson, M. W. J. (ed.), "The Structure, Development and Evolution of Reptiles," Symp. Zool. Soc. of London Academic Press, London.

Ferguson, M. W. J. 1985. The reproductive biology and embryology of the crocodiles, in: Gans, C. et al. (eds.), "Biology of the Reptilia—Volume 14," John Wiley & Sons, New York.

Ferguson, M. W. J. 1987. Post-laying stages of embryonic development in crocodilians, in: "Wildlife Management—Crocodiles and Alligators," Webb, G. J. W., et al. (eds.), Surrey Beatty and Sons, Chipping Norton, NSW, Australia.

BIBLIOGRAPHY

Finkelstein, D. 1984. Tiger of the stream. *Audubon* 86:98–110.

Fittkau, E. J. 1970. Role of the caimans in the nutrient regime of mouth-lakes of Amazon affluents (an hypothesis). *Biotropica* 2:138–42.

Fleishman, L. B. 1989. *Caiman crocodilus* does not require vision for underwater prey capture. *J. Herpetol.* 23:296.

Fogarty, M. J., Albury, J. D. 1966. Late summer food habits of small alligators from L-38 Canal, Everglades Wildlife Management Area, Ft. Lauderdale. Florida Game and Freshwater Game Commission.

Fogarty, M. J., Albury, J. D. 1968. Late summer food of young alligators in Florida. *Proc. SE Assn. Game and Fish Comm.* 21:220–222.

Foggin, C. M. 1987. Disease and disease control on crocodile farms in Zimbabwe, in: "Wildlife Management—Crocodiles and Alligators," Webb, G. J. W., et al. (eds.), Surrey Beatty and Sons, Chipping Norton, NSW, Australia.

Frey, E. et al. 1989. The axial tail musculature of recent crocodiles and its phyletic implications. *Am. Zool.* 29:857–62.

Frye, F. L. 1991. "Biomedical and Surgical Aspects of Captive Reptile Husbandry," 2nd ed. Robert E. Krieger Publishing Company, Melbourne, Florida.

Frye, F. L., Schelling, S. H. 1973. Steatis in a caiman. *Vet. Med. Small Animal Clin.* 68:143–6.

Fuchs, K. 1974. "Die Krokodilhaut," Eduard Roether-Verlag, Darmstadt.

Fuller, K. S. et al. 1987. "Latin America wildlife trade laws," 2nd ed. World Wildlife Fund, Washington, D.C.

Fuller, M. K. 1983. Growth rates and age of sexual maturity of American alligators in North Carolina, in: "Status of the American Alligator in North Carolina," North Carolina State University, Raleigh.

Gaby, R. et al. 1985. Ecology and status of a population of *Crocodylus acutus* at a power plant site in Florida. *J. Herpetol.* 19:189–98.

Galdikas, B. M. F., Yaeger, C. P. 1984. Crocodile predation on a crab-eating macaque in Borneo. *Am. J. Primatol.* 6:49–51.

Gans, C. 1976. Questions in crocodilian physiology. *Zoologica Africana* 11:241–8.

Gans, C. 1989. Crocodilians in perspective. *Am. Zool.* 29:1051–54.

Gans, C., Clark, B. 1976. Studies on ventilation of *Caiman crocodilus*. *Resp. Physiol.* 26:285–301.

Garrick, L. D. 1975. Love among the alligators or, how to court a crocodilian. *Animal Kingdom* 78:2–8.

Garrick, L. D., Lang, J. W. 1977. Social signals and behaviors of adult alligators and crocodiles. *American Zoologist* 17:225–39.

Garrick, L. D., Lang, J. W. 1977. Alligator revealed. *Natural History* 86:54.

Garrick, L. D. et al. 1978. Social signals of adult American alligators. *Bull. Amer. Mus. Nat. Hist.* 160:155–92.

Garrido, H. O., Jaume, M. L. 1984. Catalogo descripto de los anfibios y reptiles de Cuba. *Duana—Acta Vertebrata* 11:5–112.

Gatten, R. E., Jr. 1980. Metabolic rates of fasting and recently fed Spectacled caimans (*Caiman crocodilus*). *Herpetologica* 36:361–4.

Gatten, R. E., Jr. 1985. The uses of anaerobiosis by amphibians and reptiles. *Amer. Zool.* 25:945–54.

Gaunt, A. S., Gans, C. 1968. Diving bradycardia and withdrawal bradycardia in *Caiman crocodilus*. *Nature* 223:207–8.

George, J. C. 1972. "Everglades Wildguide," Natural History Series, U.S. Department of Interior: National Park Service. U.S. Govt. Printing Office (#2405-00497), Washington, D.C.

Giles, L. W., Childs, V. L. 1949. Alligator Management on the Sabine National Wildlife Refuge. *J. Wildl. Mgmt.* 13:16–28.

Gist, D. H., Kaplan, M. L. 1976. Effects of stress and ACTH plasma corticosterone levels in the caiman *Caiman crocodilus. Gen. Comp. Endocrinology* 28:413–9.

Glassman, A. B., Bennett, C. E. 1978. Responses of the alligator to infection and thermal stress, in: Thorp, J. H., Gibbons, J. W. (eds.), "Energy and Environmental Stress in Aquatic Systems," U.S. Dept. of Energy Symp. Conf. #771114— National Technical Information Service, Springfield, Virginia.

Glastra, R. 1983. Notes on a population of *Caiman crocodilus crocodilus* depleted by hide hunting. *Biol. Conserv.* 26:149–62.

Goin, C. J., Coin, C. B. 1971. "Introduction to Herpetology," W. H. Freeman Publishing, San Francisco.

Goodwin, T. M., Marion, W. R. 1977. Occurrence of Florida red-bellied turtle eggs in north-central Florida alligator nests. *Florida Scientist* 40:237–8.

Goodwin, T. M., Marion, W. R. 1978. Aspects of the nesting ecology of American alligators (*Alligator mississippiensis*) in north-central Florida. *Herpetologica* 34:43–7.

Goodwin, T. M., Marion, W. R. 1979. Season activity ranges and habitat preferences of adult alligators in a north-central Florida lake. *J. Herpetol.* 13:157–64.

Gorden, R. W. et al. 1979. Isolation of *Aeromonas hydrophila* from the American alligator, *Alligator mississippiensis. J. Wildl. Dis.* 14:239–43.

Gorman, J. 1989. Return of a reptile—Alligators in Florida. *Sports Illustrated* 70:50–2.

Gorzula, S. 1978. An ecological study of *Caiman crocodilus crocodilus* inhabiting Savanna lagoons in the Venezuelan Guyana. *Oecologica* 35:21–34.

Gorzula, S. 1984. Proposal for a photographic method for size estimates of crocodilians. *Herp. Rev.* 15:38–9.

Gorzula, S. 1987. The management of crocodilians in Venezuela, in: "Wildlife Management—Crocodiles and Alligators," Webb, G. J. W., et al. (eds.), Surrey Beatty and Sons, Chipping Norton, NSW, Australia.

Graham, A. 1968. The Lake Rudolph crocodile (*Crocodylus niloticus*) population. Report to the Kenya Game Commission, Nairobi.

Graham, A., Beard, P. 1973. "Eyelids of the Morning," New York Graphic Society, N.Y.

Gray, J. E. 1867. VII. Synopsis of the species of recent Crocodilians or Emydosaurians, chiefly founded on the specimens in the British Museum and the Royal College of Surgeons (read Dec. 9th, 1862) *Trans. Zool. Soc. Lond.* 6:(4)125–169.

Greenfield, L. J., Morrow, A. G. 1961. The cardiovascular hemodynamics of crocodilia. *J. Surg. Research* 1:97–103.

Greer, A. E. 1970. Evolutionary and systematic significance of crocodilian nesting habits. *Nature* 227:523–4.

Greer, A. E. 1971. Crocodilian nesting habits and evolution. *Fauna* 2:20–8.

Grigg, G. C., Alchin, J. 1976. The role of the cardiovascular system in thermoregulation of *Crocodylus johnstoni. Physiol. Zool.* 49:24–36.

Grigg, G. C. 1977. The body temperature of crocodiles and dinosaurs, in: Messel,

BIBLIOGRAPHY

H. et al. (eds.), "Australian Animals and their Environment," Shakespeare Publishing, Sydney.

Grigg, G. C. 1978. Metabolic rate, Q10 and the respiratory quotient (RQ) in *Crocodylus porosus* and some generalizations about low RQ in reptiles. *Physiol. Zool.* 51:354–60.

Grigg, G. C., Cairncross, M. 1980. Respiratory properties of the blood of *Crocodylus porosus. Resp. Physiol.* 41:367–80.

Grigg, G. C. et al. 1980. Survival and growth of hatchling *Crocodylus porosus* in saltwater without access to fresh drinking water. *Oecologica* 47:264–6.

Grigg, G. C. 1981. Plasma homeostasis and cloacal urine composition in *Crocodylus porosus* along a salinity gradient. *J. Comp. Physiol.* 144:261–70.

Grigg, G. C., Beard, L. 1985. Water loss and gain by eggs of *Crocodylus porosus* related to incubation age and fertility, in: "Biology of Australasian Frogs and Reptiles," Grigg, G. C. et al. (eds), Surrey Beatty and Sons, Chipping Norton, NSW, Australia.

Grigg, G. C. 1987. Water relations of crocodilian eggs: management consideration, in: "Wildlife Management—Crocodiles and Alligators," Webb, G. J. W., et al. (eds.), Surrey Beatty and Sons, Chipping Norton, NSW, Australia.

Grim, F., Bubman, G. 1978. (October 26) Saltwater croc gets last laugh. *Miami Herald* page 6C.

Groombridge, B. 1982. "The IUCN Amphibia-Reptilia Red Data Book-Part I, Testudines-Crocodylia-Rhynococephalia." IUCN, Gland, Switzerland.

Groombridge, B. 1987. The distribution and status of world crocodilians, in: "Wildlife Management—Crocodiles and Alligators," Webb, G. J. W., et al. (eds.), Surrey Beatty and Sons, Chipping Norton, NSW, Australia.

Grzimek, B. et al. (eds.) 1984. "Animal Life Encyclopedia-Volume 6—Reptiles," Van Nostrand Reinhold, New York.

Guggisberg, C. A. 1972. "Crocodiles," Stackpole Publishing, Harrisburg, Pennsylvania.

Hadley, D. 1969. Breeding of crocodiles in Livingston Game Park. *The Puku* 5:226–8.

Hagan, J. M. et al. 1983. Behavioral response of the American alligator to freezing weather. *J. Herpetol.* 17:402–4.

Hall, P. M. 1989. Variation in geographic isolates of the New Guinea crocodile (*Crocodylus novaguineae* Schmidt) compared to similar allopatric Philippine crocodile (*Crocodylus minorensis* Schmidt). *Copeia* 1989:71–80.

Hall, R. J. et al. 1979. Organochlorine residues in eggs of the endangered American crocodile (*Crocodylus acutus*). *Bull. Environ. Contamin. Toxicol.* 23:87–90.

Halliday, T., Adler, K. (eds.) 1987. "Encyclopedia of Reptiles and Amphibians," Facts-On-File, N.Y.

Harper, F. (ed.) 1958. "Travels of William Bartram: Naturalist's Edition," Yale University Press, New Haven.

Hecht, M. K., Malone, B. 1972. On the early history of the Gavialid crocodilians. *Herpetologica* 28:281–4.

Herbert, J. D. 1981. Nitrogen excretion in 'maximally' fed crocodilians. *Comp. Biochem. Physiol.* 69(B):499–504.

Herzog, H. A. 1975. An observation of nest opening by an American alligator. *Herpetologica* 31:446–7.

Herzog, H. A., Burghardt, G. M. 1977. Vocalization in juvenile crocodilians. *Z. Tierpsychol.* 44:294–304.

Hines, T. C., Schaeffer, K. 1968. Alligator research in Florida: A progress report. *Proc. SE Assn. Game & Fish Comm.* 22:166–80.

Hines, T. C., Keenlyne, K. D. 1977. Two incidents of alligator attacks on humans in Florida. *Copeia* 1977:735–8.

Hines, T. C. 1979. The past and present status of the alligator in Florida. *Proc. SE Assn. Fish & Wildl. Agencies* 33:224–32.

Hines, T. C. 1980. Nuisance alligator control in Florida. *Wildl. Soc. Bull.* 8:234–41.

Hines, T. C. et al. 1984. "American Crocodile Recovery Plan," U.S. Fish and Wildlife Service, Atlanta, Georgia.

Hines, T. C., Percival, H. F. 1986. Alligator management and value-added conservation in Florida, in: "Valuing Wildlife: Economic and Social Perspectives," Decker, D. J., Goff, G. (eds), Westview Press, N.Y. Wildlife Society, N.Y.

Hines, T. C. 1987. The management of alligators in Florida, in: "Wildlife Management—Crocodiles and Alligators," Webb, G. J. W., et al. (eds.), Surrey Beatty and Sons, Chipping Norton, NSW, Australia.

Hirschorn, H. H. 1968. "Crocodilians of Florida and the Tropical Americas," Phoenix Publishing, Miami.

Hoffman, E. 1988. Man-eaters—saltwater crocodiles. *Intl. Wildl.* 18:12–17.

Holden, C. 1977. Alligator protections loosened. *Science* 195:561.

Hollands, M. 1987. The management of crocodiles in Papua, New Guinea, in: "Wildlife Management—Crocodiles and Alligators," Webb, G. J. W., et al. (eds.), Surrey Beatty and Sons, Chipping Norton, NSW, Australia.

Honegger, R. E. (ed.) 1975. "Amphibia and Reptilia," IUCN Red Data Book. Morges, Switzerland.

Hornaday, W. T. 1891. The American crocodile in Florida. *Amer. Naturalist* 9: 498–504.

Hornaday, W. T. 1904. "The American Natural History," Charles Scribner's Sons, New York.

Horst, J. 1980. Louisiana holds brief open season on alligators after a 15-year hiatus. *National Fisherman* Jan. 1980:54.

Huggins, S. E. et al. 1968. Further study of the spontaneous electrical activity of the brain of *Caiman sclerops*: olfactory lobes. *Physiol Zool.* 41:371–83.

Hunt, R. H. 1969. Breeding the spectacled caiman, *Caiman crocodilus* at Atlanta Zoo. *Intl. Zoo Yearbook* 9:36–7.

Hunt, R. H. 1975. Maternal behavior in the Morelet's crocodile, *Crocodylus morleti. Copeia* 1975:763–4.

Hunt, R. H., Watanabe, M. E. 1982. Observations on maternal behavior of the American alligator, *Alligator mississippiensis. J. Herpetol.* 16:235–9.

Hunt, R. H. 1986. Predation of alligator nests in Okefenokee Swamp National Wildlife Refuge, Georgia. *Proc. 8th Crocodile Specialist Group, Species Survival Commission* IUCN, Quito, Ecuador.

Hunt, R. H. 1988. Nest excavation and neonate transport in wild *Alligator mississippiensis. J. Herpetol.* 21:348–350.

Hurt, H. 1987. From the Jaws of Death. *Reader's Digest* 130:116–20.

Hutt, A. 1964. The Alligator. *Fla. Wildl.* 18:12–17+34.

Hutton, J. M. 1982. Home range and territoriality in the Nile crocodile. *Zimbabwe Sci. News* 16:199–201.

Hutton, J. M. 1987. Techniques for aging wild crocodilians, in: "Wildlife Management—Crocodiles and Alligators," Webb, G. J. W., et al. (eds.), Surrey Beatty and Sons, Chipping Norton, NSW, Australia.

Hutton, J. M. 1987. Crocodile capture techniques in Zimbabwe. *Ibid.*

Hutton, J. M. 1989. Movements, home range, dispersal and the separation of size classes in the Nile crocodile. *Am. Zool.* 29:1033–49.

Hutton, J. M., Van Jaarsveldt, K. R. 1987. Crocodile farming and ranching in Zimbabwe. *Ibid.*

Hyman, R. 1985. Brazil wages war on poachers. *Intl. Wildl.* 1985:5–11.

Idress, I. L. 1946. "In Crocodile Land," Angus and Robertson, Sydney.

Iordansky, N. N. 1973. The skull of the crocodilia, in: "Biology of the Reptilia-Volume 14," Gans, C., Parson, T. S. (eds.), Academic Press, New York.

Jackson, D. D. 1987. Alligators are back. *Smithsonian* 17:36–44.

Jackson, J. F., Campbell, K. E. 1974. The feeding habits of crocodilians: validity of the evidence from stomach contents. *J. Herpetol.* 8:378–81.

Jackson, K. 1989. Las Colinas gator keeps authorities at Bay. May 23rd. *Dallas Morning News* pp. 17A, 19A.

Jacobsen, T. 1983. Crocodilians and islands: status of the American alligator in the lower Florida Keys. *Florida Field Naturalist* 11:1–24.

Jacobsen, T., Kushlan, J. A. 1984. Alligator nest flooding in the southern Everglades. *Proc. 7th Working Meeting of the Crocodile Specialist Group.* IUCN, Caracas.

Jacobsen, T. 1986. Alligator in natural areas: choosing conservation policies consistent with local objectives. *Biol. Conserv.* 36:181–96.

Jacobson, E. R. et al. 1979. Pox-like skin lesions in captive caimans. *J. Amer. Vet. Med. Assn.* 175:937–40.

Jacobson, E. R. et al. 1984. Adenovirus-like infection in two Nile crocodiles. *J. Amer. Vet. Med. Assn.* 185:1421–2.

Jayal, N. D. 1980. Crocodile conservation in India. *Tigerpaper* 7:1–3.

Jelden, D. C. 1981. Preliminary studies on the breeding biology of *Crocodylus porosus* and *Crocodylus novaeguineae* on the middle Sepik (Papua, New Guinea). *Amphibia-Reptilia* 3/4:353–8.

Jenkins, N. K. 1975. Chemical composition of the eggs of the crocodile (*Crocodylus novaeguineae*). *Comp. Biochem. Physiol.* 51A:891–5.

Jenkins, R. W. G. 1980. Crocodile comeback: problem or profit? *Australian Fisheries* 39:4.

Jenkins, R. W. G. 1987. The world conservation strategy and CITES: principles for the management of crocodilians, in: "Wildlife Management—Crocodiles and Alligators," Webb, G. J. W., et al. (eds.), Surrey Beatty and Sons, Chipping Norton, NSW, Australia.

Joanen, T. 1969. Nesting ecology of alligators in Louisiana. *Proc. Ann. Conf. SE Assn. Game & Fish Comms.* Vol. 23.

Joanen, T., McNease, L. 1971. Propagation of the American alligator in captivity. *Proc. Ann. Conf. Assn. SE Game & Fish Comms.* 25:106–116.

Joanen, T., McNease, L. 1972. A telemetric study of adult male alligators on the Rockefeller Refuge, Louisiana. *Proc. Ann. Conf. Assn. SE Game & Fish Comms.* 26:252–75.

Joanen, T., McNease, L. 1975. Notes of the reproductive biology and captive propagation of the American alligator. *Proc. Ann. Conf. Assn. SE Game & Fish Comms.* 29:407–15.

Joanen, T., McNease, L. 1976. Culture of immature American alligators in controlled environmental chambers. *Proc. Ann. Workshop World Mariculture Soc.* 7:201–211.

Joanen, T., McNease, L. 1989. Ecology and physiology and early development of the American alligator. *Am. Zool.* 29:987–98.

Joanen, T. et al. 1977. Effects of simulated flooding on alligator eggs. *Proc. Ann. Conf. SE Assn. of Fish & Wildl. Agencies.* 31:33–35.

Joanen, T., McNease, L. 1977. Artificial incubation of alligator eggs and post-hatching culture in controlled environmental chambers. *Proc. A. Workshop World Mariculture Society.* 8:483–9.

Joanen, T., McNease, L. 1978. The cloaca sexing method for immature alligators. *Proc. Ann. Conf. SE. Assn. Fish & Wildlife Agencies* 32:179–81.

Joanen, T., McNease, L. 1979. Culture of the American alligator. *Intl. Zoo. Yearbook* 19:62–66.

Joanen, T., McNease, L. 1979. Time of egg deposition for the American alligator. *Proc. Ann. Conf. SE Assn. Fish & Wildl. Agencies* 33:15–19.

Joanen, T., McNease, L. 1981. Nesting chronology of the American alligator and factors affecting nesting in Louisiana. *Proc. 1st Ann. Alligator Production Conf. Univ. of Florida, Gainesville.*

Joanen, T., McNease, L. 1981. Management of the alligator as a renewable resource in Louisiana. Georgia Department of Natural Resources, *Technical Bulletin* 5:62–72.

Joanen, T., McNease, L. 1987. The management of alligators in Louisiana, in: "Wildlife Management—Crocodiles and Alligators," Webb, G. J. W., et al. (eds.), Beatty and Sons, Chipping Norton, NSW, Australia.

Joanen, T., McNease, L. 1987. Alligator farming research in Louisiana, U.S.A. *Ibid.*

Johnsen, P. B., Wellington, J. L. 1982. Detection of glandular secretions by yearling alligators. *Copeia* 1982:705–8.

Johnson, C. R. et al. 1978. Thermoregulation in crocodilians-III Thermal preferenda, voluntary maxima and heating and cooling rates in the American alligator, *Alligator mississippiensis. Zool. J. Linnean Soc.* 62:179–88.

Johnson, L. A. et al. 1985. Alligator nuisance control program in Texas: problem and process. *Proc. 7th Grat Plains Wildl. Damage Control Workshop.*

Jollie, M. 1962. "Chordate Morphology" (reprinted 1973 w/corrections), Krieger Publishing Company, Melbourne, Florida.

Jones, F. K. 1965. Techniques and methods used to capture and tag alligators in Florida. *Proc. Ann. Conf. SE Assn. Game & Fish Comm.* 19:98–101.

Kar, S. K. 1980. Saltwater crocodile project, Orissa. *Makara* 2:7–8.

Kauffman, G. 1974. Zur Abhangigkeit der cochleapotentiale des kaimans vom stoffwechsel van aktiven transporten und von der temperatur. *J. Comp. Physiol.* 90:245–73.

Kavaliers, M., Ralph, C. L. 1980. Circadian organization of an animal lacking a pineal organ, the young American alligator. *Alligator mississippiensis. J. Comp. Physiol.* 139:287–92.

Kellog, R. 1929. The habits and economic importance of alligators. *U.S. Dept. Agriculture Tech. Bulletin* No. 147, Washington, D.C.

Kennedy, J. P., Brockman, H. L. 1965. Open heart surgery, in *Alligator mississippiensis. Herpetologia* 21:6–15.

Kent, G. 1982. "Comparative Anatomy of the Vertebrates," C. V. Mosby, St. Louis.

BIBLIOGRAPHY

Kersey, H. A., Jr. 1975. "Pelts, Plumes & Hides—White Traders Among the Seminole Indians 1870–1930," Florida Atlantic University—University Presses of Florida, Gainesville.

Khalh, F. 1958. Nitrogenous excretion in crocodiles. *J. Exp. Biol.* 35:552–5.

King, F. W., Brazaitis, P. 1971. Species identification of commercial crocodile skins. *Zoologica* 56:15–70.

King, F. W. 1972. The American alligator. *National Parks & Conserv. Magazine* (May) pp. 15–18.

King, F. W. et al. 1980. Review of the status of the American crocodile. *Proc. 5th Working Meeting, Croc. Specialist Group.* IUCN, Gland, Switzerland.

King, F. W., Burke, R. L. (eds.) 1989. "Crocodilian, Tuatara and Turtle Species of the World. A Taxonomic and Geographic Reference," Assoc. of Systematics Collections, Washington, D.C.

Kinsella, J. M. 1982. Alligator predation on round-tailed muskrats. *Fla. Field Nat.* 10:78.

Kirschner, D. 1985. Environmental effects on dorsal colouration in saltwater crocodile *Crocodylus porosus*, in: "Biology of Australasian Frogs and Reptiles," Grigg, G. et al. (eds.), Surrey Beatty and Sons, Chipping Norton, NSW, Australia.

Klause, S. E. 1983. Reproductive characteristics of the American alligator in North Carolina, in: "Status of the American Alligator in North Carolina," North Carolina State University, Raleigh.

Kleinberg, E. 1989. Entering final day—gator hunt expected to pass '88 total. *Palm Beach Post* pg. 2B, (Sept 30, 1989).

Kramer, G. 1955. Uber wachstumsbedingte proportionsanderungen bei Krokodilen. *Zool. Jahrb. Abt. Allg. Zool.* 66:62–74.

Kushlan, J. A. 1971. Observations on the role of the American alligator in the south Florida wetlands. *Copeia* 1971:993–996.

Kushlan, J. A. 1972. "An Ecological Study of an Alligator Pond in the Big Cypress Swamp of southern Florida," University of Miami, Coral Gables, Florida.

Kushlan, J. A. 1973. Observations on maternal behavior in the American alligator, *Alligator mississippiensis. Herpetologica* 29:256–7.

Kushlan, J. A., Kushlan, M. S. 1980a. Function of nest attendance in the American alligator. *Herpetologica* 36:27–32.

Kushlan, J. A., Kushlan, M. S. 1980b. Everglades alligator nests: nesting sites for marsh reptiles. *Copeia* 1980:930–32.

Kushlan, J. A., Simon, C. 1981. Egg manipulation by the American alligator. *J. Herpetol.* 15:451–4.

Kushlan, J. A., Mazzotti, F. J. 1984. Population biology and status of the American crocodile in South Florida. *Proc. 7th Meeting Crocodile Specialist Group* Caracas.

Kushlan, J. A., Mazzotti, F. J. 1989a. Historic and present distribution of the American crocodile in Florida. *J. Herpetol.* 23:1–7.

Kushlan, J. A., Mazzotti, F. J. 1989b. Population biology of the American crocodile (study period: 1977-82). *J. Herpetol.* 23:7–21.

Kushlan, J. A., Jacobson, T. 1990. Environmental variability and the reproductive success of Everglades alligators. *J. Herpetol.* 24:176–184.

Lance, V. 1981. Reproduction in the American alligator. *Proc. 9th Intl. Symp. Comparative Endocrinology.* Hong Kong Univ. Press.

Lance, V. et al. 1983. Selenium, Vitamin E and trace elements in the plasma of wild and farm reared alligators during the reproductive cycle. *Can. J. Zool.* 61:1744–51.

Lance, V. 1984. Endocrinology of reproduction in male reptile. *Symp. Zool. Soc. Lond.* 52:357–83.

Lance, V. 1987. Hormonal Control of reproduction in crocodilians, in: "Wildlife Management—Crocodiles and Alligators," Webb, G. J. W., et al. (eds.), Surrey Beatty and Sons, Chipping Norton, NSW, Australia.

Lance, V. 1989. Reproductive cycle of the American alligator. *Am. Zool.* 29:999–1018.

Lang, J. W. 1975. Thermoregulatory behavior of adult American alligators. *Amer. Zool.* 15:797.

Lang, J. W. 1976. Amphibious behavior of *Alligator mississippiensis*; roles of circadian rhythm and light. *Science* 191:575–7.

Lang, J. W. 1979. Thermophilic response of the American alligator and the American crocodile to feeding. *Copeia* 1979:48–59.

Lang, J. W. 1980. Reproductive behaviors of New Guinea and saltwater crocodiles. Abstract. "The Reproductive Biology and Conservation of Crocodiles," Soc. for the Study of Amphibians and Reptiles.

Lang, J. W. 1981. Thermal preferences of hatchling New Guinea crocodiles; effects of feeding and ontogeny. *J. Therm. Biol.* 6:73–8.

Lang, J. W. 1982. Ontogeny of thermal preference in young American alligators. *Amer. Zool.* 22:864.

Lang, J. W. 1985. Incubation temperature effect on thermal selection of hatchling crocodiles *Amer. Zool.* 25:18A.

Lang, J. W. 1987. Crocodilian behavior implications for management, in: "Wildlife Management—Crocodiles and Alligators," Webb, G. J. W., et al. (eds.), Surrey Beatty and Sons, Chipping Norton, NSW, Australia.

Lang, J. W. 1987. Crocodilian thermal selection. *Ibid.*

Lang, J. W. et al. 1989. Sex determination and sex ratios in *Crocodylus palustris. Am. Zool.* 29:935–52.

Langston, W. 1973. The crocodilian skull in historical perspective, in: "Biology of the Reptilia-Vol. 4," Gans & Parsons, (eds.), Academic Press, New York.

Lanhupuy, W. 1987. Australian aboriginal attitudes to crocodile management, in: "Wildlife Management—Crocodiles and Alligators," Webb, G. J. W., et al. (eds.), Surrey Beatty and Sons, Chipping Norton, NSW, Australia.

Larson, R. E. et al. 1983. Steatitis and fat necrosis in captive alligators. *J. Am. Vet. Med. Assn.* 1983:1202–4.

Lawson, R. et al. 1989. Allozyme variation in a natural population of the Nile crocodile. *Am. Zool.* 29:863–71.

Laycock, G. 1987. The unendangered alligator's fall from grace. *Audubon* 89:38–43.

Lazell, J., Spitzer, N. 1977. Apparent play behavior in an American alligator. *Copeia* 1977:188.

LeBuff, C. R. 1957. Observations on captive and wild North American crocodilians. *Herpetologica* 13:25–8.

LeBuff, C. R. 1957. The range of *Crocodylus acutus* along the Florida Gulf Coast. *Herpetologica* 13:188.

Lemonick, M. D. 1987. Coming back from the brink. *Time* 130:70.

BIBLIOGRAPHY

Leslie, D. G., Lang, J. W. 1977. Social signals and behaviors of adult alligators and crocodiles. *Amer. Zool.* 17: 225–39.

Letts, G. A. 1987. The management of crocodiles in Australia, in: "Wildlife Management—Crocodiles and Alligators," Webb, G. J. W., et al. (eds.), Surrey Beatty and Sons, Chipping Norton, NSW, Australia.

Lewis, J. J. 1985. "The ethology of captive juvenile *Caiman sclerops*, growth, development and sociality," PhD thesis, Northwestern Univ., Chicago. University Microfilms International, Ann Arbor and London.

Lewis, L. Y., Gatten, R. E., Jr. 1985. Aerobic metabolism of American alligators *Alligator mississippiensis* under standard conditions and during voluntary activity. *Comp. Biochem. Physiol.* 80A:441–7.

Lewis, T. A. 1987. Searching for the truth in alligator country. *Natl. Wildl.* 25:12–19.

Loveridge, J. P., Blake, D. K. 1972. Techniques in the immobilization and handling of the Nile crocodile (*Crocodylus niloticus*). *Arnoldia* (Rhod) 5:1–14.

Loveridge, J. P. 1979. The immobilization and anaesthesia of crocodilians. *Intl. Zoo Yearbook* 19:103–12.

Loveridge, J. P. 1980. Crocodile research and conservation in Southern Africa. *S. Afr. J. Sci.* 76:203–6.

Loveridge, J. P. 1984. Thermoregulation in the Nile crocodile *Crocodylus niloticus*, in: "The Structure, Development and Evolution of Reptiles," Vol. 52, Ferguson, M.J.W. (ed.), Symp. Zool. Soc. London.

Loveridge, J. P. 1987. Crocodile immobilization and anaesthesia, in: "Wildlife Management—Crocodiles and Alligators," Webb, G. J. W., et al. (eds.), Surrey Beatty and Sons, Chipping Norton, NSW, Australia.

Lutz, P. L. et al. 1980. Oxygen and water vapor conductance in the shell membrane of the American crocodile egg. *Comp. Biochem. Physiol.* 66:335–8.

Lutz, P. L., Dunbar-Cooper, A. 1984. The nest environment of the American crocodile (*Crocodylus acutus*). *Copeia* 1984:153–61.

Luxmoore, R. et al. 1985. "A Directory of Crocodilian Farming Operations," IUCN/CITES, Lausanne.

Luxmoore, R. et al (eds.) 1988. "Significant trade in wildlife: A review of selected species in CITES, Appendix II, Volume 2, Reptiles and Invertebrates," IUCN, Lausanne.

McCoy, M. 1980. "Reptiles of the Solomon Islands—Handbook Number 7," Wau Ecology Institute, Papua, New Guinea.

McIlhenny, E. A. 1934. Notes on incubation and growth of alligators. *Copeia* 1934:80–8.

McIlhenny, E. A. 1935. "The Alligator's Life History," Christopher Publishing House, Boston, reprinted 1976 by Soc. Study of Amphib. & Reps., reprinted 1987 by Ten-Speed Press, Berkeley, California.

McNease, L., Joanen, T. 1974. A telemetric study of immature alligators on Rockefeller Refuge, Louisiana. *Proc. Ann. Conf. SE Assn. Game & Fish Comms.* 28:482–500.

McNease, L., Joanen, T. 1977. Alligator diets in relation to marsh salinity. *Proc. Ann. Conf. Assn. SE Game & Fish Comms.* 31:36–40.

McNease, L., Joanen, T. 1978. Distribution and relative abundance of the alligator in Louisiana coastal marshes. *Proc. Ann. Conf. SE Assn. of Fish & Wildl. Agencies.* 32:182–6.

Magnusson, W. E. et al. 1978. A double survey estimate of population size from incomplete counts. *J. Wildl. Mgmnt.* 42:174–6.

Magnusson, W. E. et al. 1978. An aerial survey of potential nesting areas of the saltwater crocodile, *Crocodylus porosus*, on the north coast of Arnhem Land, Northern Australia. *Austral. Wildl. Resrch.* 5:401–15.

Magnusson, W. E. 1979. Dispersal of hatchling crocodiles, (*Crocodylus porosus*). *J. Herpetol.* 13:227–31.

Magnusson, W. E. 1979. Incubation period of *Crocodylus porosus. J. Herpetol.* 13:362–3.

Magnusson, W. E. 1979. Maintenance of temperature of crocodile nests. *J. Herpetol.* 13:439–43.

Magnusson, W. E. et al 1980. An aerial survey of potential nesting areas of *Crocodylus porosus* on the west coast of Cape York Peninsula. *Austral. Wildl. Resrch* 7:465–78.

Magnusson, W. E. 1980. Hatching and creche formation by *Crocodylus porosus. Copeia* 1980:359–62.

Magnusson, W. E. 1980. Habitat required for nesting by *Crocodylus porosus* in Northern Australia. *Austral. Wildl. Resrch.* 7:149–56.

Magnusson, W. E., Taylor, J. A. 1980. A description of developmental stages in *Crocodylus porosus* for use in aging eggs in the field. *Austral. Wildl. Resrch.* 7:479–86.

Magnusson, W. E., Taylor, J. A. 1981. Growth of juvenile *Crocodylus porosus* as affected by season of hatching. *J. Herpetol.* 15:242–5.

Magnusson, W. E. 1981. Suitability of two habitats in Northern Australia for the release of hatchling *Crocodylus porosus* from artificial nests. *Austral. Wildl. Resrch.* 8:199–202.

Magnusson, W. E. 1982. Mortality of eggs of the crocodile. *Crocodylus porosus* in Northern Australia *J. Herpetol.* 16:121–30.

Magnusson, W. E. 1983. Size estimates of crocodilians. *J. Herpetol.* 17:86–8.

Magnusson, W. E. et al. 1984. Sources of heat for nests of *Paleosuchus trigonatus* and a review of crocodilian nest temperatures. *J. Herpetol.* 19:199–207.

Magnusson, W. E. 1984. Economics, developing countries and the captive propagation of crocodilians. *Wildl. Soc. Bull.* 12:194–7.

Manolis, S. C. et al. 1987. Crocodile egg chemistry, in: "Wildlife Management—Crocodiles and Alligators," Webb, G. J. W., et al. (eds.), Surrey Beatty and Sons, Chipping Norton, NSW, Australia.

Martin, B. G. H., Bellairs, [A.] dA. 1977. The narial excrescence and pterygoid bulla of the gharial, *Gavialis gangeticus. J. Zool. Soc. Lond.* 182:541–58.

Mattison, C. 1982. "The Care of reptiles and amphibians in captivity," Blandford, Dorset and Sterling Publishing, N.Y.

Mazzotti, F. J., Dunson, W. A. 1984. Adaptations of *Crocodylus acutus* and *Alligator* for life in saline water. *Comp. Biochem. Physiol.* 79A:641–6.

Mazzotti, F. J., Dunson, W. A. 1989. Osmoregulation in crocodilians. *Am. Zool.* 29:903–20.

Mazzotti, F. J. et al. 1986. Field and laboratory observations on the effects of high temperature and salinity on hatchling. *Crocodylus acutus. Herpetologica* 42:191–6.

Mazzotti, F. J. et al. 1988. Dessication and cryptic nest flooding as probable causes of egg mortality in the American crocodile *Crocodylus acutus* in Everglades National Park in Florida. *Florida Scientist* 51:65–72.

Medem, F. 1960. Notes on the Paraguay caiman, *Caiman yacare* DAUDIN. *Milt eilungen aus de Zoologische Museum* Berlin. 36(1):129–42.

Medem, F. 1980. Caimans and crocodiles—a tale of destruction. *Oryx* 15(4):390–1.

Medem, F. 1981. "Los crocodylia de Sur America, Vol. I. Los crocodylia de Colombia," Universidad Nacional de Colombia, Bogota.

Medem, F. 1983. *Ibid.*—Volume II (Venezuela, Trinidad, Guyana, Ecuador, Peru, Brazil, Surinam, Paraguay, Argentina, Bolivia, Uruguay, French Guiana).

Mertens, R. 1943. Die rezenten Krokodile des Natur-Museums Senckenberg, *Senckenbergiana* 26(4):252-312.

Mertens, R. 1960. "The World of Amphibians and Reptiles," McGraw-Hill Book Company, New York.

Messel, H., Stephens, D. R. 1980. Drug immobilization of crocodiles. *J. Wildl. Mgmnt.* 44:295–6.

Messel, H. et al (1979-1984). "Surveys of tidal river systems in Northern Australia and their crocodile populations," Monographs 1 thru 18. Pergamon Press, Sydney.

Messel, H., Vorlicek, G. C. 1987. A population model for *Crocodylus porosus* in the tidal waterways of Northern Australia: management implications, in: "Wildlife Management—Crocodiles and Alligators," Webb, G. J. W., et al. (eds.), Surrey Beatty and Sons, Chipping Norton, NSW, Australia.

Methren, B. 1989. Gator hunt. *Fins and Feathers* (Winter Issue-1989) p.15.

Metzen, W. D. 1977. Nesting ecology of alligators in the Okefenokee National Wildlife Refuge. *Proc. Ann. Conf. SE Assn. Game & Fish Comms.* 31:39–42.

Minnich, J. E. 1972. Excretion of urate salts by reptiles. *Comp. Biochem. Physiol.* 41:535–49.

Minton, S. A., Minton, M. R. 1973. "Giant Reptiles," Chas. Scribner's Sons, New York.

Mittleman, M. B., Brown, B. C. 1948. The alligator in Texas. *Herpetologica* 4:195–6.

Modha, M. L. 1967. The ecology of the Nile crocodile (*Crocodylus niloticus*) on Central Island, Lake Rudolph. *East African Wildl.* 5:74–95.

Modha, M. L. 1968. Crocodile research project. *East African Wildl. J.* 6:148–50.

Montage, J. J. 1981. His crop is crocodiles. *Intl. Wildl.* 11:21–8.

Montage, J. J. 1983. Influence of water level, hunting pressure and habitat type on crocodile abundance in the Fly River drainage, Papua, New Guinea. *Biol. Conserv.* 23:309–339.

Montage, J. J. 1984. Morphometric analysis of *Crocodylus novaeguineae* from the Fly River drainage, Papua, New Guinea. *Austral. Wildl. Resrch.* 11:394–414.

Mook, C. C. 1921. Skull characteristics of recent crocodilia. *Bull. Amer. Mus. Nat. Hist.* 44:123–268.

Mook, C. C. 1923. Skull characteristics of *Alligator sinensis*. *Ibid.* 48:553–62.

Moore, J. C. 1953. The crocodile in the Everglades National Park. *Copeia* 1953: 54–59.

Mount, R. H. 1975. "The Reptiles and Amphibians of Alabama," Auburn University, Auburn, Alabama.

Murphy, P. A. 1981. Celestrial compass orientation in juvenile American alligators. *Copeia* 1981:638–645.

Murphy, T. M., Fendley, T. T. 1973. A new technique for live trapping of nuisance alligators. *Proc. Ann. Conf. SE Assn. Game & Fish Comms.* 27:308–11.

Murphy, T. M., Coker, J. W. 1983. "American alligator population studies in South Carolina," Study completion report: [10/79]–[9/83]: South Carolina Wildlife & Marine Resources Dept., Charleston, S. C.

Myers, N. 1982. Africa's massive crocs. *Intl. Wildl.* 12:32–7.

Neil, W. T. 1946. Notes on *Crocodylus novaeguineae. Copeia* 1946: 17–20.

Neil, W. T. 1971. "The Last of the Ruling Reptiles: Alligators, Crocodiles and their kin," Columbia University Press, New York.

Nichols, J. D., Chabreck, R. H. 1980. On the variability of alligator sex ratios. *Am. Nat.* 116:125–37.

Nichols, J. D. et al. 1987. Population models and crocodile management, in: "Wildlife Management—Crocodiles and Alligators," Webb, G. J. W., et al. (eds.), Surrey Beatty and Sons, Chipping Norton, NSW, Australia.

Nietschmann, B. 1976. Nicaraguan skin connection. *Nat. Hist.* 86:28.

Norell, M. A. 1989. The higher level relationships of the extant crocodylia. *Jour. Herpetol.* 23:325–35.

Norman, G. 1980. Gators. *Esquire Magazine* (October 1980) 94:112–14.

Nowak, R. M. 1976. Wildlife of Indochina: tragedy or opportunity? *National Parks & Conserv. Magazine* 50:13–18.

Obst, F. J. et al. (eds.) 1988. "The completely illustrated Atlas of Reptiles and Amphibians for the terrarium," T. F. H. Publications, Neptune City, N.J.

Ogden, J. C. 1971. Survival of the American crocodile in Florida. *Animal Kingdom* 74:7–11.

Ogden, J. C., Singletary, C. 1973. Night of the crocodile. *Audubon.* 75:32–37.

Ogden, J. C. 1978. Status and nesting biology of the American crocodile, *Crocodylus acutus* in Florida. *J. Herpetol.* 12:183–96.

Ogden, J. C. 1978. American crocodile, in: "Amphibians and Reptiles. Rare and Endangered biota of Florida": Volume III, McDiarmid, R. W. (ed.), University of Florida Press, Gainesville.

Oliver, J. A. 1955. "The Natural History of North American Amphibians and Reptiles," Van Nostrand, Princeton, New Jersey.

Onions, J. T. V. 1987. Crocodile farming and ranching in Australia, in: "Wildlife Management—Crocodiles and Alligators," Webb, G. J. W., et al. (eds.), Surrey Beatty and Sons, Chipping Norton, NSW, Australia.

Packard, G. C. et al. 1979. Water vapor conductance of testuidinian and crocodilian eggs. *Can. J. Zool.* 63:2422–9.

Packard, G. C., Packard, M. J. 1980. Evolution of the cleiodic egg among reptilian antecedents of birds. *Amer. Zool.* 20:351–62.

Palmisano, A. W. et al. 1973. An analysis of Louisiana's 1972 experimental alligator harvest program. *Proc. Ann. Conf. SE Assn. Game & Fish Comms.* 27:184–206.

Parker, I. S. C., Watson, R. M. 1970. Crocodile distribution and status in the major waters of western and central Uganda in 1969. *E. African Wildl. J.* 8:85–103.

Parsons, L. C., Huggins, S. E. 1965. Effects of temperature on the EEG of the caiman. *Proc. Soc. Esp. Biol. & Med.* 120:422–6.

Pérez-Higareda, G. et al. 1989. Comments on the food and feeding habits of Morelet's crocodile. *Copeia* 1989(4):1039–1041.

Perrero, L. 1975. "Alligators and Crocodiles of the World—Disappearing Dragons," Windward Publishing, Miami.

Perry, S. F. 1988. Functional morphology of the lungs of the Nile crocodile; non-respiratory parameters. *J. Exp. Biol.* 134:99–117.

BIBLIOGRAPHY

Pooley, A. C. 1962. The Nile crocodile, *Crocodylus niloticus*: notes on the incubation period and growth rates of juveniles. *Lammergeyer.* 2(1):1–55.

Pooley, A. C. 1969. Preliminary studies on the breeding of the Nile crocodile *Crocodylus niloticus* in Zululand. *Lammergeyer* 3:22–44.

Pooley, A. C. 1969. Some observations on the rearing of crocodiles. *Lammergeyer* 3:45–57.

Pooley, A. C. 1973. Conservation and management of crocodiles in Africa. *J. So. Afr. Wildl. Mgmnt. Assn.* 3:101–3.

Pooley, A. C. 1974. How does a baby crocodile get to water? *African Wildl.* 28:8–11.

Pooley, A. C., Gans, C. 1976. The Nile crocodile. *Scientific American* 234:114–24 (April 1976).

Pooley, A. C. 1977. Nest opening of the Nile crocodile, *Crocodylus niloticus. J. Zool. London* 182:17–26.

Pope, C. H. 1935. "The Reptiles of China—Roy Chapman Andrews Expedition," American Museum of Natural History, New York.

Pope, C. H. 1960. "The Reptile World," Alfred A. Knopf, New York.

Potter, F. E., Jr. 1981. "Status of the American alligator in Texas," Texas Parks and Wildlife Dept., Austin.

Pough, F. H. 1983. The advantages of ectothermy in vertebrates. *Am. Nat.* 115: 92–112.

Ramirez, Y. et al. 1977. Conservation: Venezuelan crocodile project. *Herp. Rev.* 8(4):130.

Rand, A. S. 1968. Dessication rates in crocodile and iguana eggs. *Herpetologica* 24:178–80.

Reese, A. M. 1907. The breeding habits of the Florida alligator. *Smithsonian Misc. Coll.* 50:381–6.

Reese, A. M. 1908. The development of the American alligator (*Alligator mississippiensis*). *Smithsonian Misc. Coll.* 51:1–66.

Reese, A. M. 1915. "The Alligator and its Allies," G. P. Putnam's Sons, New York.

Reese, A. M. 1921. The structure and development of the integumental glands of the crocodilia. *Jour. Morph.* 35:581–611.

Reese, A. M. 1931. The ways of alligators. *Sci. Month.* 33:321–55.

Reese, A. M. 1947. Bibliography of the crocodilia. *Herpetologica* 4:43–54.

Reese, A. M. 1948. Hibernation of the alligator in an artificial environment. *Herpetologica* 4:127–8.

Rhodda, G. H. 1984. Movements of juvenile American crocodiles in Gaton Lake, Panama. *Herpetologica* 40:444–51.

Ricciuti, E. R. 1972. "The American Alligator," Harper & Row, New York.

Ricciuti, E. R. 1976. Gators! *Natl. Wildl.* 14:4–11.

Romer, A. S. 1976. "The Osteology of the Reptiles," University of Chicago Press, Chicago.

Ross, C. A., Franklin, D. R. 1924. The caudal scalation of central crocodylus. *Proc. Biol. Soc. Wash.* 87:231–4.

Ross, C. A., Garnett, S. (eds.) 1989. "Crocodiles and Alligators," Facts-On-File Publications, New York.

Roth, J. J. 1980. Nonpineal melatonin in the alligator (*Alligator mississippiensis*). *Science* 210:548–50.

Roth, J. J. 1980. Alligator rhythm without a pineal. *Sci. News* 118:279.

Ruckel, S. W., Steele, G. W. 1984. Alligator nesting ecology in two habitats in Georgia. *Proc. SE Assn. Fish & Wildlife Agencies* Vol. 38.

Ruckel, S. W. 1987. The status of the American alligator in Georgia. *Third Symp. SE Nongame Endangered Wildlife Conf.* Athens, Ga.

Rudloe, J. 1982. Master of my lake (Attack on dog in Otter Lake). *Audubon* 84:5–6.

Sargeant, F. 1982. Jaws that are real. *Outdoor Life* 169:54–5.

Schaller, G. B., Cranshaw, P. G. 1982. Fishing behavior of the Paraguayan caiman (*Caiman crocodilus*). *Copeia* 1982:66–72.

Schmidt, K. P. 1922. The American alligator. *Field Mus. Nat. Hist. (Chicago)* Leaflet #3.

Schmidt, K. P. 1924. Notes on Central American crocodiles—reports on results of Captain Marshall Field Expedition. *Field Mus. Nat. Hist. Chicago.*

Schmidt, K. P. 1928. Notes on South American caimans: reports on results of the Captain Marshall FIeld Expedition—Publ. No. 252, Zool. Ser: V. 12, No. 17 *Field Mus. Nat. Hist. Chicago.*

Schmidt, K. P. 1928. A new crocodile from New Guinea. *Field Mus. Nat. Hist.* Zool. Series 12:176–81.

Schmidt, K. P. 1935. A new crocodile from the Philippine Islands. *Ibid.* 20:67–70.

Schmidt, K. P. 1938. History of a paratype of *Crocodylus mindoriensis. Copeia* 1938:89.

Schmidt, K. P. 1952. Crocodile hunting in Central America. Chi. Nat. Hist. Mus. Popular Series, No. 15.

Schmidt, K. P., Inger, R. F. 1957. "Living Reptiles of the World," Doubleday, Garden City, New York.

Schmidt-Nielsen, B., Skadhauge, E. 1967. Function of the excreatory system of the crocodile (*Crocodylus acutus*). *Am. J. Physiol.* 212:973–80.

Seidal, M. R. 1979. The osteoderms of the American alligator and their functional significance. *Herpetologica* 35:375–80.

Seymour, R. S., Ackerman, R. A. 1980. Adaptations to underground nesting in birds and reptiles. *Amer. Zool.* 20:437–47.

Seymour, R. S. et al. 1985. Blood gas tensions and acid-base regulation in the saltwater crocodile *Crocodylus porosus* at rest and after exhaustive exercise. *J. Exp. Biol.* 118:143–59.

Seymour, R. S. et al. 1987. Effect of capture on the physiology of *Crocodylus porosus*, in: Wildlife Management—Crocodiles and Alligators," Webb, G. J. W. et al. (eds.), Surrey Beatty and Sons, Chipping Norton, NSW, Australia.

Shaw, J. F. 1981. There's only one Harry Messel-Thank goodness. *Intl. Wildl.* 11:12–15.

Shortt, W. H. 1921. A few hints on crocodile shooting. *J. Bombay Nat. Hist. Soc.* 28:77.

Sill, W. D. 1968. The zoogeography of the crocodilia. *Copeia* 1968:76–88.

Sinba, K. 1987. Village and community attitudes to the management of crocodiles in Papua, New Guinea, in: "Wildlife Management—Crocodiles and Alligators," Webb, G. J. W., et al. (eds.), Surrey Beatty and Sons, Chipping Norton, NSW, Australia.

Singh, L. A. K. 1987. Public involvement in the Indian crocodile conservation program. *Ibid.*

Smith, A. M. A., Webb, G. J. W. 1985. *Crocodylus johnstoni* in the McKinlay River Area, N.T. VII. A population simulation model. *Austral. Wildl. Resrch.* 12:541–54.

BIBLIOGRAPHY

Smith, E. N. 1975. Thermoregulation of the American alligator *Alligator missis-sippiensis. Psysiol. Zool.* 48:177–94.

Smith, E. N. 1979. Behavioral and physiological thermoregulation of crocodilians. *Amer. Zool.* 19:239–48.

Smith, H. M. 1893. Notes on the alligator industry. *Bull. U.S. Fish Comm. (1891)* 11:343–5.

Smith, M. A. 1931. "The Fauna of British India including Ceylon and Burma," Reprinted 1973, Ralph Curtis Books, Sanibel Island, Florida.

Spencer, S. L. 1986. Alligators in Alabama. *Conservation* 56(5):9.

Spotila, J. R. et al. 1972. The biophysical ecology of the alligator: heat energy budget and climate space. *Ecology* 53:1094–1102.

Spotila, J. R. et al. 1977. Mouth gaping as an effective thermoregulatory device in alligators. *Nature* 265:235–6.

Spotila, J. R., Standora, E. A. 1985. Energy budgets of ectothermic vertebrates. *Amer. Zool.* 25:973–86.

Staton, M. 1975. Studies on the dry season biology of *Caiman crocodilus croco-dilus* from the Venezuelan Llanos. *Mem. Soc. Cienc. Nat. La Salle* 35(101): 237–66.

Staton, M. 1977. Breeding biology of the spectacled caiman, *Caiman c. crocodilus* in the Venezuelan Llanos. *U.S. Fish & Wildl. Serv. Wild. Resrch.* #5.

Steel, R. 1989. "Crocodiles," Christopher Helm (publishers) London.

Stoneburner, D. L., Kushlan, J. A. 1984. Heavy metals in southern Florida crocodile eggs. *J. Herpetol.* 18:192–3.

Stuart, K. 1987. Crocodiles survive in power plant cooling canals. *South Dade Leader* November 2, 1988, page 13.

Stutzenbaker, C. D. 1973. Alligator Holes. *Texas Parks & Wildlife* 31(5):20–22.

Stutzenbaker, C. D. 1979. When 'gators come to town. *Texas Parks & Wildlife* 37(6):6–7.

Subba Rao, M. V. 1977. On breeding crocodiles. *Sci. Today* 12(4):29–33.

Subba Rao, M. V. 1987. Incubating eggs of the gharial (*Gavialis gangeticus*) for conservation purposes, in: "Wildlife Management—Crocodiles and Alliga-tors," Webb, G. J. W., et al. (eds.), Surrey Beatty and Sons, Chipping Norton, NSW, Australia.

Sullivan, B. 1989. 266 will be allowed to kill total of 3,990 gators in September hunt. *Palm Beach Post* July 15, 1989, p. 18A.

Sunquist, F. 1988. The private passion of Tomas Blohm-breeding of endangered Orinoco crocodiles in Venezuela. *Intl. Wildl.* 18:20–4.

Suvanakorn, P., Youngprapakorn, C. 1987. Crocodile farming in Thailand, in: "Wildlife Management—Crocodiles and Alligators," Webb, G. J. W., et al. (eds.), Surrey Beatty and Sons, Chipping Norton, NSW, Australia.

Taplin, L. E., Grigg, G. C. 1981. Salt glands in the tongue of the estuarine crocodile *Crocodylus porosus. Science* 212:1045–7.

Taplin, L. E., Grigg, G. C. 1989. Historical zoogeography of the eusuchian croco-dilians. *Am. Zool.* 29:885–901.

Taplin, L. E. et al. 1982. Lingual salt glands in *Crocodylus acutus* and *Crocodylus johnstoni* and their absence from *Alligator mississippiensis* and *Caiman crocodilus. J. Comp. Physiol.* 149:43–7.

Taplin, L. E. 1984. Drinking of freshwater but not seawater by the estuarine crocodile *Crocodylus porosus. Comp. Biochem. Physiol.* 77A:763–7.

Taplin, L. E. 1984. Evolution and zoogeography of crocodilians: a new look at an ancient order, in: "Vertebrate Evolution and Zoogeography in Australasia," Archer, M. Clayton, G. (eds.), Hesperian Press, Perth.

Taplin, L. E. 1984. Homeostasis of plasma electrolytes, sodium and water pools in the estuarine crocodile, *Crocodylus porosus* from fresh, saline and hypersaline waters. *Oecologica* 63:63–70.

Taplin, L. E. 1987. The management of crocodiles in Queensland, Australia, in: "Wildlife Management—Crocodiles and Alligators," Webb, G. J. W., et al. (eds.), Surrey Beatty and Sons, Chipping Norton, NSW, Australia.

Tarsitano, S. F. et al. 1989. The evolution of the Crocodilia: a conflict between morphological and biochemical data. *Am. Zool.* 29:845–56.

Tarver, J. et al. 1987. "Fur Animals, Alligators and the Fur Industry in Louisiana," Louisiana Dept. of Wildlife & Fisheries, Baton Rouge.

Taylor, D. 1984. Management implications of size class frequency distribution in Louisiana alligator populations. *Wildl. Soc. Bull.* 12:312–19.

Taylor, J. A. 1976. The foods and feeding habits of subadult *Crocodylus porosus* in Northern Australia. *Austral. Wildl. Resrch.* 6:347–59.

Taylor, J. A. 1978. Methods of obtaining stomach contents from live crocodilians. *J. Herpetol.* 12:415–7.

Terpin, K. M. et al. 1978. Observations on ketamine hydrochloride as an anesthetic for alligators. *Copeia* 1978:147–8.

Thompson, B. C. et al. 1984. "Management Plan for the American alligator in Texas," Texas Parks & Wildlife Dept., Austin.

Thompson, R. L., Gidden, C. S. 1972. Territorial basking counts to estimate alligator populations. *J. Wildl. Mgmt.* 36:1081–8.

Thorbjarnarson, J. B. 1990. Notes on the feeding behavior of the gharial under semi-natural conditions. *J. Herpetol.* 24:99–100.

Toops, C. 1979. "The Alligator—Monarch of the Marsh," Florida Parks & Monuments Assn., Homestead, Florida.

Toops, C. 1982. Gator hunt (Everglades). *National Parks* 56:9–11.

Townsend, P. S. 1978. Can the croc come back? (The American crocodile). *Natl. Parks & Consv. Magazine* 52:13–15.

Valentine, J. M., Jr. et al. 1972. Alligator diets on the Sabine National Wildlife Refuge, Louisiana. *J. Wildl. Mgmt* 36:809–15.

Valentine, L. et al. 1983. Selenium, vitamin E and trace elements in the plasma of wild and farm-reared alligators during the reproductive cycle. *Canadian J. Zool.* 61:1744–51.

Valentine, L. 1989. Reproductive cycle of the American alligator. *Am. Zool.* 29:999–1018.

Van Brunt, J. F., Menzies, R. A. 1971. Synthesis of serum calcium-protein lipophosphoprotein complex by South American alligators (*Caiman latirostris*) in response to 17-estradiol. *Proc. Fed. Amer. Soc. Exp. Biol.* 30:1160.

Van Meter, V. B. 1987. "Florida's Alligators and Crocodiles," Florida Power & Light Co., Miami.

Vanzolini, P. E., Gomes, N. 1979. Notes on the ecology and growth of Amazonian caimans. *Papeis avulsos de Zool.* 32(17):205–16.

Verona, L. S. 1980. Protection in Cuba. *Oryx* 15(3):282–4.

Vliet, K. A. 1989. Social displays of the American alligator. *Am. Zool.* 29:1019–31.

BIBLIOGRAPHY

Voeltzkow, A. 1892. On the oviposition and embryonic development of the crocodile. *Ann. Mag. Nat. Hist.* (Ser. 6) 9(49):66–72.

Vogel, Z. 1964. "Reptiles and Amphibians, their care and behavior," Viking Press,
New York.

Wallach, J. D. et al. 1967. Hypoglycemic shock in captive alligators. *J. Amer. Vet. Med.
Assn.* 151:893–6.

Wallach, J. D., Hoessle, C. 1968. Steatitis in captive crocodilians. *Ibid.* 153:845–7.

Waller, T. 1987. Registro de las localidades de distribucion de las especies del
genero caiman en Argentina, *Amphibia y Reptilia* 1(3):68–75.

Walsh, B. P. 1987. Crocodile capture techniques in the Northern Territory of
Australia, in: "Wildlife Management—Crocodiles and Alligators," Webb, G. J.
W., et al. (eds.), Surrey Beatty and Sons, Chipping Norton, NSW, Australia.

Watson, R. M. et al. 1971. A comparison of four East African crocodile populations.
East African Wild. J. 9:25–34.

Webb, G. J. W. 1977. The natural history of *Crocodylus porosus*, in: "Australian
Animals and their Environment," Messel, H., et al. (eds.), Shakespeare, Sydney.

Webb, G. J. W., Cooper-Preston, H. 1989. Effects of incubation temperatures on
crocodiles and the evolution of reptilian oviparity. *Am. Zool.* 29:953–71.

Webb, G. J. W., Messel, H. 1977. Crocodile capture techniques. *J. Wildl. Mgmt.*
41:572–5.

Webb, G. J. W. et al. 1978. A record of a *Crocodylus porosus* attack. *J. Herpetol.*
12:267–8.

Webb, G. J. W. et al. 1978. Growth rates of *Crocodylus porosus* from Arnhem Land,
Northern Australia. *Australian Wildl. Research* 5:385–99.

Webb, G. J. W., Messel, H. 1978. Morphometric analysis of *Crocodylus porosus* from
the north coast of Arnhem Land, Northern Australia. *Austral. J. Zool.* 26:1–27.

Webb, G. J. W., Messel, H. 1979. Wariness in *Crocodylus porosus. Austral. Wildl.
Rsrch.* 6:227–34.

Webb, G. J. W. 1979. Comparative cardiac anatomy of the reptilia III. The heart of
crocodilians and an hypothesis on the completion of the interventricular
septum of crocodiles and birds. *J. Morph.* 161:221–40.

Webb, G. J. W., Gans, C. 1982. Galloping in *Crocodylus johnstoni*—a reflection of
terrestrial activity? *Rec. Aust. Mus.* 34:607–18.

Webb, G. J. W. et al. 1982. *Crocodylus johnstoni* in the McKinlay River area, N.T. I.
Variation in the diet and a new method of assessing the relative importance
of prey. *Aus. J. Zool.* 30:877–99.

Webb, G. J. W. et al. 1983. An interim method for estimating the age of *Crocodylus
porosus* embryos. *Aus. Wildl. Research* 10:563–70.

Webb, G. J. W. et al. 1983. *Crocodylus johnstoni* in the McKinlay River area, N.T. II.
Dry season habitat selection and an estimate of the total population size.
Ibid. 10:378–82.

Webb, G. J. W. et al. 1984. Cloacal sexing of hatchling crocodiles *Ibid.* 11:201–2.

Webb, G. J. W., Smith, A. M. A. 1984. Sex ratio and survivorship in the Australian
freshwater crocodile *Crocodylus johnstoni*, in: "The Structure, Development and Evolution of Reptiles," Ferguson, M. J. W., (ed.), Academic Press,
London.

Webb, G. J. W. et al. 1986. The possible relationship between embryo orientation,
opaque banding and the dehydration of albumen in crocodile eggs. *Copeia*
1986:252–7.

Webb, G. J. W. et al. 1987. The management of crocodiles in the Northern Territory of Australia, in: "Wildlife Management—Crocodiles and Alligators," Webb, G. J. W., et al. (eds.), Surrey Beatty and Sons, Chipping Norton, NSW, Australia.

Webb, G. J. W. 1987. Life history parameters, population dynamics and the management of crocodilians. *Ibid.*

Webb, G. J. W. et al. 1987. Methods for retrieving and examining crocodilian embryos. *Ibid.*

Webb, G. J. W. et al. 1987. Crocodilian eggs: a functional overview. *Ibid.*

Webb, G. J. W. et al. 1987. The effects of incubation temperature on sex determination and embryonic development rate in *Crocodylus johnstoni* and *Crocodylus porosus*. *Ibid.*

Webb, G., Manolis, C. 1988. "Australian Saltwater Crocodiles"/"Australian Freshwater Crocodiles," G. Webb Pty. N. T. Australia.

Weinheimer, C. J. et al. 1982. Peripheral circulation in *Alligator mississippiensis*: effects of diving, fear, movement, investigator activities and temperature. *J. Comp. Physiol.* 148:57–63.

Weisburd, S. 1988. New look at the sprawl in gator's gait (re: research by J. M. Parrish). *Science News* 133:71.

Welman, J. B., Worthington, E. B. 1943. The food of the crocodile, *Crocodylus niloticus*. *Proc. Zool. Soc. Lond.* 13:108–12.

Wermuth, H. 1953. Systematik der rezenten krokodile. *Mitt. Zool. Mus. Berlin* 29:375–514.

Wermuth, H., Mertens, R. 1961. "Schildkroten. Krokodile. Bruckenechsen," Veb. Gustav Fischer Verlag, Jena.

Westergaard, B., Ferguson, M. W. J. 1986. Development of the dentition in *Alligator mississippiensis*. Early embryonic development in the lower jaw. *J. Zool.* A210:575–97.

Wever, E. G. 1971. Hearing in the crocodilia. *Proc. Natl. Acad. Sci. (U.S.)* 68(7):1498–1500.

Whitaker, R., Whitaker, Z. 1977. Notes on natural history of *Crocodylus palustris*. *J. Bombay Nat. Hist. Soc.* 74:358–60.

Whitaker, R., Whitaker Z. 1978. A preliminary survey of the saltwater crocodile *Crocodylus porosus* in the Andaman Islands. *Ibid.* 75:43–9.

Whitaker, R., Daniel, J. C. 1978. The status of Asian crocodilians. *Tiger Paper* 5:12–17.

Whitaker, R. 1979. Crocodile egg collection in Tamil Nadu. *Indian Forester* 105:121–8.

Whitaker, R., Whitaker Z. 1979. Preliminary crocodile survey—Sri Lanka. *J. Bombay Nat. Hist. Soc.* 76:297–316.

Whitaker, R. 1982. A taxonomic note on Mugger subspecies (*Crocodylus palustris*). *Ibid.* 79:426–7.

Whitaker, R., Basu, D. 1983. The gharial (*Gavialis gangeticus*) A review. *Ibid.* 79:531–48.

Whitaker, R., Whitaker Z. 1984. Reproductive biology of the mugger. *J. Bombay Nat. Hist. Soc.* 81:297–316.

Whitaker, R. 1987. The management of crocodiles in India, in: "Wildlife Management—Crocodiles and Alligators," Webb, G. J. W., et al. (eds.), Surrey Beatty and Sons, Chipping Norton, NSW, Australia.

Whitehead, P. J. 1987. Respiration of *Crocodylus johnstoni* embryos. *Ibid.*

BIBLIOGRAPHY

Whitworth, J. 1971. Notes on the growth and mating of American alligators, *Alligator mississippiensis* at the Cannon Aquarium, Manchester Museum. *Intl. Zoo Yearbook* 11:144.

Wieber, C. G. 1960. Effect of temperature on the heart of the alligator. *Am. J. Physiol.* 198:861–3.

Wilkinson, P. M. 1983. "Nesting ecology of the American alligator in coastal South Carolina," (August 1978-September 1983), South Carolina Wildlife and Marine Resources Department, Charleston.

Williams, J. 1985. How to avoid close encounters of the wrong kind. *Texas Parks & Wildl.* 43(8):15.

Williamson, L., Williford, L. 1979. Alligators—Are they back to stay? *Ibid.* 37(6):2–5.

Williston, S. W. 1914. "Water reptiles of the past and present," University of Chicago Press, Chicago.

Woodward, A. R., Marion, W. R. 1978. An evaluation of factors affecting night-long counts of alligators. *Proc. Ann. Conf. SE Assn. Game & Fish Comms.* 32:291–302.

Woodward, A. R. et al. 1984. Spacing patterns in alligator nests. *J. Herpetol.* 18:8–12.

Woodward, A. R. 1987. Alligator ranching research in Florida, in: "Wildlife Management—Crocodiles and Alligators," Webb, G. J. W., et al. (eds.), Surrey Beatty and Sons, Chipping Norton, NSW, Australia.

Wright, D. E., Moffat, L. A. 1985. Morphology and ultrastructure of the chin and cloacal glands of juvenile *Crocodylus porosus*, in: "Biology of Australasian Frogs and Reptiles," Grigg, G. C., et al. (eds.), Surrey Beatty and Sons, Chipping Norton, NSW, Australia.

Wyman, J. 1870. On the existence of a crocodile in Florida. *Amer. J. Sci. Arts* 49:105.

Yadnav, R. N. 1979. A further report on breeding the mugger crocodile. *Intl. Zoo Yearbook* 19:66–8.

Zander, H. C. 1988. On the Billabong with Crocodile Max translated from *Stern*, in: *World Press Review* (February) 35(2):32–3.

Zappalorti, R. T. 1976. "The Amateur Zoologists Guide to Turtles and Crocodiles," Vol. I. Stackpole Books, Harrisburg, Pennsylvania.

Appendix I

Illustrated Identification Key
to the Crocodilia

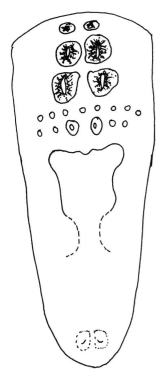

Alligator mississippiensis
(*after Mook*)

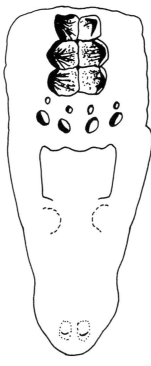

Alligator sinensis
(*after Mook*)

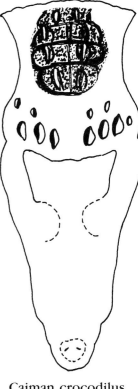

Caiman crocodilus
(*after Mook*)

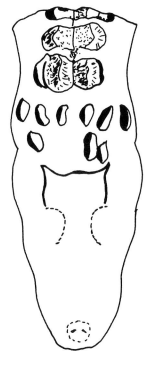

Caiman latirostris
(*after Natterer*)

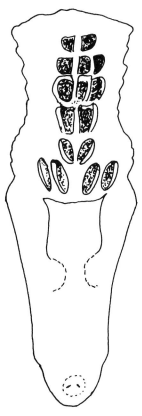

Paleosuchus palpebrosus
(*after Natterer*)

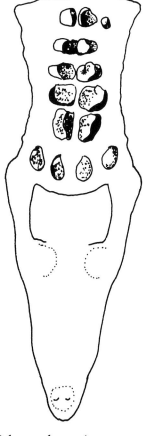

Paleosuchus trigonatus
(*after Natterer*)

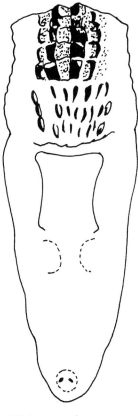

Melanosuchus niger
(*after Natterer*)

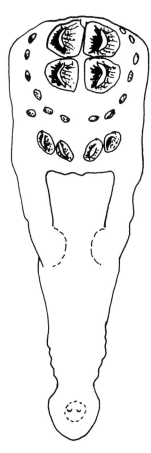

Crocodylus acutus
(*after Wermuth*)

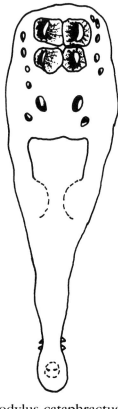

Crocodylus cataphractus
(*after Wermuth*)

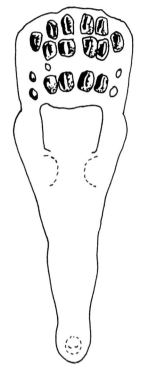

Crocodylus intermedius
(*after Wermuth*)

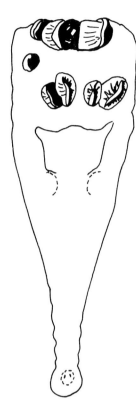

Crocodylus johstoni
(*after Gray*)

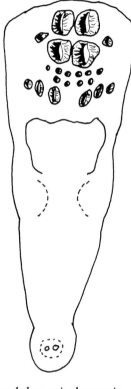

Crocodylus mindorensis
(*after Hall, 1989*)

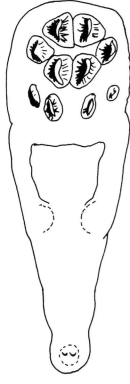

Crocodylus morelettii
(*after Wermuth*)

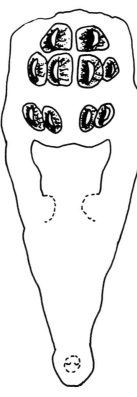

Crocodylus niloticus
(*after Wermuth*)

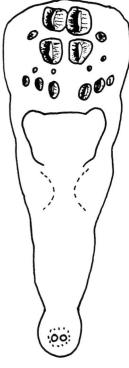

Crocodylus novaeguineae
Southern form
(*after Hall, 1989*)

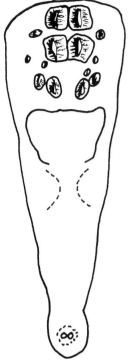

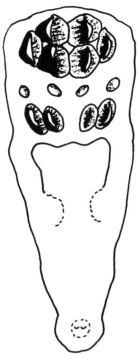

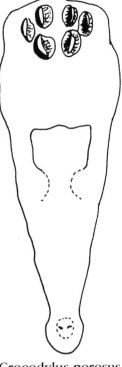

Crocodylus novaeguineae
Northern form
(*after Hall, 1989*)

Crocodylus palustris
(*after Wermuth*)

Crocodylus porosus
(*after Wermuth*)

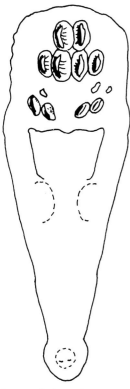

Crocodylus rhombifer
(*after Wermuth*)

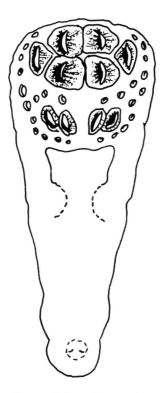

Crocodylus siamensis
(*afater Wermuth*)

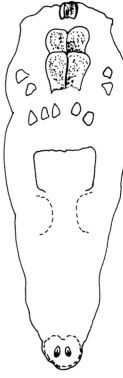

Osteolaemus tetraspis
(*after Strauch*)

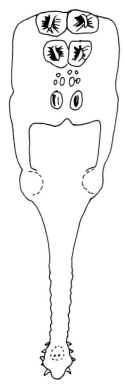

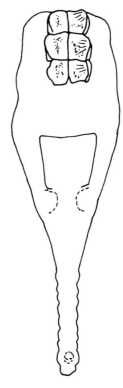

Gavialis gangeticus
(*after Wermuth*)

Tomistoma schlegelii
(*after Wermuth*)

APPENDIX II
MEASUREMENT CONVERSION FACTORS

Measurement Conversion Factors

When you know—	Multiply by—	To find—
Length:		
Millimeters (mm)	0.04	inches (in)
Centimeters (mm)	0.4	inches (in)
Meters (m)	3.3	feet (ft)
Meters (m)	1.1	yards (yd)
Kilometers (km)	0.6	miles (mi)
Inches (in)	2.54	centimeters (cm)
Feet (ft)	30	centimeters (cm)
Yards (yd)	0.9	meters (m)
Miles (mi)	1.6	kilometer (km)
Area:		
Square centimeters (cm^2)	0.16	square inches (sq. in.)
Square meters (m^2)	1.2	square yards (sq yd)
Square kilometers (km^2)	0.4	square miles (sq mi)
Hectares (ha)	2.5	acres
Square inches (sq in)	6.5	square centimeters (cm^2)
Square feet (sq ft)	0.09	square meters (m^2)
Square yards (sq yd)	0.8	square meters (m^2)
Square miles (sq mi)	1.2	square kilometers (km^2)
Acres	0.4	hectares (ha)
Mass (Weight):		
Grams (g)	0.035	ounces (oz)
Kilograms (kg)	2.2	pounds (lb)
Ounces (oz)	28	grams (g)
Pounds (lb)	0.45	kilograms (kg)

Measurement Conversion Factors (*Continued*)

When you know—	Multiply by—	To find—
Volume		
Milliliters (ml)	0.03	fluid ounces (fl oz)
Liters (L)	2.1	pints (p)
Liters (L)	1.06	quarts (qt)
Liters (L)	0.26	U.S. gallons (gal)
Liters (L)	0.22	imperial gallons (gal)
Cubic centimeters (cc)	16.387	cubic inches (cu in)
Cubic meters (cm^3)	35	cubic feet (cu ft)
Cubic meters (cm^3)	1.3	cubic yards (cu yd)
Teaspoons (tsp)	5	millimeters (ml)
Tablespoons (tbsp)	15	millimeters (ml)
Fluid ounces (fl oz)	30	millimeters (ml)
Cups (c)	0.24	liters (L)
Pints (pt)	0.47	liters (L)
Quarts (qt)	0.95	liters (L)
U.S. gallons (gal)	3.8	liters (L)
U.S. gallons (gal)	231	cubic inches (cu in)
Imperial gallons (gal)	4.5	liters (L)
Imperial gallons (gal)	277.42	cubic inches (cu in)
Cubic inches (cu in)	0.061	cubic centimeters (cc)
Cubic feet (cu ft)	0.028	cubic meters (m^3)
Cubic yards (cu yd)	0.76	cubic meters (m^3)

Temperature:		
Celsius (°C)	multiply by 1.8, add 32	Fahrenheit (°F)
Fahrenheit (°F)	subtract 32, multiply by 0.555	Celsius °C)

Note: The practice of leaving units of measurement in the same form as found in the original source has been used in this book. Readers will find both metric and English (Std. U.S.) methods in the text. Therefore, this conversion chart is provided.

INDEX

( ) indicates illustration.

INDEX

INDEX

INDEX